Dear Reader:

The book you are abou[t] ... [fro]m the St. Martin's True [Crime Library, what the Ne]w *York Times* calls "the l[eader in true crime!" We] offer you a fascinatin[g account of a sensa]tional crime that has captured the national attention. St. Martin's is the publisher of bestselling true crime author and crime journalist Kieran Crowley, who explores the dark, deadly links between a prominent Manhattan surgeon and the disappearance of his wife fifteen years earlier in THE SURGEON'S WIFE. Suzy Spencer's BREAKING POINT guides readers through the tortuous twists and turns in the case of Andrea Yates, the Houston mother who drowned her five young children in the family's bathtub. In Edgar Award-nominated DARK DREAMS, legendary FBI profiler Roy Hazelwood and bestselling crime author Stephen G. Michaud shine light on the inner workings of America's most violent and depraved murderers. In the book you now hold, MURDER IN PARADISE by Lisa Pulitzer, you will learn that tragedy can strike even in the most unlikely of places . . .

St. Martin's True Crime Library gives you the stories behind the headlines. Our authors take you right to the scene of the crime to show you what really happened. St. Martin's True Crime Library paperbacks are better than the most gripping thriller, because it's all true! The next time you want a crackling good read, make sure it's got the St. Martin's True Crime Library logo on the spine—you'll be up all night!

Charles E. Spicer, Jr.
Executive Editor, St. Martin's True Crime Library

"Seal Off the Area!"

Officer Rhymer steered the SUV three hundred to four hundred feet east on Sir Francis Drake Highway, taking her cues from the anxious preteen in the passenger seat.

"Right here," Sheena announced, pointing to a spot a fair distance out on the rocks.

In response to the girl's directive, Rhymer navigated the vehicle across the single white line that divides the two-lane highway, then parked on the road's shoulder, just below the home of the Skelton family. Climbing out of the driver's seat, a paste of mud and crabgrass underfoot, the officer directed her attention to the beach, and the location that Sheena was now indicating. And then she spotted it: the body of a white female lying stone-still at the edge of the shoreline.

Rhymer could feel her throat getting dry as she stepped carefully over the boulders to get a closer look. She sensed the presence of the officers who had accompanied her to the scene, but did not turn to look at them. Instead, she forged ahead. Nearing the body, she swallowed hard.

"Mr. George, Mr. Farrington, seal off the area!" Rhymer barked her orders to the other two constables. . . .

ST. MARTIN'S PAPERBACKS TRUE CRIME LIBRARY
TITLES BY LISA PULITZER

A Woman Scorned

Fatal Romance

Murder in Paradise

MURDER IN PARADISE

The Mystery Surrounding the Murder of American Lois Livingston McMillen

LISA PULITZER

St. Martin's Paperbacks

Printed in the United States of America

St. Martin's Paperbacks edition / November 2003

10 9 8 7 6 5 4 3 2 1

I dedicate this book to Lois Livingston McMillen, an innocent soul, whose life was taken in a senseless act of violence and aggression.

Let it be known that her spirit lives on in all of the people whose lives she touched. None can ever forget her goodness, and her caring ways.

It is my wish that Lois' family find peace and comfort in knowing that all who knew her considered her an angel in their midst.

ACKNOWLEDGMENTS

I wish to thank the following people for their help, time, and cooperation:

Russell and the late Josephine McMillen, whose pain I cannot comprehend. May the family find peace and comfort in knowing that Lois was loved by so many.

To Lois' aunt, Phyllis Cobb, I say thank you for sharing her love of Lois with me.

To Michael Spicer of Charlottesville, VA, Alexander Benedetto of New York, NY, and Evan George of San Francisco, CA, for cooperating with me and for sharing their pain and their triumphs. I also wish to thank Chris Matthews of Watertown, NY, for her honesty and candor. I admire the way Mrs. Matthews stood by her brother, Michael Spicer, and for her courage in showing the world how much she loves him.

I extend a heartfelt thank you to Deputy Commissioner of Police John Johnston and his wife, Irene. Mr. Johnston headed up the investigation into the murder of Lois McMillen as second in command of the Royal Virgin Islands Police Force. He was cooperative in the writing of this book, as well as gracious and hospitable. He and Irene welcomed me into their charming home in the Highlands of Scotland and treated me with the utmost respect and kindness.

I would also like to extend a special thanks to Mr. Terrence Williams of the Attorney General's office. Mr. Williams was also most cooperative, giving up several Sundays and talking to me instead of watching the cricket matches he so adores.

Gratitude to former Commissioner of Police Vernon Malone and Commissioner of Police Barry Webb of the Royal Virgin Islands Police Force.

An important source in the writing of this book was journalist John Springer, whose reporting on the case was fair and accurate. When I had questions about facts pertaining to this case, I relied upon Mr. Springer's published accounts on CourtTV.com and was in touch with him frequently. I want to thank him for his time, cooperation, and excellent coverage of this story.

To Beulah and Joseph Wellington Romney, I am grateful. I thank Joseph for encouraging his wife to speak with me, and I thank Beulah for finding the courage to meet and talk with me, a stranger. I know from our lengthy interviews that Mrs. Romney is most disturbed by what happened to Lois Livingston McMillen outside of her home on the night of January 14, 2000. I also know that she holds Russell and Josephine McMillen in her prayers.

To Clinton Romney, my taxi driver, keep up the good work. During one of our many taxi rides, Mr. Romney shared with me how he volunteers his time to help and provide guidance to schoolchildren of Tortola, an important role that will shape futures.

To Joseph Archibald and Oscar Ramjeet of J.S. Archibald & Co., I extend a heartfelt thank you for their time, cooperation, and insights.

To Jay Salpeter of Jay Salpeter Investigations of Great Neck, thank you for sharing your thoughts and observations with me.

To the McDonalds of Old Inverness, Scotland, thank you for making my stay in your country a wonderful one. To Sharon, Liz, and the staff at the Sugar Mill Hotel, I will never forget your kindness and hospitality.

As always, I extend my gratitude to my wonderful and patient editor, Charles Spicer of St. Martin's Press. Thank you, Charlie, for believing in me, and for giving me countless extensions!

"I couldn't have done it without you!" is what I want to say to Joshua Rivkin, the best editor I have ever had the pleasure of working with. Let it be known that it was Mr. Rivkin's brilliant editing and countless hours of revision work that made this book shine. Also, special thanks to Henry Kaufman, Esq., Richard Onley and John Rounds.

And then there are my literary friends, Cynthia Blair, Gilbert Matthews, Amy Wapner, and Barbara Young, all of whom helped in the writing of this book.

Other important people who deserve a "thank you" are Jeffrey Plante of Plano, Texas, "Shannon," Andrew O'Mar Mullin of Jamaica, Michael Griffith of Southampton, NY, Bomba Callwood of Bomba's Shack, Louis Schwartz of the Jolly Roger Inn, James Morris, Bernard Barboza of Southampton High School, Dennis Finnerty of Southampton, NY, Angela Rogers of Lynn University, Lisa McCown of Washington and Lee University Library in Lexington, Virginia, fellow crime writers Marion Collins and Kieran Crowley, and television journalist Jane Cassidy.

Most of all, I would like to thank my faithful babysitter, Domenica Petrizzo, who tirelessly cared for my two young children as I typed away in an upstairs office. And hugs to babysitter Jenny Studenroth, who loved my daughters and kept the peace.

And finally, kisses to my daughters, Francesca and Juliet, who tolerated the long absences of their mother, and who every day bring sunshine into my heart; and to my husband and editor, Douglas Love, for being there every step of the way.

I would also like to thank the people of Tortola, who welcomed me to their tiny slice of paradise and treated me with the utmost kindness and respect.

As always, a special thanks to my agent, Madeleine Morel of 2M Communications.

Author's Note: William Labrador declined to speak with me. Through his mother, I was informed that he and his family did not intend to participate in the writing of this book in any fashion.

AUTHOR'S NOTE

This book is based upon dozens of interviews, court transcripts, police affidavits, and numerous other documents obtained during a lengthy investigation in the United States, on the British Virgin Island of Tortola, and in Scotland.

In some cases, people who were involved in the case disagreed about what actually transpired on certain days and times. In those cases, I have relied primarily upon official court documents and sworn testimony from police officers and other involved parties. I have also tried to incorporate opposing views when and where possible.

PROLOGUE

A woman's spine-tingling screams just before midnight sent
Beulah Romney racing to the window of her pink-and-white
hilltop house. Seconds before, she had heard the screech of
car tires as a vehicle braked to a halt on the deserted stretch
of Sir Francis Drake Highway, which runs along the water's
edge just below her home on the sleepy Caribbean island of
Tortola. Concerned, the thick-set grandmother in the sleeve-
less housecoat peered out into the darkness. For a split second, an eerie silence fell over the beach. Then the screaming
resumed. Leaning against the windowsill, Beulah anxiously
fought to see around the towering tree that graced her front
yard. But the leafy palms were obscuring her view. Frustrated, she stood stone-still and listened, trying to figure out
who was shrieking. She could make out no words, just frantic cries that seemed to be coming from somewhere along
the shoreline a few hundred feet away.

It was not uncommon to hear the heated arguments of
neighbors, whose domestic disputes might spill out onto the
street. But on this particular night—January 14, 2000—
Beulah did not recognize the cries as those of any neighbor.

Tearing herself away from the window, fifty-four-year-
old Beulah hurried to summon her husband from the
shower. She grew increasingly upset as she crossed the living room, noting that the high-pitched wails from the beach
were taking on a more desperate, more urgent tone.

"Zoom Boy!" she shouted, using the nickname that Joseph Wellington Romney had had since grade school. "Zoom Boy, come out and hear the screaming," Beulah said, pounding her fist on the bathroom door.

"What did you say?" Joseph Wellington Romney struggled to wrap a towel around his compact body, still wet from the shower. He tried to explain to his wife that he couldn't hear her over the running water. But Beulah was not listening. Grabbing his hand, she pulled him toward the window.

"Somebody's out there screaming," she announced, and pointed a thick finger toward the shoreline.

Staring out at the darkened roadway, they both listened. But the commotion had given way to a peaceful calm. The only thing that Beulah and her husband could hear was the gentle slapping of the waves against the rocky shoreline.

Beulah sensed that something was terribly wrong, and for a brief moment, she thought about summoning the police. But she decided against it, assuming that it was her neighbors at it once again. She did not want to get involved in someone else's personal affair. Not on this tiny island where everybody knew everybody else's business.

Besides, she assumed that the police would have heard everything she'd heard, since the West End substation was just a few yards up the highway. Surely one of the officers would have gone out to check.

Still feeling slightly uneasy, Beulah turned in for the evening. Her decision not to call police that night was one that she would regret for years to come.

CHAPTER ONE

The Discovery

It was just before seven on Saturday morning the fifteenth of January in the year 2000 when Winsome Manning left her husband's house in Huntums Ghut, a small community set high in the hills of the mountainous Caribbean island of Tortola. Temperatures had already climbed into the mid-70s and the sweet scent of hibiscus filled the air as the Jamaican dressmaker set out for one of the palm-lined territory's most popular restaurants, Pusser's Landing. It was located at the Soper's Hole wharf on the western end, in one of the island's three main ports of entry. Winsome intended to grab a cup of coffee and some breakfast before beginning work at the seaside establishment, with its open-air bar, plenitude of tables topped with colorful umbrellas, and unobstructed views of the ferry dock across the harbor.

Visiting her husband, who was employed on the island, Winsome had remained to enjoy the lively Millennium celebrations, turning her Christmas sojourn into an extended holiday. Since she did not have a car at her disposal, she began her early morning journey on foot—never dreaming that her lengthy trek to the island's West End would take a grisly turn.

The handsome woman stayed close to the road shoulder as she descended the steep route into town from her house's position at fifteen hundred feet above sea level. She sensed that she was nearing the shore when the prickly cacti and wild tamarind covering the hillside slowly gave way to a profusion of wild frangipani and leafy palms.

She was nearly thirty minutes into her walk when she reached the waterfront area of the capital city of Road Town, a jumble of tourist shops, churches, and off-shore banks, with flocks of chickens roaming its winding streets like the stray cats of the Greek islands. Wasting no time, she hitched a ride from a passing motorist who took her as far as Big Ben's filling station on the Sir Francis Drake Highway, the island's principal east–west road. Tortola was a British Territory on which traffic followed British rules, with drivers on the left side of the road. Big Ben's marked the halfway mark on her trip. From there, she continued on foot, ambling at a leisurely pace.

As she proceeded west on the sea side of the highway, Winsome listened to the songs of the hummingbirds that hid among the mangroves, mango trees, and enormous red flowers that sprang from the bounty of bougainvillea sprouting all over the island. A warm breeze blew steadily off the sea as she strolled along, passing houses trimmed in pretty white gingerbread with lovely stucco terraces facing the sea.

It was a few minutes past eight when she spotted the cement-block building that houses the West End police station, about one hundred feet ahead, and perched atop a small rise on the opposite side of the highway. And then she saw it—the motionless body that lay face up on the rocky shoreline, sprays of seawater splashing onto it.

Winsome immediately stopped on a grassy patch of road shoulder, staring out at the rocky beach in disbelief. She shuddered involuntarily as she studied the lifeless figure sprawled on the boulders at the edge of the seashore. She felt momentarily sickened as she stood paralyzed on the roadway, unable to come to terms with what she was slowly beginning to realize wasn't merely a figment of her imagination. Taking a moment to compose her thoughts, she drew a deep breath of salty sea air, and again directed her attention toward the disturbing sight. From where she stood, she could see that the body was that of a white female.

The coastal area where the body lay was a beach made up of rough sand and coral gravel. It was not an area where people would come to swim. And it was difficult to negotiate on foot because of the boulders that had been put down to protect the road from erosion by the sea.

The seamstress noted the woman's stylish clothing, her three-quarter pants and expensive-looking gold-and-white blouse. Red nail polish adorned the tips of her long fingers. Her blouse was pulled up, exposing one of her breasts. She appeared to be young, and worse, she appeared to be dead.

Trudging breathlessly up the dusty driveway of the police station just across the way, she rushed into the two-story headquarters through a pair of open doors.

"Hello, my name is Winsome Manning," she began, and then paused to take a deep breath. "While walking between the filling station and here I saw what looked like a body. It was near to the water, not in the water. The water was splashing on it."

The uniformed officer behind the desk listened intently as the woman detailed her finding.

Winsome described the location, and then remained to fill out a report. Meanwhile, West End constables, armed with the information, hastened out of the building to look for the body on the beach. But police were not immediately able to confirm Winsome's report, and it wasn't long before another individual, this time a very young girl, came running into the stationhouse claiming that she, too, had spotted a body lying at the water's edge.

Woman Police Constable No. 61, Jocelyn Rhymer, was there to take the report when the visibly shaken girl rushed in at ten minutes to ten. Rhymer had been on duty at the West End headquarters for a little more than an hour, having arrived just after eight thirty.

"Yes, can I help you?" the sturdy officer in the gray-and-white uniform asked. Rhymer recognized the child as Sheena Andrews, the niece of one of her fellow constables. It troubled her to see the young girl so distraught.

Rhymer listened intently as Sheena, in between pants of

breath, related the details of her early morning discovery. "I was walking to my math class at Romney Estate around nine o'clock this morning," the slender, clear-skinned adolescent began in a shaky voice. "I looked over on the shore side and saw something like a manikin, a doll. Its face was purple. So I noticed it was real.

"At the same time, I saw a white man on a bicycle coming down the road. I wanted to stop him, but I didn't. I turned back around and . . ."

"Yes." Officer Rhymer nodded to show she was listening carefully. "Go on."

The policewoman was unaccustomed to reports of dead bodies washing up on the beaches of Tortola. There was the occasional drowning victim, but even then, the appearance of a body usually followed a report of a missing person. Rhymer, her hair tied back in neat braids, paid close attention as Sheena continued her story, struggling to remain focused even though she was clearly upset.

"The body was part on the shore and part in the sea," Sheena went on. "When the waves came in, they were making the body sway. I think her head was facing to the west and her feet to the east. I think she was wearing white long pants and a white shirt."

"Come with me. I'd like you to show me." Grabbing the keys to the department's Mitsubishi, Officer Rhymer shepherded the girl into the gray four-wheel-drive vehicle. She signaled to two colleagues to hop in the back seat and accompany her to the location the girl had described.

The female officer steered the SUV three hundred to four hundred feet east on Sir Francis Drake Highway, taking her cues from the anxious preteen in the passenger seat.

"Right here," Sheena announced, pointing to a spot a fair distance out on the rocks.

In response to the girl's directive, Rhymer navigated the vehicle across the single white line that divides the two-lane highway, then parked on the road's shoulder, just below the home of the Skelton family. Climbing out of the driver's seat, a paste of mud and crabgrass underfoot, the officer directed her attention to the beach, and the location that Sheena was now indicating. And then she spotted it: the body of a white female lying stone-still at the edge of the shoreline.

Rhymer could feel her throat getting dry as she stepped carefully over the boulders to get a closer look. She sensed the presence of the officers who had accompanied her to the scene, but did not turn to look at them. Instead, she forged ahead. Nearing the body, she swallowed hard. But not even her police training prepared her for the horror of the disfigured, bloated, partially nude woman that lay before her.

Kneeling beside the body, she instinctively placed two fingers on the woman's carotid artery to check for a pulse, but found no sign of life. She remained on the ground for several seconds, studying the body and at the same time struggling to maintain her composure in the face of such a sickening discovery. It was difficult to keep her focus on the woman's face, which was swollen and grotesquely distorted, probably as a result of its exposure to the briny seawater.

Continuing her assessment, the officer noted that the young lady was barefoot, and that there was a red fluid, probably blood, running from her left ear. She observed that, as the girl had reported, the woman was attired in lacy white capris and an expensive-looking blouse with gold Greco-Roman designs, which was pulled up to expose her left breast. Her delicate flesh-colored brassiere was also showing.

Scanning the woman's torso, her attention was immediately drawn to several dark marks to the left of her ribcage, and two red scratches in the same general area. A single gold-colored shoe lay on the shore about seven feet from her head. It was a shoe with a heel, a shoe that its owner would just slip on, she noted.

"Mr. George, Mr. Farrington, seal off the area!" Rhymer jumped to her feet and barked her orders to the other two constables. She had no reason to suspect foul play, and thought that the death was a drowning. Yet her police training told her that she must take proper precautions. She knew she needed to protect the scene until the medical examiner arrived to make an assessment.

Once Rhymer saw that they had everything under control, she started back to the West End police station to retrieve the crime-scene tape. As she navigated the boulders back toward the road, she noticed that a woman in a passing car had stopped to speak to her. She recognized the driver as a nurse who worked at the hospital in Road Town.

Rhymer would later explain that the woman had provided her with a colorful sheet, which she placed over the lifeless body—never imagining that the gesture of respect would later be called into question.

CHAPTER TWO

Taking Charge

Deputy Police Commissioner John Johnston cranked down the window of his Mitsubishi Montero, resting one arm on the door to enjoy the warm Caribbean sun on his tanned skin. His day off, a Saturday, was shaping up to be another perfect day in paradise. His wife, Irene, sat beside him in the front seat, chatting happily; and like him, anticipating a day of sun and snorkeling, topped off with a quiet picnic on a secluded beach.

Johnston had just passed through Road Town, which was abuzz with Hawaiian-shirt–clad cruise ship passengers milling about the windy streets to the steel drum tunes blaring from the harbor-front restaurants. He was heading east toward the beach when a message came over the police radio that was bolted to his dashboard and never turned off. "The body of a white woman has been found on the beach," a dispatcher announced.

The fifty-four-year-old Scotsman could feel the whole tenor of the day shift as he listened in to the desk officer on duty at Road Town police headquarters relaying details to West End units.

Johnston, the department's second in command, grimaced and turned to look at Irene. "I'm going to have to go to this one because it just doesn't sound right.

"Funny," he mused. "Nobody filed a Missing Person's Report last night."

Johnston and his men often responded to drowning accidents. Drownings were fairly commonplace on a popular Caribbean resort island like Tortola where vacationers spent a portion of each day swimming, snorkeling, scuba diving, or boating. But experience also told him that in those cases, there was inevitably a frantic call to the police department from a friend, family member, or some other involved party who was anxious to report the accident and summon emergency personnel.

That wasn't the case this time.

Dropping Irene back at their villa, Johnston raced toward the West End. "I'm on my way," he said in a clear voice, his thick Scottish accent immediately identifying him to the desk officer monitoring the police radio. "Get the other senior officers informed, and have them report to the location as soon as they can get there!"

In his three decades with the Scottish police, Johnston had served in a variety of high-profile roles, including providing protection for members of England's Royal Family. He had supervised the security detail for the Queen Mother, Prince Charles, and Princess Diana, and Prince Andrew and Duchess of York Sarah "Fergie" Ferguson, during their visits to the Highlands where Queen Elizabeth had a summer home. He also helped to provide protection for the UK's first nuclear power plant and a submarine testing facility maintained by the British.

Johnston drove for nearly fifteen minutes on the Sir Francis Drake Highway, known locally as Drake's Highway, before reaching the spot where Winsome Manning and Sheena Andrews had sighted the motionless body. There were no traffic lights on Tortola. Instead speed bumps, stop signs, and roundabouts were used to regulate the flow and pace of traffic. As he neared the Drake's Highway location, he could see two of his officers from West End standing on the rocks about four hundred feet east of the police station. Several bystanders were watching them from the road.

Parking on a patch of grass near the home of a local taxi driver, the trim, well-toned commander jumped from his

vehicle and hurried over to speak with the officers on the
scene. One of the men directed his attention to the sheet-
covered body lying on the foreshore behind a long strip of
yellow police tape. He ambled over and nodded to the officer standing nearby.

When Woman Constable Rhymer lifted the colorful bed
linen, Johnston winced. He had seen dozens of dead bodies
during his career. But the condition of this woman was difficult even for him to view. Her face was so bloated and purple that she looked like she was wearing some sort of
ghoulish scarlet mask. Strands of her lengthy platinum hair
were drenched with seawater.

Remaining at a safe distance so as not to disturb anything, the commander pulled the sunglasses from his eyes
and slowly scrutinized the disfigured corpse. Squinting
against the bright tropical sun, he observed that the manner
in which the woman's blouse and brassiere were pushed up
suggested that there might have been some sort of physical
struggle. He also noted that she was lying on her back in a
couple of inches of water. It was an odd position for a
drowning victim and one that immediately confirmed his
suspicions that something was not right. Glancing out at the
ocean, Johnston noticed that there was no sea running—
the water was quietly lapping the shoreline, which meant
that the body hadn't been turned over because of big waves
coming in.

The veteran commander continued his visual inspection.
He observed that a small amount of blood appeared to be
oozing from the woman's left ear, although he could not see
any particular wound in the area. His attention was drawn to
what looked like scratches on the palms of her hands, and he
noted that her fingers were blanched—a whitish coloration
that signaled that she had been lying in the water for some
time.

"This isn't somebody who's just fallen in the water and
drowned," Johnston declared, his expression grim. "There's
something more to this. Something happened."

His own experience was telling him that, while this

woman had the appearance of a drowning victim, the unusual redness of her face and the absence of froth and mucous around her mouth and nose suggested otherwise. Because she was lying on her back—and not face down in the water, as you would expect to find a person who has drowned—he reasoned that drowning did not appear a logical explanation for her death. Her legs were outstretched, and the tips of her feet were slightly overlapped; it was almost as if someone had posed the dead woman at the water's edge after her death, the commander thought.

Johnston stepped back from the body, the thick rubber soles of his sandals gripping the rocks for balance, and raised his arms to draw his officers' attention. "Look, get these people back away from the scene," he barked. He directed the handful of police personnel that had gathered at the location to push everyone back about two hundred yards on either side of the body. "Everybody needs to stay back until the Scenes of Crime people get here."

"Hands in pockets!" Johnston commanded next. He had learned early in his career that one of the key things to do when you go to a crime scene is to put your hands in your pockets and not touch anything. Already, one of his constables had foolishly draped the woman's body with a sheet—an action he wished had not been taken.

But it was difficult for him to remain angry. Many of his officers were unaccustomed to handling homicides, since the murder record on Tortola had been at a rate of less than one a year for over a decade. Since 1996, the British Virgin Islands—situated east of Puerto Rico between the Atlantic Ocean and the Caribbean Sea—had only seen six murders, and none of them involved a visitor. In a rare instance, two murders had occurred on Tortola in 1999. It was a remarkably low number, considering that just across the way on St. Thomas, the rate was between twenty and forty a year. It was five hundred a year on the large, bustling island of Puerto Rico, which was located only sixty miles away. And while the officers lacked hands-on experience in homicide investigations, they had received added training from retired officers like Johnston, who had come to Tortola from the United Kingdom with three decades of experience to share with members of the force. Agents from the US Federal Bureau of Investigation stationed in Puerto Rico routinely visited the BVI as well and conducted workshops for officers.

"We need a doctor on the scene immediately!" Johnston yelled to WPC Rhymer, who was clearly shaken over the discovery. "We don't want to touch anything until we get a doctor to pronounce life extinct." Although it was fairly obvious that the woman was dead, Johnston knew that he needed a medical person to make the ruling before he could proceed with the investigation.

"We're going to have to close off the road," the commander directed the handful of traffic officers who had been summoned to the scene. Johnston realized that his command would effectively shut down Tortola's main highway, the principal road that runs from west to east and carries virtually all of the island's traffic from the West End ferry terminal to Road Town. He knew that his order was certain to snarl traffic, perhaps for hours. Tourists driving rental cars would never find, or want to use, the treacherous back roads that wound their way around the island. But that was not among his top worries. As the first senior officer to arrive, his priority was to protect the crime scene until it could be fully examined.

About fifteen minutes passed before the first members of the Criminal Investigations Division (CID) began arriving at the Drake's Highway location. During his nineteen months with the department, Johnston had determined that the Royal Virgin Islands Police Force had a number of competent officers, capable of delivering effective police service to the territory. But he felt there were areas in which they could benefit from more training. A handful of the investigators were highly specialized in the area of drug intervention and in the investigation of financial crimes, such as money laundering and commercial fraud—important skills since the island was fast becoming a center for offshore banking. But murder was a different story.

From his position on the shore, Johnston could see the department's senior officials assembling along Drake's Highway. The first investigator to arrive on the scene was Sergeant Duncan Williams. Soon after, Johnston's second in command, Chief Inspector of Police Jacob George, approached him for an orientation. Johnston waved as the officer with the thin moustache mouthed a "Hello," his glass eye concealed behind thick sunglasses. George wore it like a badge of honor, a testament to his bravery on the job.

Inspector George had been with the department for more than thirty years, coming to Tortola from the eastern Caribbean island of Dominica. Even though he'd spent most of his adult life on Tortola, he was still considered a "Visitor" by local folk, who labeled themselves "Belongers."

After a brief conversation with the tall, athletic inspector, Johnston pointed out the location of the woman's body, which was still hidden beneath the multicolored sheet, its edges wet from seawater.

Soon, Johnston spotted several more members of the investigative team pulling up along Drake's Highway. Roy Stoutt, the head of the Crime Management Unit, and other senior investigators in plainclothes stood out among the sea of constables in uniform. Station Sergeant Julian Harley, who had trained for crime-scene management in the United Kingdom, clutched a 35mm camera and a case full of crime-scene equipment.

The morning sun warmed the beach as the wiry commander led the team out onto the rocky shore. While slightly built, Johnston's authoritative manner left people with the impression that he was much larger than he actually was. No one uttered a word as CI George removed the sheet to reveal the woman beneath it, strands of her golden hair swaying in the gentle waters. Several of the officers gasped at the sight of the lifeless form, its eyes wide open, its face unrecognizable as a woman.

The officers collectively reached the same conclusion:

that this was no accident. The bull's eye–like marks on the woman's arms and torso were later determined to be sea urchin bites, and their location indicated that her clothing must have been hiked up before she died, possibly during a violent struggle, or in an attempted sexual attack. From the way the body was "staged"—on its back, legs touching at the ankles—police suspected that the woman had been face down at some point during the fight that ended her life and that her attacker may have moved the body after her death.

The next step was identifying the body, which Johnston and the others knew would be difficult given its condition. It appeared that an attacker had savagely ground the woman's face into the sand. The vicious assault, combined with the bloating effects of the seawater, had left her face nearly featureless. With no pocketbook, no form of identification, and no report of a missing person, Johnston knew that he had to forge ahead with the investigation and hope that he and his men would recover something that would help them crack the case.

"We've got a tricky one on our hands," Johnston told the investigators gathered at the edge of the shoreline. "Because we've got to first figure out who the hell she is, and then start to work through and figure out 'What where her movements?' and 'How did she come here?'"

At nearly quarter past ten, the men still had no idea about this woman's identity, and Johnston feared that her horrific condition would make it close to impossible to get an ID. But all that was about to change.

CHAPTER THREE

Inch by Inch

"West End Police, how can I help?"

The officer manning the phones was expecting a routine report, such as an irate farmer accusing his neighbor of stealing one of his cows or a desperate plea from a hotel manager whose patron was threatening to check out unless the rooster in the hills behind his room was quieted. Tourism was the main business on this twenty-one-mile stretch of paradise, and keeping the tourists happy was a big part of the job for the constables of the Royal Virgin Islands Police Force.

But the voice on the other end of the line was not a familiar one.

"Hello, Officer," the man began in a strained tone. "My name is Russell McMillen. Would you check and see if there have been any reports about car accidents? My daughter hasn't turned up and we're worried that she's been in an accident."

Russell McMillen and his wife, Josephine, had been awake and dressed since well before dawn, waiting for and worrying about their thirty-four-year-old daughter. It was not like her to stay out all night. They feared the worst: that she had been in a car crash and was lying in a ditch somewhere, unable to call for help.

Car accidents were the one thing the McMillens worried

about when Lois went out alone in the evening. Family holidays had been a lot less complicated when they first bought their vacation villa on Tortola in 1979. Back then, Lois was just fourteen and too young to drive. The situation changed, however, when she got her license, and began asking for the keys to the car. Her parents were aware that the roads on Tortola were treacherous. Most of the routes to the local bars and nightclubs were unlit and chock-full of precipitous curves. The Ridge Road on the island's north side, the route to Quito's Gazebo restaurant and bar, one of Lois' favorite hangouts, was particularly challenging, with no guardrails to prevent vehicles from veering off the steep cliffs and into the ocean below.

"I have the license plate number of the car right here," Russell McMillen told the officer on the other end of the phone. He had retrieved the car rental receipt from his dresser before placing the call, and he dictated all of the pertinent information to help the police in their search for Lois. "It's a Daihatsu, a four-door vehicle. It's black, and the license plate is RT 0564."

"Can you please hold on?" the officer asked. "I'll be right back to you, sir."

Mr. McMillen held the line and waited, his heart racing. The elder man was unaware that the dispatcher was radioing Johnston at the crime scene to alert him to the call. The deputy commissioner and his men were on the beach. They were about to begin their fingertip search of the area that had been cordoned off with crime-scene tape when a constable approached Johnston with the news.

"Sir." The uniformed officer interrupted the meeting. "We've just received a message from the West End police station. An American couple by the name of McMillen has just telephoned to say that their daughter has not returned home after leaving the previous night, and they are concerned about her."

Johnston grimaced. He had been on the scene for nearly an hour, having just completed an impromptu crime-scene

conference with members of the department's Criminal
Investigations Division. He and Chief Inspector George
were busy assigning officers to various teams that would
carry out different aspects of the investigation.

"Whom do you want on your team?" the wiry commander had just inquired of Jacob George, who towered
over him at more than six feet in height.

"I want Anderson Blackman under my command, sir,"
George announced, referring to the veteran sergeant in
charge of the West End police station.

Blackman was not a member of the department's Criminal Investigations Division. Still, Johnston believed that the
relationship he had forged with residents of West End made
him a logical choice for the job. Sergeant Blackman had
been contacted at his home in Road Town earlier in the day
and alerted to the discovery of the body on the beach.

A veteran detective, Blackman knew the West End area
well. But more important, he understood the people who
lived there. Tortola's West End had a special cachet, in part
because it was populated by wealthy foreigners who maintained upscale residences in the private Belmont Estates section. The West End, too, was home to several first-class
hotels and restaurants and was a popular destination for
yachters, who often dropped anchor in its picturesque harbor
at Soper's Hole. Deputy Commissioner Johnston was always
surprised by the amount of intelligence that Blackman and
his constables were able to glean from locals who lived in
the area.

"Constable, tell the McMillens that someone will be right
up to see them," Johnston said, instructing the officer who
had delivered news of the McMillens' phone call. He then
turned his attention to Anderson Blackman.

"Anderson, go up and see these people," he directed the
lanky officer with the moustache and goatee. "Get a description of the girl and, if possible, get a photograph of her. Let's
try and get an initial identification of the body.

"It may or may not be her, so be careful, Anderson, as to

how you deal with the McMillens," the commander warned
the sergeant. "You can't go in there and say, 'We've found
your daughter dead,' because we have no idea who she is."

Johnston liked Anderson Blackman, although he found
the forty-something detective somewhat restrained. He
watched as the investigator made his way along the craggy
beach toward the roadway. He remained cautiously optimistic that they might yet be able to identify the body on the
beach.

As the most senior officer present, Deputy Commissioner
Johnston's role was to instruct the investigators on the different tasks required in a criminal inquiry and to make sure
all necessary actions were being taken. Once the process
was safely under way, he would let the other senior officers
take control.

He stood by the water watching Inspector George take
charge of the crime scene. The men followed the inspector's
orders to extend the yellow police tape to include a greater
area of the shoreline.

"Everybody fall in line single file!" Inspector George
called out. "We are going to begin a fingertip search of the
scene."

The inspector and six of his constables fell into position,
preparing to use their fingertips to comb for clues. Following police protocol, Sergeant Harley, a forensics expert and
one of the most highly trained officers in the department,
took the lead. Harley had attended a number of "scenes of
crime" courses sponsored by the US Justice Department at
schools on the islands of Jamaica, Antigua, and Barbados,
learning how to search a crime scene for physical and trace
evidence, and then label, mark, preserve, and transport it for
laboratory examination.

Harley, his close-cropped hair and bristly sideburns a distinguished mix of black and gray, began by delegating various duties, which included scouring the area for clues,

taking measurements, collecting exhibits, and logging them in a record book. He chose areas on both sides of the highway and along the rocky shoreline to be searched. Next, he decided that the men would begin on the road's north side and work their way east toward where the woman's body lay on the shore, now uncovered and exposed to the midmorning sun.

Almost immediately, the officers spotted the black skid marks of a braking vehicle, along with a hubcap.

"I've found something!" Sergeant Williams' declaration sent Harley racing to his side. Along the north side of Drake's Highway, Williams had spotted a shiny brass-colored item between some rocks. It was a delicate necklace with a dainty heart-shaped pendant dangling from its chain. Not far away, on the edge of the highway, was a lady's white hair tie commonly called a "scrunchie."

Using spray paint, Sergeant Williams painted a bold green circle around each item, marking the evidence that Sergeant Harley would later document on film.

Each additional piece of evidence added to investigators' picture of what might have happened on the beach. It appeared a violent struggle had begun somewhere on the landward side of Drake's Highway, near the place the first hair tie was found. Time and time again an assailant had grabbed for the woman's long hair and clothing, and at her neck. She'd managed to break free, running across the highway toward the beach. The struggle left a trail of personal items strewn across the road: the scrunchies, a fragment of gold chain, its missing link across the road in some thicket. It was possible the woman had been trying to make it just a few hundred feet down the highway to the West End police station.

Crossing to the south side of the highway, Sergeant Williams continued his inch-by-inch examination, methodically scanning the bushes and the bluish-gray boulders that formed a sea wall. He noticed that some of the underbrush along the road shoulder was uprooted and the grass had been pulled out. He also saw what appeared to be bloodstains on some of the rocks in the sea wall.

He followed the trail of tiny red blotches toward the water, where he spotted a second brass-colored neck chain with the same design.

Not far from the necklace, on the grass, was a black hair tie similar to the white one he had already found. A few yards farther on, about ten feet from where he had first noticed the bloodstains, he discovered a can of Mace—the first true indication that the woman may have attempted to defend herself against an attacker. Close by was a woman's shoe, gold with a fancy Pierre Dumas label, no doubt a match to the left shoe that had been found near the body.

"Gentlemen, we are beginning to confirm our initial suspicions that this was not a natural death," Johnston announced to the officers in his thick Scottish brogue. "We are beginning to establish that there is some sort of flight; that a struggle has taken place; that the girl has been wounded in some sort of way because there are blood spots. The can of Mace would indicate that she had been attempting to defend herself.

"The Mace is used. She loses a shoe, then she loses the other shoe, and she is stumbling and falling as she runs down on the rocky shore," Johnston continued. He noted that the evidence found suggested she had briefly eluded her attacker, running for about seventy-five yards before she was captured. "Clearly we've got a flight sequence before the girl is done to death. It would appear that indeed this girl has met a violent end."

As the investigators continued their examination of the crime scene, word of the grisly discovery began to circulate among local residents. Beulah Romney was roused from bed by the frantic shouts of her next-door neighbor. She had been out much earlier in the morning, chauffeuring tourists in her taxi minivan, and had lain down for a quick nap.

"Girl, where are you?" It was Beulah's sister-in-law rapping on the front door. "Beulah! Come quick!"

"What is it? What's going on?" When Beulah answered the knock, her sister-in-law grabbed her hand and dragged her outside. She could not believe what she was seeing. More than a dozen police officers milling about. A sick feeling came over her.

"Haven't you heard? They found a woman's body!"

Beulah remembered the screams she had heard the previous night. Now, she felt nauseated.

CHAPTER FOUR

Where's Lois?

It was close to ten thirty when Mr. McMillen heard the constable's voice on the other end of the phone line once again.

"Sir. . . ." The constable's tone was officious.

"Yes?" Mr. McMillen responded.

"Stay right there. We'll be right over."

Ten minutes seemed an eternity as the couple waited at the kitchen table where Lois, a fledgling artist, had been working on her latest piece. It was a work in progress, a collage of odd items: a Queen of Hearts playing card, glittery cut-outs of stars and moons, and a page from the Old Testament that was torn in two. She had pasted the images onto a canvas and was in the midst of painting over them in a pattern of colorful pastels.

For more than a week, her father had watched her from his favorite wicker chair, the one with the upholstered cushions in a tropical scene. He had been spending a lot of time in that chair. Russell was in his early 80s and had recently been diagnosed with bladder cancer, and a secondary muscular disorder that was affecting his nervous system. The illness made it difficult for him to walk or stand, so he had created a comfortable place in the house to spend his days. The wicker chair was strategically placed in a corner of the living room that allowed him to enjoy spectacular views of the ocean from the room's floor-to-ceiling windows, and to view the television set that sat on a small table just across the

way. In fact, the reason Lois had made a point of spending
the holidays with her parents was that she feared this Christmas might be his last.

The McMillens' home had an open, airy feeling that was
welcoming to guests, with its multiple levels and few doors
separating the rooms. The décor was a tasteful mix of natural wicker and wood furniture, floors of terra cotta tile, and
rooms adorned with potted palms. Its white stucco walls
were hung with mirrors and the exotic artwork the McMillens had collected over the years. Scattered among them
were paintings that Lois had done.

Some of her canvases had a spiritual theme. Fanciful and
bursting with bright iridescent color, they depicted angels and
castles and clouds. Others were of a more serious nature, like
the one of a dagger piercing a woman's bare breast, addressing Lois' commitment to end violence against women.

As Russell McMillen sat waiting for the police to arrive, the
painting that Lois had been working on caught his attention.
He thought back to how he had marveled at the way she
moved around the canvas, eyeing it carefully before dabbing
a speck of paint here, or a swirl of the brush there. He
admired her concentration, and noted her ability to remain
focused on the art project, appreciating how unusual it was
for his daughter to persevere.

The McMillens started at the sound of Anderson Blackman rapping on the front door.

"Come in." Josephine McMillen sprang from the kitchen
chair to show the tall investigator into the villa. The detective was attired in shirtsleeves and slacks and accompanied
by two uniformed constables.

"I'm Station Sergeant Anderson Blackman." The slender
officer with the moustache and goatee extended his hand to
the auburn-haired woman who had answered his knock. He
introduced the two uniformed officers who accompanied
him, Constable Rhymer and another officer from the West
End substation.

"Yes, hello." The refined, well-dressed American smiled nervously. "I'm Jo McMillen." Even as she worried for her daughter's safety, Lois' mother remained composed and gracious. A woman of great reserve, she found it difficult to reveal the anxiety she was feeling over her daughter's failure to return home.

"We have some good news and some bad news." Blackman's tone remained steady as he blurted out the facts. "There's been a problem on the Drake's Highway. We've found a body of a woman out in the water . . . who's dead."

The officer's words hit the couple like a slap. If this woman was Lois, they reasoned, then there could be no good news.

"Would you describe your daughter to us?" the officer went on, seemingly oblivious to their shock. Despite his orders, his own discomfort with the situation prevented him from presenting the news as smoothly as he could have. "Can you tell us, what was she wearing when she went out last night? What clothing she had on?"

"I don't know," Lois' eighty-two-year-old father responded in a shaky voice. "I went to bed before she went out."

Blackman nodded at the tall, slightly stooped man with the graying hair and piercing green eyes, and then turned to Mrs. McMillen. "Do you remember if she was wearing gold-colored shoes?"

"How smashed up was the car?" Mr. McMillen interrupted. He assumed that there had been a horrific car crash and that his daughter had died as a result.

"It wasn't smashed up at all."

Mr. McMillen's eyes widened. He looked at the officer in astonishment, as he tried to comprehend what he was hearing. "Not smashed up at all?" His tone was a mixture of surprise and horror as he wondered, How could that be? If what the sergeant is saying is true, if it was Lois' body that they'd discovered along Drake's Highway, then how could it be possible that her car was undamaged?

"Sir," Blackman repeated, "do you know if your daughter was wearing gold shoes when she went out last night?"

"I don't know," Mr. McMillen answered, barely able to focus on the question. "I don't know." Slowly it was beginning to dawn on him that his assumption that there had been a car accident was wrong.

"Can you tell us where your daughter was going when she left the house last night?"

Everything was blurry. Mr. McMillen could make no sense out of what the sergeant was asking of him. The last thing he could remember about his beautiful daughter was her standing over the kitchen table stroking a paintbrush on the broad canvas that was now propped on the wall just beside where he was standing.

"Sir?" the investigator prodded. "Can you . . ."

Josephine McMillen jumped in. "She was going to the Jolly Roger to listen to some music," the seventy-five-year-old woman began.

Mrs. McMillen never worried about Lois' safety at the Jolly Roger Inn. The rambling two-story establishment, painted in the bright hues of the Caribbean, was owned by Louis Schwartz, one of their neighbors from the Belmont Estates complex. Schwartz had relocated to Tortola from Long Island, New York, after several extended vacations to the island. A successful restaurateur, he was tired of the hustle and bustle of New York life and was ready to make a change. He opened a small restaurant in a ramshackle building at the end of Drake's Highway once inhabited by modern-day pirates. The McMillens and many of their neighbors from the Belmont Estates area were regular patrons of the popular turquoise-and-white eatery that was topped by a pirate's flag, a white skull and crossbones on a threatening black backdrop. The restaurant drew an eclectic mix of well-heeled homeowners, a variety of locals, and tourists of all ages. It was the kind of place where young children dining with their parents could jump up and dance along to the local bands that performed there on Friday and Saturday nights.

"A blues band was playing there, and Lois knew one of the performers," Mrs. McMillen told Blackman. "Lois said that she wanted to get out for a few hours, because it was

Friday night, you see. She didn't want to stay at home with her parents on a Friday night.

"She said she wanted to find someone to go sailing with, someone other than her mother," she quipped. "Lois loves to sail."

Mrs. McMillen remained poised as she related the details of the excursion that she and Lois had made to St. John the previous day to shop at the boutiques and enjoy the sights. She told the officers that they had caught an early morning ferry to the fashionable United States Virgin Island, once home to industrialist and philanthropist John D. Rockefeller. Lois was in good spirits when the two women departed Tortola that morning.

"We took the late ferry back," she explained. "We got into West End about six ten. Russ picked us up and we went back to the villa. I fixed a light supper for the three of us. It was about eight o'clock.

"After supper my husband and I went upstairs and left Lois doing the dishes. She left home at about nine thirty. She took the car."

"Ma'am, can you tell us who your daughter has associated with since arriving on the island?" Blackman asked.

Mrs. McMillen explained that her daughter had been sick with the flu for much of their vacation and had barely left home. The only people Lois had seen, as far as she knew, were the boys staying at another vacation villa called Zebra House, just up the hill. She had run into her neighbor, Michael Spicer, and his friends at a bar called Bomba's Surfside Shack on Wednesday evening, two nights before, and had given them a ride home. She explained that Michael and his mother rarely rented a car when they visited the island. They usually called for a taxi when they wanted to go out. She said that Michael had then called the villa on Thursday at around four o'clock to speak to Lois. He'd invited her up to Zebra House for a cocktail and a swim in the pool.

But Lois had declined. She explained that her father was not feeling well, and that she was going to take him to the beach at Smuggler's Cove, a secluded stretch of soft white sand reached by a rough dirt road through Belmont Estates, to swim and relax in the shade beneath the palm trees. She did say that she would try to stop over at Zebra House when she returned.

When Michael phoned back an hour later, it was Mrs. McMillen who answered the call. She explained that Lois had not yet returned home. She told the officers she was pleased when Michael apologized for keeping her daughter out so late the previous evening, and was happy to hear him promise to have her home early if she joined them again that night.

"Can you tell Lois that since it's already late, we'll go to Pusser's instead?" Mrs. McMillen recalled Michael's request. He wanted Lois to pick them up at Zebra House late Thursday afternoon and drive everybody to the restaurant at Soper's Hole.

"That sounds fine. I'll tell her," Mrs. McMillen said before hanging up.

Lois' mother then explained that Lois picked up the men at Zebra House sometime after five thirty. She drove them to Pusser's Landing at Soper's Hole wharf, where one of Michael's guests, a man named William Labrador, treated everyone to a bottle of wine and a platter of chicken wings.

"She asked me, 'Mother, do you think it's okay to let William Labrador pay for my meal?'" The well-spoken woman recalled the conversation she had with her daughter as they had crossed the channel on their way to St. John. "She said that he'd charged it to his credit card. I told her, 'Yes, I think it's okay. After all, you're the one doing all the driving.'"

Blackman listened attentively, noting bits of the information on a small pad that he carried in his back pocket. "Ma'am, can you describe your daughter to us?"

"My daughter is about five-foot-five, slender." The woman was articulate and spoke in deliberate tones. "She weighs about one hundred and twenty to one hundred and twenty-five pounds."

"Do you have a photograph of her?" Blackman was

following Johnston's orders. While it seemed likely that the woman on the beach was Lois McMillen, it was necessary to the investigation that they make absolutely certain.

The inspector and the two uniformed officers waited in the foyer as Mrs. McMillen disappeared up a short flight of steps and then returned with a photograph. He noted that the woman's delicate, manicured fingers were trembling as she handed the color picture of Lois to him.

A terrible sense of dread came over Blackman the moment he glanced at the snapshot. He recognized her immediately. She had been the woman who sat next to him on the plane ride to a neighboring island several months before. He recalled that he had enjoyed chatting with the bubbly blond during the short flight, and remembered her excitement at the prospect of helping to crew a friend's sailboat in a popular Caribbean regatta. The gorgeous woman smiling at him from the picture bore no resemblance to the bloated, distorted victim he had seen on the beach. He needed something more conclusive. Russell McMillen had already said that he had not seen his daughter before she departed for the Jolly Roger. Perhaps her mother had.

Blackman was careful not to react as he asked, "Mrs. McMillen, can you tell us what your daughter was wearing when she left the house last night?"

"When she went out last evening, she had on white three-quarter-length pants and a white blouse with swirls of color on the front. It was a Versace blouse. We bought it yesterday at a boutique on St. John." The woman paused, and then nervously smiled at the investigator before continuing the description. "She was wearing a pair of clear plastic shoes with a little gold on the heel. And she was wearing a delicate heart necklace that her father had given her for Christmas. . . ."

Sergeant Blackman struggled to keep from responding. He wasn't yet ready to reveal the fact that the items of clothing that Mrs. McMillen was listing fit the exact description of those recovered at the crime scene.

CHAPTER FIVE

Identifying Lois

Deputy Commissioner John Johnston was relieved when he spotted the local doctor from Peebles Hospital in Road Town pulling up in her car, and waited as she made her way out onto the beach. Accompanying her past the crime-scene tape, he looked on as Dr. Nandale Ramvaki knelt down beside the body and felt for a pulse.

This would be the second time in three months that the doctor had been called to the island's south shore to work a case with Johnston and his investigators. In November, a promising local athlete named Jason Bally had been gunned down as he stood talking on a pay phone outside of a gas station along Drake's Highway. The after-dark murder had occurred less than two miles from their present location, in an area called Sea Cow Bay. Police suspected that the thieves who had just burglarized the gas station had killed him, fearing that Bally was calling cops to alert them to the heist. But a police investigation turned up no suspects and the crime remained unsolved.

Now, just 15 days into the New Year, Johnston feared that he and his men were confronting what was beginning to look like another homicide.

In 1999, there had been three murders in the BVI; two had been solved, but the Bally case remained open. Previously, there had not been a murder since 1996, when there had been two—both of which had been solved.

The BVI had also seen a spike in violent crimes, especially armed robberies, since October. The islands' police commissioner, Vernon Malone, attributed the upswing to drug trafficking. Malone believed that a close-knit gang was operating in the BVI. He feared that catching the crooks was going to be a continuing challenge because members of the community were, either knowingly or unwittingly, providing alibis or helping them to hide weapons.

It was nearly eleven thirty a.m. when Dr. Ramvaki made her pronouncement on the beach.

"She's dead." The doctor's declaration came as no surprise to Johnston or the other officials on the scene, yet it gave them the green light to move in closer to the body—albeit not to touch it—and begin their investigation.

Up until this point, the police had been working under the assumption that this woman had drowned, as the first officer to take the report had said. And the doctor's determination that "life was extinct" did not put them any closer to determining the cause of death. Ramvaki was not a pathologist, and it was not her job to make that determination. For the moment, it was the role of the officers on the scene to figure out how this young woman had died, and whether her death was accidental or the result of foul play—as many already suspected.

At Johnston's request, Dr. Ramvaki stayed on the scene for several minutes. In a small notepad, she jotted down her observations, commenting on the bruising on the woman's arms, neck, and face, and the presence of blood around the ears. She also recorded that all of the signs she would associate with drowning were present.

A warm breeze tousled the curls of Julian Harley's graying hair as he moved within inches of the lifeless figure to capture its condition on film. Raising the 35mm camera to his eye, the forensics expert focused his lens on the bluish spots that marked the woman's arms, and then snapped the first of a number of photos. Next, he focused on her stomach, and listened to the click of the shutter as he recorded the dark-colored bruises that marred her abdomen. He also

documented the elegant gold ring with the three white stones
she wore on her left middle finger, and the tiny cuts on both
of her hands. The cuts appeared to be classic defense
wounds—evidence that she may have been trying to ward
off an attacker.

It was nearing noontime when Phillip Davis of the Davis
Funeral Home arrived with one of his employees to begin
the grim task of removing the woman's body from the
beach. Her identity was still a mystery to the investigators
on the scene, who had been hoping to find a purse or at least
a wallet during their inch-by-inch sweep of the scene.

Inspector George watched as the funeral director, assisted
by several police officers, placed the woman's remains in a
body bag and then loaded it into the hearse. He would take it
to his place of business in the center of Road Town, where the
McMillens would soon be arriving to determine if this lifeless
woman found on the beach was in fact their precious Lois.

"You'll have to come and see if it's your daughter." Sergeant
Anderson Blackman stunned Russell and Josephine McMillen
when he suddenly announced that he wanted them to go to
the morgue in Road Town to examine the body of the white
woman he now suspected was Lois. His manner greatly
upset Lois' father, who was still struggling to comprehend
what might have happened to his daughter.

Reeling from Blackman's remarks, the McMillens fought
to compose themselves, before getting on the telephone to call
neighbors and see if there was someone available who could
drive them to the funeral home. They did not have a car; Lois
had taken their rental when she went out the previous evening.
Within minutes, several friends appeared at the front door.

Motioning toward the foyer of the couple's spacious,
well-appointed vacation villa, Blackman announced that he
intended to pay their neighbor Michael Spicer a visit.

"Don't bother," Mr. McMillen advised him. "I've already
phoned him several times this morning, and there's no one at
home."

Lois and Michael had known each other for more than a decade; their parents' villas were just a few doors apart in the secluded Belmont Estates section. Their friendship was casual, and they only saw each other when they both happened to be vacationing on the island. Lois would sometimes go up to Zebra House for a swim in the Spicer family's pool, or go out for a meal with Michael at a local pub.

Even though he had been up since before 6 a.m., Mr. McMillen's first call to Zebra House was at 8:30 that morning. Russell McMillen was always a gentleman, and it would have been improper to call any earlier—no matter how worried he was about his daughter. He was hoping that Michael had run into Lois at one of the local hangouts. He thought if maybe he could tell the police where she was last seen, they would have an easier time finding her. He told Blackman and the other officers that he had hung up when the answering machine picked up, and then waited about fifteen minutes before trying the number again. He decided to telephone the police station when his third call was greeted by a recorded voice.

The sergeant nodded in acknowledgment, then stood on the pavement outside the charming Mediterranean-style villa, which boasted an authentic red-tile roof and was planted with leafy green shrubs and shaded by lofty palms. Blackman watched as the elderly couple climbed into the back seat of their neighbor's car, and then remained on the cement driveway until the vehicle disappeared down the steep hill.

Clutching the photograph of Lois McMillen, he reached inside his Montero for the police radio.

"This is Blackman. Get me the West End." The dispatcher immediately patched the radio transmission to the crime-scene location.

"Is it her?" Johnston yelled out to the officer working the radio.

"He thinks it's her," the officer shouted back at the commander. "But he says that she had a car, a rental Jeep, license number RT 0564."

Johnston strode to the roadway and immediately assembled the traffic officers who were tending to the lengthy tie-
ups the road closure was creating. "Listen up," he cracked,
and then paused to make eye contact with each officer standing at attention before him. "I want you to search every road
in Tortola, from west to east, until you find this Jeep."

The thirty-minute ride to Road Town seemed surreal to
Russell and Josephine McMillen. The couple sat in the back
seat of their neighbor's car, and watched out the window as
views of Peter Island and Salt Island shifted to flashes of
Virgin Gorda, an exclusive stretch of tropical heaven just
across the Sir Francis Drake Channel. The island of Virgin
Gorda was a favorite destination of yachters who anchored
in its protected harbors, and of wealthy vacationers drawn to
its understated Little Dix Bay resort, where, for $1,000 a
night, they could enjoy a beachfront bungalow with all the
amenities. The elegant resort was founded by Laurence
Rockefeller in the late 1970s and marked the beginning of
upscale tourism to the second largest of the British Virgin
Islands.

Several of the McMillens' neighbors followed behind the
couple in separate vehicles. They were anxious to provide
moral support to their longtime friends. It seemed that
everybody in the private cluster of vacation houses had been
alerted to Lois' disappearance early in the day, and throughout the morning they had phoned the McMillens at Belmont
Grove Villa No. 4 to offer their help.

Missing was a call from Michael Spicer.

Sergeant Blackman had learned a bit about Lois' longtime
friend during the interview he had just conducted with the
McMillens at their villa. Trying to establish their daughter's
movements since her arrival on Tortola, he had been told that
she had been in the company of Spicer and his friends several times over the past week. He decided that he would begin
his investigation by speaking to them. He took a quick look
around the perimeter of the McMillens' villa and gestured to

Constables Jocelyn Rhymer and Dennis Jones to jump into the Montero for the short drive on the private road and then up the extremely precipitous driveway to Zebra House. The approach included two switchbacks that forced Blackman to turn the wheel sharply to navigate the bends.

Zebra House literally clung to a hillside. The location of the front door was not obvious at first. Most visitors gained entrance to the property by a small flight of steps that led to a stone-and-tile patio with spectacular views of the waters below Belmont Estates and the rocky silhouettes of several small islands in the distance. The most outstanding feature of the expansive terrace area, which was planted with bougainvillea bushes and dotted by patio furniture and mini-palms in ceramic planters, was the rectangular swimming pool that separated the two buildings of the residence, the home's main quarters and a guest cottage.

"Yes, can I help you?"*

Blackman recalled that it was Michael Spicer who answered their call. "Good morning, sir," the investigator began in measured tones. "I am a police officer in plain clothes. This is Constable Rhymer, and this is Constable Jones."

Blackman was surprised to find the gentleman at home— especially since Mr. McMillen had just told him that his repeated phone calls to the hilltop residence earlier in the day had gone unanswered. "Mr. Spicer," the investigator contin- ued, "can you tell us when you last saw Lois McMillen?"

"Yes," the American man with the pale blue eyes and dark chiseled features responded at once. "It was last Thursday around eleven at night when she dropped my houseguest Evan and myself off here."

"Sir, the body of a female has been found along the shoreline at the West End area. It appears the woman is dead . . . and it is possible that the body is that of Lois McMillen."

*The following account of the investigators' visit to Zebra House is written based on the signed deposition of Inspector Blackman.

Michael's eyes widened. "How did she die?" His tone was one of surprise.

"I don't know." Blackman paused. "That is what we're trying to find out."

The investigator and the two uniformed constables waited on the terrace. They watched the courtly American disappear into the main house through a large sliding glass door and then return with a much younger gentleman he identified as Evan George. Blackman listened intently as the amiable man with the aristocratic air informed his sandy-haired friend what he had just been told. He noted that Evan, too, reacted with surprise.

A warm, steady breeze created ripples across the water in the turquoise pool as Blackman and the two uniformed officers lingered on the patio waiting to speak to a third man who was staying in the boxy tan-and-brown guest house adjacent to the pool. A veteran of the police department for more than ten years, the sergeant instinctively carried out what had been ingrained in him since joining the force. In a casual manner, his eyes studied the deck area around the pool, which was tastefully finished in tan ceramic tiles and ornamented with palms in expensive-looking basket-weave pots. His attention was immediately drawn to several pairs of wet and sandy sneakers that were lined up near the south side of the pool.

An unsettling feeling overcame him as he waited with the two men for the other houseguest to join them on the patio. He had felt a similar reaction before. In fact, he had experienced it many times during his career as a law enforcement officer. It was an intuitive feeling, an unexplainable perception that was telling him to raise his antennae and pay close attention.

He watched carefully as the new arrival, an olive-skinned gentleman with thick, bushy eyebrows, appeared on the veranda. The man, who identified himself as William Labrador, was advised of the possibility that the dead body of a woman police had found on the beach that morning might be that of Lois McMillen. The sergeant observed that the fellow immediately raised his hand to his mouth in what seemed a moment of shock.

"The police will be in contact with you again later today." Blackman nodded to Spicer, and then turned to leave. His two officers followed closely behind. As he walked back to his vehicle, a policeman's hunch was telling him that something was not right.

There was something about the attitude of the men from Zebra House that troubled Blackman, though he couldn't put a finger on anything specific.

Meanwhile in Road Town, Sergeant Duncan Williams was waiting at the entrance to the Davis Funeral Home, a family-owned business tucked away on a narrow side street. He was there to meet the car carrying Josephine and Russell McMillen. They had been instructed by Blackman to report to the small, sparsely equipped funeral parlor in Road Town to confirm that the body that had been found on the beach was that of their daughter Lois. There was no police mortuary on the island, only the privately run funeral home of Mr. Davis, which was behind the busy local supermarket in the center of town.

Sergeant Williams had been charged with accompanying the dead body to the mortuary. He knew the task that lay before the American couple was one that all parents dreaded. How does one come to terms with burying one's own child? he wondered to himself.

As he waited in the small parking area in back of the Rite-way supermarket, Williams took in the pleasant aroma of fresh bread wafting from the *boulangerie* just up the road, and watched as the community went about its day. It was a Saturday, which meant that most of the offices in town were closed. Many of the meandering streets were bustling with sightseers in vividly colored attire. They had wandered onto the lively back street after browsing the handful of boutiques and outdoor T-shirt stands that lined the main drag along the water. Mixed in with the tourists were local islanders out to do their grocery shopping, and of course, the packs of wild chickens that roamed freely about the town. The style of dress on Tortola is traditionally English, with women in knee-length skirts and dresses and men in lightweight slacks and shirtsleeves. It would be rare to see a townsperson in shorts or a tank top.

The uniformed sergeant tipped his hat when the McMillens nervously walked past him, then up the steps and into the funeral parlor. He waited in the small entrance foyer, which was furnished in wood and wicker, as the couple spoke in hushed tones. They were accompanied by a small group of American friends they knew from Belmont Estates.

Mr. Davis and several officers had a brief conversation with the couple, and explained what lay ahead. Officers were not surprised when Russell McMillen announced that he would make the identification alone, without his wife. When Jo McMillen first started down the hall on her husband's arm, she seemed fine, but when she entered the room and glimpsed the outline of the human figure beneath a sheet on the cold slab of cement, she stopped abruptly. In a gentle voice, she announced that she could not handle viewing her only child in the "broken" state that police had described to them.

Lois' mother went to wait with friends, and watched as Russell, gripping the brass handle of a wooden cane for balance, slowly disappeared into the cramped room where the woman whom police had found on the beach lay covered.

Swallowing hard, the elder McMillen made his pronouncement. "Okay, I'm ready."

As the funeral worker pulled back the cloth, the gray-haired McMillen involuntarily recoiled in horror. He could feel his body trembling as he looked down at this person he barely recognized. He noted the flesh on her face was all but gone. What remained was barely a human being. This could not be the beautiful woman who had accompanied him to the beach just days before.

He wanted to reach out and stroke strands of her silky yellow hair, to tell her it would be all right. But he was immobilized, unable even to raise a finger.

"Yes, it's Lois." His voice cracked as he affirmed his daughter's identity for Sergeant Williams.

The policeman did not utter a word. Like him, most of the officers on the force had families and children of their own. He could feel a lump welling up in his throat, and he fought to hide his own devastation as he watched the grown man standing before him suddenly break down sobbing over the body of his child.

CHAPTER SIX

Rounding Up the Suspects

Upon returning to the crime scene, Sergeant Blackman sought out Deputy Commissioner John Johnston. He was feeling uneasy about his visit with the three men at Zebra House, and wanted to discuss his findings.

"Something's not right here," Blackman mumbled, as was his habit. "These guys are not right."

"What makes you think that?"

"Because the McMillens said that for the last three or four days, their daughter has been going out with these four guys so that she had company, so that she wasn't going out on her own."

Johnston listened intently as the sergeant spelled out his concerns. What troubled Blackman at first was that Spicer and his guests at Zebra House had failed to answer the phone that morning as Mr. McMillen called time and again in his search for Lois. He couldn't understand why they hadn't picked up when they were all at the house. In addition, Blackman told the commander while the men seemed surprised at the news, their reactions did not seem sincere. He was troubled by what he described to Johnston as the men's eagerness to accept, as fact, that the yet-unidentified woman police had found along Drake's Highway was their Belmont neighbor, Lois McMillen. It was as if they already knew that Lois was dead, Blackman reported.

It was clear to Johnston that the detective's conversation

with the men at Zebra House raised suspicion about their possible involvement in the case.

"Follow it up, Anderson!" The commander thought back to his own days as a detective. He recognized Blackman's reaction as one that he had had himself numerous times in the past. It was a gut reaction for a detective who is observing people and listening to what they are saying. He remembered what it was like, picking up on those subtle cues that you cannot really explain scientifically or otherwise. You just know that the person in front of you either knows more about what they are saying, or else they are telling you lies, when the facts just don't add up. It was sort of a sense that officers gain from their experience dealing with people, with interviewing them time and again. It's the feeling that telegraphs, "These guys know more about this than they're telling."

It was 12:05 p.m. when Johnston received word that the rental vehicle Lois McMillen had been driving had been found about three miles west of their present location on Drake's Highway.

"I'm at the West End ferry dock, and I've located a black, four-door Daihatsu SUV, registration number R-T-0-5-6-4," Constable Kendolph Bobb radioed to West End units. "It's parked on the seaward side, facing Frenchman's Cay."

"Mr. Harley!" Johnston yelled to the forensics expert kneeling by the roadside. "We've located the vehicle."

Sergeant Harley still had several more tasks to complete before he could leave the crime scene. He and several of his team members were on the roadway near the spot where investigators believed that a struggle had taken place.

Reaching inside his tote, the seasoned forensics expert pulled out an evidence-collection kit and carefully unwrapped the paper coating of the sterile swabs he would use to scrape samples of the reddish-brown substance that had been found on the rocks. Next, he collected several soil samples from both sides of the road, and some specimens of the sand from close to where the body was found. Marking the location was a bright green ring that Sergeant Williams had spray-painted. His final task was to snap a photograph of the rocky shoreline.

Nearby, Anderson Blackman was conferencing with Chief Inspector George. Temperatures had risen into the eighties, and a light breeze was cooling the beach as the sergeant related the details of his visit to Zebra House.

Inspector George had been back on the job for just fourteen months—having returned to active duty after almost two years of intense rehabilitation for a gunshot wound that nearly took his life. Yet, in his new position as head of the Criminal Investigations Division, police protocol dictated that Deputy Commissioner Johnston turn the case over to him and remain in the background to play a more supervisory role in the investigation. Johnston had learned much about George's undercover drug investigation—and the shoot-out that nearly ended his life—soon after his arrival on Tortola. As part of his duties, Johnston had become involved in the investigation of a number of Colombian drug runners known as the "Island Boys," who had set up shop on Tortola and were using the island as a transit point to deliver cocaine to the United States.

The gang's presence on the island could be traced back to 1995. The police had first heard about their activities in 1991, four years before they surfaced on Tortola. They had learned that the Colombian drug lords had recruited a group of West Indians to transport kilos of the white powder from Colombia through the Eastern Caribbean and into the United States via the US Virgin Islands and Puerto Rico. By 1995, they had set up a highly sophisticated operation on Tortola. Investigators from the British Virgin Islands police's intelligence unit managed to infiltrate the organization.

One night in July of 1996, the undercover police received word that a large shipment of cocaine was to move through Road Town en route to the US Virgin Islands. George was placed in charge of a ten-man team that was to set up a road check to intercept it. Members of his unit successfully stopped the vehicle carrying the drugs, but were unprepared for what followed. A spray of gunfire pierced the air as the drug runners attempted to flee, leaving behind 1200 kilos of cocaine, a cache of sophisticated weaponry, satellite telephones, and radio scanners. The cocaine carried an estimated street value of forty-four million dollars. Its destination was a town in Georgia, and it would be the last of more than thirty drug runs of similar size and street value that had been routed through the islands.

During the melee, Inspector George was struck in the head by one of the men's bullets. His comrades didn't know if he would live or die as medical personnel ordered that he be airlifted to Puerto Rico for treatment. Doctors and surgeons there were able to save his life, but not his left eye. George's recovery was miraculous, and his bravery was rewarded with his elevation to a higher post in the department. Yet, upon his return to duty in 1998, he refused to carry a firearm, and continued to police the islands without a gun.

After a brief conversation with Blackman, Inspector George instructed him to join the corps of officers now waiting in police vehicles along the edge of the highway. It was twelve thirty p.m. when the team navigated the steep driveway to Zebra House.

The subjects of their inquiry—Michael Spicer, Evan George, and William Labrador—had been sitting on furnishings in the sun-drenched living room since Sergeant Blackman's visit more than one hour earlier. Alex Benedetto, another guest at Zebra House, was not at home when the investigator came calling. Michael and his friends assumed that he had gone out for a walk, or to the beach for an early morning swim. Michael reported that he, Evan, and William were "in shock" at news that Lois' body had been found on the beach.

"Do you think we should call the McMillens?" Spicer later reported that he had inquired of his two houseguests.

William Labrador, a muscular, dark-haired, thirty-six-year-old man from Southampton, Long Island, was seated on one of the room's upholstered wicker sofas. Like the rest of the house, the cushions in the living area of the modest two-bedroom ranch were sewn in a zebra motif. On the stark white walls of the spacious salon were a number of drawings of the black-and-white-striped animals.

Michael's mother was absolutely mad about zebras and

she celebrated her love of the animal by incorporating it into the décor throughout the comfortable vacation residence. From the bedding in the master suite to the glassware in the small, ceramic-tiled kitchen, zebras dominated the surroundings. Ernesteene "Teena" Spicer had even found animal-print dishtowels on one of the many jaunts that she and her lawyer husband had taken. The couple had traveled extensively, visiting exotic destinations on every continent. Some could argue that the zebra motif was overdone. Mrs. Spicer even had switch plates in the animal pattern covering every light switch in the house.

No matter what the décor, William Labrador loved staying with Michael at the rambling hillside house—in part because he did not have to pay a cent for his lodging. Money was always an issue with William. Growing up in the fashionable Hamptons, Long Island's summer playground of the rich and famous, William tended to surround himself with people who were wealthy and belonged to all the right clubs. He had long aspired to be rich himself, but as he celebrated his thirty-seventh birthday, his bank account still did not match his dreams or his lifestyle.

Yet he was convinced that his latest business venture would improve his portfolio. He and his boyhood friend, Alexander "Alex" Benedetto, had just launched a model management agency called Bella Management, and were operating on a $600,000 start-up loan that Alex's father had extended them. Their plan for the new company was to represent A-list actresses and models for print and runway work.

Alex, the handsome, fair-haired son of a wealthy New York book publisher, was impressed with William's past job as a handler at Men Women Model Management in downtown Manhattan. His duties had included managing the day-to-day affairs of several of the agencies' hottest talents, and he was responsible for everything from booking the women's photo shoots to accompanying them to trendy nightclubs and parties. Among the rising stars the agency claimed to have discovered was the model Kate Moss.

Alex loved to listen to William's stories, and desperately

wanted to be part of his circle. The glamorous world of modeling was not unfamiliar to the publishing heir. His mother, Karin, was born to a prominent family in Düsseldorf, Germany, and had enjoyed a successful career as a model in the 1960s, represented by New York's famous Ford agency. The shapely beauty was also a champion tennis player. Alex shared her milky complexion and natural golden hair. Yet his father's Italian roots were apparent in his chiseled Roman nose and strong chin.

Alex and William had all but lost touch since their teenage summers at the elite Southampton Bath and Tennis Club on Gin Lane where they first met. The exclusive members-only facility was on the ocean, in the heart of Southampton's estate section. Membership included amenities such as cabanas and lockers, an oceanfront restaurant, tennis lessons, club tournaments and a day camp for children.

Many of its members were residents of Manhattan who kept summer houses in the Hamptons, as was the case with Alex's family. The Benedettos owned a lovely residence in the quiet enclave of Water Mill, where celebrities including *Today* show co-anchor Katy Couric have homes.

Back then, Alex did not consider himself a friend of William Labrador, who was two years his senior and was labeled a tough guy by the other kids at the beach club. At fourteen years old in 1978, Alex found himself more an adversary than an admirer of the older boy whom he considered a bully. He did not like that the brawny teen targeted children who were younger and weaker, and found William's mean-spirited teasing a turn-off. Yet there was something magnetic about the way he carried himself. William had an air of arrogance and self-confidence that commanded attention.

In many ways, William did not fit in with the summer crowd at the fashionable beach club. The powerful, dark-haired youth was a "townie" who had moved with his mother and sisters to the chic East End town of Southampton while still a youth.

William Labrador, Sr., was Filipino, and already had five children from his first marriage when he met Barbara in San

Francisco. Their marriage was brief, and ended when William was in grade school. Tall and athletic, William shared his father's East Asian features. After William's parents divorced, his mother had to raise him and his two sisters, Barbara Jean and Lara, almost exclusively on her own.

Barbara Labrador worked hard to provide her three children with a good life. Intelligent and outspoken, the sturdy bottle-blond did everything from cleaning people's homes to answering phones for a local lawyer to stay on top of the bills. Her appointment to the town's zoning board of appeals in October 1979 gave the family clout and position in the close-knit community. Barbara Labrador became one of five people charged with ruling on requests from property owners to build everything from swimming pools and tennis courts to additions on houses worth millions of dollars.

When Alex ran into William Labrador on Long Island in 1992, he was astonished to learn of the glamorous lifestyle that his childhood acquaintance was leading. Alex had just returned to Manhattan from San Diego, California, and was enrolled in classes at the downtown campus of New York University. He was surprised to run into William at an ocean beach in Southampton one summer weekend. The two rekindled their friendship at the beach and during an evening out at Nell's, the trendy Upper East Side nightclub to which they had gone to for some fun. It was not unusual to see such famous faces as Barbra Streisand, Woody Allen, and even former President Bill Clinton at the 85th Street haunt.

Alex noted that his old summer chum was impeccably dressed and in the company of several beautiful young women whose modeling careers he managed. What began as a rekindled friendship quickly blossomed into a business partnership. After accompanying his friend to the posh parties attended by New York's hip and trendy, Alex began to dream of a career in this exciting field.

In 1996, he joined his father's company, Camex, a small book and music publishing house in lower Manhattan. The business was quite successful, and owned the rights to some popular music. But for twenty-seven-year-old Alex, the job of editor did not have the same cachet as his friend's work. He loved being in the company of the gorgeous front-page head-turners, and jumped when William suggested they start their own company.

Alex was convinced that his friend's contacts in the industry would catapult their new firm, Bella Management, into the limelight and give them entrée to the exclusive galas that most people could only read about in the gossip section of the *New York Post*, called Page Six.

When they started the company in late 1997, it was decided that Alex would play a minor role in the business, while William would be designated president. They set up a desk in the Fifth Avenue office suite from which Alex's father ran his publishing company. There, William had access to a phone and fax machine, and did not have to worry about steep Manhattan rent.

The small boutique firm struggled for the first two years, with William amassing a large amount of debt. By the end of 1999, Alex reported that it was starting to generate some revenue, but not enough to allow the two men to enjoy a first-rate vacation. In an effort to save money, they decided to forgo their usual winter jaunt to the ultra-deluxe French West Indian isle of St. Bart's and enjoy a more frugal Caribbean holiday on balmy Tortola.

At first, Alex was not comfortable with the idea of spending his entire vacation on the small, mountainous island. He had been there before, and recalled that he did not feel comfortable or welcome. He and William had visited Tortola together in January of 1997 and had stayed at the Jolly Roger Inn, which has four rooms to let above its restaurant. They used the island as a stopping ground—a place to get a base tan and shed a few pounds before heading to the glitzy French Isle of St. Barts.

Alex said he found the quiet island of Tortola boring, and hoped that he and William would again continue on to St. Bart's for their Millennium holiday. He longed to celebrate on the ritzy French isle where the two men, along with Michael Spicer, had enjoyed a wonderful vacation in late

January of 1997. There, they had splurged on champagne, indulged in fine food, and partied until dawn at wild, trendy nightclubs. Even their accommodation was spectacular. They had stayed at the chic Carl Gustaf, a small, upscale hotel overlooking the main part of town that boasted breath-taking views of the charming harbor of Gustavia. Life on Tortola was more low-key, and contrasted sharply with the international party scene on St. Bart's that Alex so adored. Alex complained that the sleepy British Territory did not have the same cachet as the bustling French isle where high-fashion boutiques, elegant perfumeries, and expensive eateries line the capital's narrow sidewalks. Alex later recalled that William reminded him of their financial situation, urging him to consider the amount of money they would be saving by staying with Michael at his mother's hillside Tortola dwelling.

The plan was to meet Michael at the ferry dock when he arrived on the third of January. Since they did not want to miss the wild Millennium celebration at Foxy's Bar on the nearby island of Jost Van Dyke, they arranged to depart New York on the morning of December 30. The popular ocean-side hotspot drew locals from neighboring islands, as well as boatsmen, yachters, and jet-setters anxious to sample the beachside barbecue fare and dance till dawn to the sounds of live Caribbean bands. Alex and William were among the barefoot revelers at Foxy's who welcomed in the year 2000 with a raucous all-night party and fireworks extravaganza. They had called ahead to reserve rooms at the Jolly Roger Inn in Tortola's West End. As they had done in the past, they spent three nights in the cramped, second-floor accommodations, and then moved their belongings to the Spicers' vacation house, where they enjoyed the remainder of their tropical holiday.

Their first days at Zebra House were delightful. William was given a one-bedroom cottage adjacent to the pool that had its own bathroom and kitchenette. Alex took the master bedroom in the main house. There was even talk of a jaunt to St. Bart's. That all changed when Michael announced that he

had invited a new friend to join them at Zebra House. Both
William and Alex received the news with disappointment. In
the past, it had been just the three of them on their tropical
vacations. But this holiday would be different.

When Michael learned that his mother was ill and would
not be flying with him to Tortola, he opted to invite his
twenty-two-year-old friend, Evan George, to join the group.
Michael met Evan in 1997 while visiting San Francisco on
business. Evan was employed as a house cleaner by Michael's
old friend Justin Cohen.

When Michael announced that he would return to the
East Coast, he invited Evan to join him. A benefactor of a
trust fund set up by his affluent lawyer father, Michael could
easily afford to keep the well-toned young man with the
strong chin and deep-set brown eyes in a comfortable studio
apartment in Washington, DC. The single-room residence
where Evan lived was located in an upscale area near
Georgetown, in the same building where Michael owned
several other flats. He spent four or five nights a week there
with Evan, all the while keeping the relationship secret from
just about everyone; it has been reported that several
members of his immediate family did not know that he was
gay.

On the nights he was not staying in the city with Evan,
Michael went home to Charlottesville, Virginia, where he
resided in a wing of his mother's majestic home. The family's regal red-brick residence was the kind of house featured in an F. Scott Fitzgerald novel. It was set on five
sprawling acres in one of the most exclusive neighborhoods
of Virginia and was protected by a towering wrought-iron
gate. Michael had moved his mother to the dignified house
on Lake Drive in Albemarle County from his childhood
home in Watertown shortly after he graduated from law
school in 1990. He paid about $600,000 for the prime slice
of property adjacent to the exclusive Farmington Country
Club. Visitors were often surprised when they learned that
the estate had nine bathrooms.

Michael's father, Lewis, had died of complications of

Parkinson's disease just days after Michael's high school graduation. Although his father was wheelchair-bound for much of his son's childhood, Michael recalled that he shared a close relationship with the man who once played professional basketball for the Providence Steamrollers. Theirs was a cerebral relationship that revolved around discussions of current events, politics, and books of interest.

While his father's death was not unexpected, it cast a negative shadow on what should have been a happy occasion for Michael. At the time, he was the only one of his three siblings still living at home, and he willingly took on the role of caretaker to his grief-stricken mother.

Michael and Evan had been friends for more than two years when Michael celebrated his thirty-sixth birthday on January 1, 2000. But the two men did not spend that day together. Michael opted to return home to Charlottesville to ring in the New Year with his mother, while Evan stayed behind to enjoy the elaborate fireworks show in the Capital City. Besides, Michael and his mom were booked to leave for Tortola on the third of January, and it seemed appropriate that Michael give her a hand to prepare for the journey. But at the last minute, Teena Spicer announced that she was not feeling well enough to accompany her son to the island. Since the early 90s, Michael had been taking care of his mother who, family members said, was frail and sometimes confused.

Two days later, Michael was alone on a plane to St. Thomas, where he would catch a ferry for Tortola. Evan was ecstatic when Michael called him on the fifth of January to invite him to the island. Yet Evan's first journey outside the United States was fraught with difficulties. Unaccustomed to international travel, he did not realize that he would need proof of citizenship to visit the British Virgin Islands. He had left home on the tenth of January without a passport, or any other acceptable form of identification. In fact, he did not even have any luggage, just the shirt on his back. Michael had told him not to worry about packing, that he kept enough clothing on the island for the two of them to share.

When his plane landed in Puerto Rico, Evan was informed that he would not be able to continue on to Tortola without additional documentation.

Frustrated, he remained in San Juan overnight, and then traveled to St. Thomas the following morning. Upon arrival in the steamy US territory, he was told that he would be permitted to travel to the British Virgin Island of Tortola by ferryboat on a sworn affidavit. He quickly obtained the official paper from a law firm in the bustling port city of Charlotte Amalie, and then climbed aboard a departing ship.

Michael, William, and Alex were waiting at the ferry terminal when Evan's boat sailed into the West End harbor on January 11, three days before Lois McMillen died. The quaint, gingerbread-trimmed building where passengers pass through customs was small enough that the men could hear the Immigration official telling Evan that he needed additional documents to remain in the BVI.

Evan was relieved when the officer agreed to let him stay on the island for twenty-four hours—if he promised to return the following day with a faxed copy of his driver's license or voter's registration card. He celebrated his landing with two rounds of drinks at a nearby restaurant. Then he and his friends enjoyed a leisurely walk along the craggy dirt road to pristine Smuggler's Cove beach. There, the four men shared several beers and some cookies they bought from a young American who peddled candy, soft drinks, and trinkets beneath the lofty palms.

As the day wore on, it became increasingly clear that William and Alex were not pleased with Michael's new houseguest. As they'd feared, having Evan in the mix changed the threesome's usual chemistry. Suddenly, it did not feel like it had on previous trips, when the men had fashioned themselves after "The Three Musketeers."

Contrary to Blackman's official police statement that he had been introduced to Evan George on his first visit to Zebra House, Michael contended that Evan had not yet met the investigator.

In fact, Michael recalled that it was William Labrador,

and not he, who had actually answered the sergeant's call earlier in the day. William had been sitting on a lounge chair by the pool reading a novel when the officers arrived. They told him that they wanted to speak to Michael to inform him of what had taken place in West End.

"Michael, the police are here," is what William announced when he poked his head through the terrace door.

Michael said that he and Evan had been dozing in the second bedroom's twin beds when William made the announcement. Michael had already been awakened several times that morning by the ringing of the telephone, but had not bothered to get up to answer it.

Instead, he had waited for the answering machine to pick up so that he could hear who was calling. Back home, he detested the solicitations of telemarketers and made a habit of letting the machine screen them out. When he heard the click of the person hanging up on the answering machine, he rolled over and went back to sleep. So far as he was concerned, if the calls were important, the person dialing his number would either leave a message or call back later. Besides, he, Alex, and Evan had stayed up into the wee hours of the morning, watching the movie *Vertigo*. It was after four a.m. when they finally went to bed.

"I wish I had answered the phone," Michael would later say, insisting that if he had heard Mr. McMillen's voice on the machine, he would have jumped up to answer the call.

Michael reported that while he and William sat on deck chairs talking with Sergeant Blackman, he heard Evan get up to use the bathroom. He said that it was not until police left the residence that Evan learned why they had come.

"From now on, we walk in pairs," was the way Evan responded when Michael informed him of the police's grisly discovery. "It's clear it's not safe to go out alone."

Michael and William had nodded in agreement. They, too, were worried about what Lois' death would mean for the future of the island. For Michael, it seemed almost surreal. He had been coming to Tortola for nearly twenty years,

and for the most part, had felt safe and protected on the subtropical paradise.

His mother, however, had grown increasingly uncomfortable about visiting Zebra House. In recent years, she had
expressed fear of staying alone at the family's remote
Caribbean hideaway, and had limited her visits to the times
when Michael or his sister and brother-in-law accompanied
her. Their vacations were usually limited to days spent by the
pool or at the nearby beach and then quiet dinners at home.
Since her husband's death in 1981, Teena Spicer had stopped
visiting Zebra House on her own, in part because the home
was in a secluded location, tucked away on a sloping hillside
and out of earshot of the neighbors. Another reason was that
in more recent years, she had heard about a number of bur-
glaries in the Belmont Estates section and worried that her
home might be targeted.

It was rare for Michael and his mom to venture out of the
West End. On occasion they'd call for a taxi to take them to
the gourmet restaurant at the Sugar Mill Hotel in Apple Bay,
or to Pusser's Landing at West End for a burger and fries.
When they needed provisions, they'd usually hitch a ride to
Road Town with one of their neighbors. Otherwise, they
tended to remain at Belmont Estates.

It was only when a visitor was coming to Zebra House
that Michael and his family felt compelled to leave their safe
haven and give their guests a whirlwind tour. That had been
the case on this trip. Michael had wanted to show Evan a
good time.

"This is it for Tortola and me," Michael recalled thinking
when police first delivered the news about Lois. "The neighbor has been killed. The island's unsafe."

Michael again contemplated a call to her parents, but
hesitated.

The men were uncertain about what to do. As they sat in
the living room sipping coffee, they recalled Blackman telling
them that Josephine and Russell were on their way to the
funeral home. That meant that even if they phoned, there
would be no one at the McMillen home to receive their call.

"I think it's too soon," one of the men declared.

"What about if we call Kay Carpenter Doyle?" Michael inquired next, referring to the mature woman who lived two doors away from him in the Belmont Estates complex. "Or maybe we should call Clifford."

His suggestions of contacting Kay or their friend Clifford, who was staying at Equinox House, the residence at the base of Michael's driveway, were rejected as "too gossipy."

"I don't think you should interfere, because it's a criminal investigation," William reportedly advised Michael.

The sound of an engine revving on the driveway of Zebra House just after lunch on Saturday afternoon alerted Michael to an approaching vehicle. Rising to his feet, he ambled to the sliding glass door that led to the terrace. He stepped out into the moist afternoon heat, and then made his way past the pool to the stone patio area. He grew alarmed when he saw the cortège of officers trailing behind the lofty investigator making their way up the staircase to the right of the guesthouse. Michael counted at least three in uniform, and as many in plainclothes. The number of police immediately telegraphed to him the serious nature of their visit.

Rays of midday sun bathed the patio where Inspector Jacob George and his team were now standing. Michael noticed that the heavy-set female constable in uniform who had visited earlier in the day was in the group. He remembered her because of the way she had been skulking along the side of the house, trying to peer in the windows of the kitchen and back bedroom. Her behavior had immediately cued him that this was not a routine call.

In fact, Michael later recalled that when he first saw the handful of officers on his terrace earlier that morning, he had wondered if they were lost, or perhaps in hot pursuit of a burglar who had run up the hill. In the twenty years that his family had owned the house, police had never had reason to call on him there. He knew, though, that police had been to Zebra House before. Guests who had rented the property from the family had been burglarized and had called them to the residence.

Michael recalled that it was not until they mentioned Lois that he realized that something terrible had happened. Now, a second team was back with more questions—and grim news.

"I am Chief Inspector Jacob George."

Michael noted the forceful tone of the investigator's voice.

"I am making inquiries into a report where the body of Lois McMillen was found on the beachside at West End. I would like you to assist me with my investigation because the information I have is that you are familiar with the deceased."

"Of course." Michael was polite, and appeared upset at news that the woman police had found on the beach was, in fact, Lois.

Inspector George scanned the patio area, looking for anything that seemed suspicious. His gaze immediately fixed on the three pairs of wet, sandy sneakers lined up on the tiled area that rimmed the pool. "Gentlemen, to whom do those shoes belong?" he inquired.

"Those are mine," Michael announced, pointing to a well-worn pair of K-Swiss sneakers at the pool's edge.

"The pair of Kastels is mine." Evan George flagged the blue-and-white sneakers next to the ones Michael had just identified.

"The Adidas belong to me," William responded.

"May I ask, how did the shoes get so wet and sandy?"

Evan's explanation was that he had gone to Quito's, a popular beachfront bar and restaurant on the north side of the island in the Cane Garden Bay area. He said that he and Michael had taken a moonlit stroll along the beach, and had stepped in the briny seawater that was washing up on the shore.

Michael agreed with Evan's pronouncement, offering little in the way of new information.

William Labrador was silent.

The investigator waited, noting that Labrador, who was standing beside the two other men on the patio, did not immediately respond to the question. "I went hiking the day before and believe that's how my shoes got wet," he said finally.

"When were you last wearing the shoes?" Inspector George asked, referring to the pair of white sneakers with the blue-and-gray accents on the pool deck that William had just identified as his.

"Friday night," William replied.

The inspector studied the athletic-looking man with the coal-black hair that was slicked back off his face. He observed that he had a small, fresh cut on the bridge of his nose. "What happened to your nose?"

"I probably got it when I went hiking."

"Mr. Labrador, what were you wearing last night?"

"The same clothes I'm wearing now."

Inspector George noted his garish maroon-colored pants and short-sleeve polo shirt. Next, he turned his attention to Michael Spicer.

"Mr. Spicer, what were you wearing last night?" He observed that the slender, tanned gentleman was having difficulty remembering.

"You were wearing a blue long-sleeve shirt," Evan jumped in.

His comment prompted Michael to disappear inside the house. When he returned, he was holding a favorite light blue button-down shirt that he had purchased at Banana Republic, which he handed to the inspector.

The officer's face revealed nothing as he studied the item, focusing on a small red stain the size of a quarter on the chest area of the garment, just above the pocket. To him, the mark appeared to be blood.

"What is this stain here?" the investigator asked, pointing to the one-inch splotch.

Michael was silent.

"I would like to take this shirt into custody," Inspector George announced.

"That's fine." Michael smiled, the deep dimples of both cheeks discernible. He felt he had nothing to hide, and had already given the investigators a green light to look around.

"Mr. George, what were you wearing last night?"

"What I'm wearing now," Evan responded in a soft voice.

"Would you gentlemen please accompany me to the West End police station?"

"Of course." Michael wanted to help the officers in their investigation. But he also wanted to get to the beach. It was nearing two o'clock when the investigative team led by Inspector George started back to the West End substation; in tow were Michael, Evan, and William. Alex had still not returned from his outing. The investigator had instructed the men to accompany him to the West End headquarters under the guise that their help was needed in the ongoing investigation.

Michael sat in the rear of the police cruiser next to his friends, watching out the partially open window as tanned bathers frolicked in the cool blue Caribbean waters in front of the elegant Long Bay hotel, just down the road from his home. He hoped the police inquiry wouldn't eat up their entire afternoon.

CHAPTER SEVEN

Trouble in Paradise

Deputy Commissioner Johnston continued to oversee the investigation after leaving the crime scene at West End—and always stayed in the background. As the inquiry evolved, he coordinated the work of the various investigators and oversaw attempts to bring in a pathologist to conduct the autopsy. But throughout the process, he was careful to let his officers and other personnel stay out front and run the investigation.

Many who were involved in the case, including the McMillens, Alex Benedetto, William Labrador, Michael Spicer, and Evan George never even saw or talked to Johnston. None of them had any idea that the man overseeing the investigation was not one of the local police officers, but a seasoned professional from the Scottish police.

After more than three hours at the Drake's Highway location, Johnston had returned home to his Road Town residence for lunch with his wife. Over sandwiches, he shared the incredible events of the morning with Irene, all the while listening for the phone for updates from the four teams he had working the case.

He had divided the labor by creating separate contingents to handle the various inquiries and administrative tasks facing the investigators. For the rest of the afternoon, he remained in regular contact with the inquiry teams by landline, cell phone, and police radio. He had arranged a full briefing for four p.m. at police headquarters in Road Town that would include the heads of all four investigative teams and his boss, Vernon Malone. He knew that the commissioner of police would be back from St. Thomas by that time, and would take over the unfolding investigation.

Malone had been on his way to the ferry dock to catch a boat for St. Thomas when he received word of the body on the beach. The message had sent him straight to the Drake's Highway location.

Malone had been the commissioner for close to six years when Johnston arrived on Tortola. A bear of a man at well over three hundred pounds, Malone was the first native of the British Virgin Islands ever to hold the post. All of his predecessors had been Englishmen, appointed to a term by Her Majesty the Queen. Because Tortola is a territory of the United Kingdom and is under the control of the British government, Malone was often looked upon as a figurehead; much of the day-to-day operations fell on the deputy commissioner, who is selected by representatives of the Queen.

While he liked Malone, Johnston found his style of policing very different from his own. Yet in spite of their differences, the two men managed to work out a system that allowed them to operate the department effectively without stepping on each other's toes.

The department's top brass had been at the Drake's Highway location for less than thirty minutes. Malone's goal of making certain that the scene had been properly secured and that his men were following police procedure had been satisfied. And he was certain that Johnston would bring him up to date upon his return from St. Thomas that afternoon.

It was nearing two o'clock when Inspector George ordered the small procession of police vehicles carrying Michael, Evan, and William to stop at the Bomba Shack. He had reason to believe that they might be able to pick up Alex Benedetto before continuing on to the police station. No one had seen the thirty-four-year-old Benedetto that Saturday morning. It appeared that he had gotten up early and had gone out before any of the men had awakened. His friends at Zebra House suggested that he might have gone to Bomba's to body-surf the waves adjacent to the rickety bar. Tourists and locals regularly used the small beach to ride the two- to three-foot breakers.

The ramshackle beach bar was located about two miles from Zebra House in Apple Bay on the island's north side, where groves of mango and banana trees covered the landscape. The investigators would soon learn that it was at this small roadside shanty that Alex first met Lois McMillen.

Bomba's had always been one of Lois' favorite hangouts, despite its questionable reputation. The structure is a true shack, cobbled together from an odd assortment of driftwood and old construction timbers. It has no real floor, just the sand of the seashore.

Its owner, Charles "Bomba" Callwood is proud of the bras and panties that hang from its rafters. The undergarments had been given to him in lieu of the three-dollar payment for a cup of Bomba Punch, a potent concoction of pineapple, orange, and passion fruit juices, coconut cream, and super-proof rum that is blended by Bomba himself. Graffiti, old license plates, and handwritten messages cover the pieces of wood that are nailed together to create walls. One large scrawled message on a plank of wood talks of the Bomba Shack's infamous Full Moon Parties:

> WHAT IS A FULL MOON PARTY? FULL MOON PARTY IS A GROUP OF PEOPLE GET TOGETHER ONCE A MONTH HAVIN FUN AND DANCIN IN THE SAND DRINKIN, EATIN, BRING IN FRIENDS DRINKIN BOMBA PUNCH AND EATIN MUSHROOMS PLAYING WITH THE ONE YA LOVE SITTIN NAKED ON BOMBA'S LAP GETTING YOUR TITTIES SQUEEZED AND JUST BEIN FRIENDLY. RELEASE STRESS ONCE A MONTH?

A woman from Santa Cruz, California, had signed the placard.

It was at one of these wild gatherings in January of 1997 that Alex and William had first struck up a conversation with the dazzling, flaxen-haired Lois McMillen. Michael had returned to Washington, DC, for a real estate closing, and was not on the island the day that Alex met the pretty Connecticut woman.

In fact, Lois had given the two men a ride back to their accommodation that night. But she was not the best driver, and steered the vehicle into a fence in front of the Long Bay hotel, an upscale complex on the beachfront road that leads to Belmont Estates. No one had been seriously hurt, but there was damage to the car.

Michael and the others waited in the rear of the police vehicle, its engine idling, while a uniformed officer went inside Bomba's to check for Alex. The three men watched from the Montero's open window as the constable scrutinized the tiny shack. It did not take five minutes to determine that their friend was not inside, nor among the handful of sunbathers on the seashore.

From there, the small motorcade made its way along Zion Hill Road, the winding north-to-south route that intersects Drake's Highway. The men watched the sea rising in front of them as the officer at the wheel of the SUV negotiated the serpentine curves of the constricted two-lane road.

As they turned right onto Sir Francis Drake Highway, Michael took in the view through the vehicle's rear window. The seascape across the channel had always been his favorite. He loved the picturesque panoramas, the dramatic colors of the ever-changing sky, and the jagged contours of the islands across the way.

As the officer steered the gray SUV up the rocky driveway of the West End police station, Michael noticed a group of uniformed officers milling about outside the headquarters. He had never seen so many constables in one location on the tiny island. Michael and the others expected to give their statements to police when they arrived and then be released. But that did not happen. Instead, they were shepherded into various rooms, and told to wait.

• • •

It was earlier that afternoon, about 12:30 p.m, when Julian
Harley, the forensics expert, had finally gathered up his
equipment at the Drake's Highway location and set out for
the West End ferry dock where he met Constable Kendolph
Bobb. He found the uniformed detective standing next to a
dark green four-wheel-drive vehicle in the lot just off the
south side of Drake's Highway. It was the parking area east
of the West End Jetty, where tourists and locals alike take the
ferries departing for St. Thomas and the other islands of the
BVI.

Several taxi drivers watched the officers conversing from
the rickety front porch of the small shingle house across the
highway. It was the location of the West End taxi stand,
where the cabbies sat playing card games and sharing stories
as they waited for fares to arrive on the incoming ferries.

Harley noted that the rental vehicle was parked with its
front end facing the sea. Placing his hand on the grill, he felt
for heat from the engine. It was cold. On the ground beneath
one of the rear tires, he noticed that there was a muddy patch
of earth. He noted that all four of the vehicle's windows
were closed, but the Jeep was not locked.

Peering inside, he was surprised to see that the key was
still in the ignition switch. He also noticed that there was a
variety of paraphernalia on the passenger seat. There was an
unopened can of Budweiser, a bottle of Windex glass cleaner,
and a lady's gold handbag on the passenger-side floor. On
the seat was a copy of a local entertainment guide and a purple hairbrush and mirror set. He observed that the *Limin'*
Times magazine was not crumpled, which led him to suspect
that the woman had not had a passenger in the vehicle. On
the floor, he found a single gold earring and a brass-colored
heart pendant similar to the one found on the road. A yellow-
and-white beach chair was in the rear cargo area.

Glancing across the vehicle to the driver's side, he noticed
that the floor mat beneath the steering wheel was wet and a
little sandy. It was the only area of the interior that was damp

and speckled with tiny sand granules. A small crowd gathered as Harley pulled a camera from his bag and began to photograph the items, which he then collected and catalogued as evidence. Next, he checked the interior for fingerprints, examining the steering wheel, gearshift lever, door handles, dashboard, and other areas where prints would normally be found. But there were no prints on any of those surfaces—not even one belonging to Lois McMillen. It appeared that the inside of the car had been carefully wiped clean.

What he did find was a shoe print on the inside rear door panel.

After returning to the West End police station, Harley retreated to a back office with the samples he had collected. Among them were samples he had vacuumed from ten areas of the interior of the McMillen girl's rental car, as well as the vehicle's five floor mats. As he catalogued the items, Inspector Jacob George joined him in the rear office and presented him with three pairs of sneakers he had taken from Zebra House. The inspector told Harley he had just visited the hilltop home and had three of its occupants in tow.

Harley noted in a small ledger that the Kastels belonging to Evan George and the Adidas of William Labrador were "very wet and sandy." But he made no notation about the pair of white K-Swiss shoes owned by Michael Spicer.

"We have the men from Zebra House at West End, sir," Sergeant Anderson Blackman spoke into the phone to Deputy Commissioner John Johnston. He had called the commander at his home to give him an update on the investigation.

"What else do you have, Anderson?" Johnston inquired, hoping to hear that his men had found something of substance.

"Well, we are getting a search warrant, sir, to search the premises at Zebra House." Blackman told him that he had been charged with obtaining the document from the local court.

"Keep me informed," the commander responded in

between bites of a sandwich. "Let me know what you find."

Johnston took another call—this one from a member of his administrative team. As he listened to the officer on the other end of the line, it was slowly becoming clear that he was about to hit his first major roadblock.

Johnston knew that he needed to get hold of a pathologist, and fast. He had a dead body, and suspected foul play. Yet, he also knew that Tortola and the British Virgin Islands did not have a resident pathologist. Instead, the government used the services of a pathologist in the US Virgin Islands.

"It's a Saturday, sir, and it appears that no one is answering the phone at the doctor's office." The constable was one of three people assigned to the case's administrative team and was working out of police headquarters in Road Town.

He had been trying to make contact with Dr. Francisco Jose Landron at his office on St. Thomas. Johnston knew that Landron was under contract to the department to conduct all the medical examinations and autopsies carried out in the British Virgin Islands. The BVI had no need for a full-time pathologist because there were so few criminal or suspicious deaths in which autopsies had to be performed. To reduce cost, the government contracted with Landron.

"Sir, we can't make contact with the pathology department at all," the officer told Johnston. "We just can't get ahold of anybody. We're stuck."

Johnston was realizing that the problem was bigger than he had initially suspected. It was a Saturday, and the start of the three-day Martin Luther King weekend in the United States. "We're not going to get ahold of anybody in the pathology department there until Tuesday at the earliest," the commander reasoned. "That's not good enough. Keep trying, and let's start looking elsewhere. Where is there another pathologist in the Caribbean that we can get ahold of?"

"Barbados, sir."

"Call them and let me know what you find."

Johnston wiped the sweat from his brow, and turned to Irene, who was sitting across the table from him finishing her sandwich. He knew from experience that Tortola had long had a problem getting a pathologist to the island on a timely basis. Sometimes the problem had been especially bad and the department had been forced to keep corpses on ice for up to three weeks before they could be examined. He realized that the hurdle he was now facing was to be expected; it was just one of the difficulties with being a police officer on a small, remote island. He also knew that in the United States, and just about anywhere in Europe, you could call in a forensic pathologist and the doctor would be there within thirty minutes. The pathologist would take charge of the body, and within hours investigators would have information in relation to his analysis of the final moments of that person's life, and the cause of death.

The ring of the telephone startled Johnston from his musing. It was the officer at the Road Town police station calling back.

"Sir, the pathologist from Barbados is in Grenada doing autopsies. He says that he can't get here until Thursday or Friday of next week."

"Let's keep looking. Try to track down Landron at his home in Puerto Rico."

Meanwhile, Lois McMillen's body lay in cold storage at the funeral home in Road Town. Johnston believed that she had been murdered after a violent struggle, but without a pathologist to examine the body, he had no way of knowing for sure.

CHAPTER EIGHT

Executing the Search

It was nearing three o'clock when Inspector George entered the back office of the West End police station where Michael Spicer had been waiting. In measured tones, he advised the slender dark-haired man of the warrant that police had obtained to search his home. It was not the news that Michael was expecting. He did not know what to make of the investigator's decision to search Zebra House, but did not take the move too seriously. He assumed that it was routine police protocol and part of the way that police conducted investigations on the tiny island, and he did not object. In fact, he and William Labrador were asked to accompany the team to Zebra House, while Evan was told to remain at the West End substation.

Climbing back into the police vehicles, Michael and William took their places in the rear of the Montero for the ten-minute ride back to Belmont Estates. Members of the crime-scene examination team, led by forensics expert Julian Harley, followed behind in separate vehicles. A warm breeze swayed the leafy palms along the hillside as the caravan traversed the steep Zion Hill Road, passing the roadside stand where Nan Thomas sold arts and crafts. Thomas, a painter from America, had talked art with Lois over the years, and the two were friends. Her tiny wooden booth was located at the base of the road leading to Belmont Estates.

The procession next passed Sebastian's hotel, and the

tiny convenience store where Spicer and his houseguests regularly shopped for provisions, such as canned goods, toothpaste, and cigarettes.

Farther down was the sprawling Long Bay hotel, with its oceanfront bungalows and vacation villas tucked amongst palm trees on the hillside across the street. Uniformed guards were posted at various points around the property to provide guests with a degree of security. There had been a number of thefts at the hotel, and the guards were there to help prevent a recurrence. A small sign marked the entrance to Belmont Estates. Passing the McMillens' villa on the right, the procession continued up the precipitous approach to Zebra House, parking at odd angles along the bumpy dirt driveway.

William was ordered to remain in the police vehicle, while Michael was instructed to accompany Inspector George and his team into the house. As the two men climbed the cement stairs beside the guest cottage, they noticed Alex sitting on a lounge chair by the pool reading a book.

"Hello, I'm Inspector George." The tall, plainclothes official stepped in front of Michael to introduce himself to the fair-haired Benedetto. "The body of a white blond woman has been found on the rocky shoreline on the southern coast of the island. And we believe it to be Lois McMillen."

"What?" Alex jumped up in stunned disbelief. "What happened? What happened? Guys, what happened?"

Alex clutched the novel in his hands as he looked first at the officer with the thin moustache, and then at his friend Michael for an explanation. Suddenly, he broke down in tears. "Is she dead?"

"Yes," the inspector replied dryly.

"How did she die?" Alex asked in between sobs.

"That's why I'm here seeking your assistance to find out how she came by her death," Inspector George explained. "Mr. Benedetto, we'd like to talk with you about your relationship with Miss McMillen. We'd like you to help us to understand what was going on in Lois McMillen's head.

"This is Inspector Charles," Inspector George gestured at

the slender man standing beside him. "He is going to speak with you today."

Over the next hour, Alex and Inspector Charles sat by the pool on white lounge chairs, discussing the publishing heir's relationship with Lois McMillen. Alex seemed happy to oblige, and appeared to speak openly about his island romance with the stunning blond.

Rays of late afternoon sun warmed the spacious patio as he told the inspector that it was during his first trip to the island in 1997 that he met Lois McMillen. He and William Labrador had been staying at the Jolly Roger Inn and had gotten a ride to Bomba's Shack to celebrate with revelers at one of the bar's Full Moon Parties.

"She wasn't introduced to me by anyone," he recalled. "We just met and talked because she was alone at the time.

"She told me that she was living at Belmont Estate, just like Michael. She also told me that she's known Michael for twenty years. Michael and I became friends about four years ago, when I first came to Tortola with William."

Alex admitted that he was taken with the thirty-one-year-old head-turner. "After our initial meeting in Tortola in January '97, we had an intimate relationship which lasted for about three months," he explained, his blue eyes focused on Inspector Charles as he spoke.

He told the officer that after his visit to Tortola, where he had worked on his base tan and body-boarded at the beach behind Bomba's, he had continued his vacation on St. Bart's, where he, William, and Michael had spent another week. Upon returning to the States, he said that he continued to see Lois. After they had been dating for several months, he invited her to New York to spend the weekend with him at his posh Fifth Avenue apartment. But Alex said he noticed that Lois was behaving very strangely.

He explained that she spoke incessantly of the supernatural and, at one point, declared that she had infiltrated a witches' coven. He admittedly found her preoccupation with the paranormal alarming, but was convinced that she truly believed all that she was relating to him.

"She had a continuous blank stare on her face and in her eyes," Alex recounted in an animated fashion, his arms flailing, his tone a mix of seriousness and laughter. He further explained that when she was not ranting about the mystical world, she seemed off in fantasy.

"She was always very slow to respond when asked a question, she dressed outlandishly, she would speak as though she was better than everybody else, and she called herself 'one of God's children' and everybody else was not," he told George.

He explained that during the visit, Lois invited him to Connecticut to meet her parents. But he declined the invitation.

"I didn't accept the offer because I noticed that she was behaving very strangely, the things she said, the way she dressed, the feeling she gave off, and the way she acted made me scared, as well as other people," he recalled. "It made me anxious to get away from her. I told her that I couldn't continue with the relationship and asked her to go home and not to see me again."

Alex recalled that even though he had admonished Lois not to contact him again, she appeared at his office some weeks later.

"She went to my office asking for me, but I wasn't there," he said.

Instead, it was Alex's father, Victor, who met Lois in the waiting area. The elder Benedetto was unaware that Lois had just come from a march on the United Nations, in which she was protesting violence against the women of Bosnia. To dress the part, she and the other protestors had worn burquas, the traditional garb of Muslim women. Lois was still dressed in the black sheath when she'd arrived at the offices of Bella Management.

"My father told me that she was at my office acting very strangely and making people in the office feel very uncomfortable." Alex recounted that his dad and several of his employees told him that Lois put them off with her odd apparel and vacant stare.

"Mr. Benedetto, when did you see Lois again after that?" Inspector Charles was curious about the man's contact with the dead woman during his current visit to Tortola. He inquired about the time the two might have spent together on the island over the last several days.

"The next time I saw her was last Wednesday night at Bomba's Shack around eleven p.m.," Alex recalled. He and the other guys staying at Zebra House had gone to the twice-weekly beach barbecue where for ten dollars, patrons could help themselves to as much chicken, ribs, and rice as they could heap on their plates. A calypso band played accompaniment to the sizzling sounds of the meat grilling on the open pit. "We had a very peaceful, kind, and sympathetic conversation. She was alone at the time and I was with Michael and Evan."

Alex said that he talked with Lois for about an hour, maybe two.

"When we were ready to leave Bomba's Shack, Lois gave us a ride to the driveway of Zebra House," he continued. "This was about one o'clock in the morning. I gave her a hug and wished her well with her father and that was the last time I saw Lois McMillen."

Julian Harley, the forensics expert, was in charge of the examination of Zebra House, and was overseeing the evidence collection. His primary function was to make certain that the items seized from the premises were properly gathered, and to photograph them as they were being amassed.

His officers began in the small wooden guest cottage where William Labrador had been staying. Michael was on hand as the team went through the cabana-like accommodation. He watched as the investigators methodically moved about the bright white room with the tan tile floor. It was decorated in the same whimsical zebra motif as the house's main quarters. Michael knew that in addition to his mother's love of zebras, she had another reason for using the theme. She felt the animal's colors, black and white, were indicative of the racial harmony that existed on Tortola.

Michael casually posted himself in the doorway just off the pool, which was painted a dark shade of brown. Leaning against the frame of the sliding doors, he looked on in a perfunctory manner as the officers gingerly folded the brown-and-black animal print sheet from the queen-size bed and then placed it in a plastic evidence bag. Next, they scanned the tops of the small white nightstands on either side of the mattress before stopping to collect hair samples from William Labrador's suitcase.

Crossing to the opposite side of the room, they carefully inspected the small kitchen area, and then brushed past a large round table, scanning it as they moved toward the lavatory. It was draped in a lacy white cloth, and provided a place for important provisions such as a flashlight and a spray bottle of bug repellent. Above the table on the wall was a large circular mirror framed in white wicker. An exact replica hung in between the two single beds of the spare bedroom where Michael was staying in the main house.

Michael noticed that one of the officers emerged from the toilet clutching the small beige garbage pail that usually sat near the sink. Inside the garbage bag, the officer noted that there were a number of stained tissues, and pieces of clipped fingernails. But Michael did not appear too worried. Instead, he was musing about how thorough the investigators were being in their efforts. His years on Tortola had taught him that things moved at a slow pace in the BVI. He believed it best to cooperate with island officials, and to be patient. He recognized that the officers were just doing their job, and were working at a typical rate of speed for the Caribbean in an attempt to figure things out. He was certain that their search was just a formality, and that they would soon catch the person responsible for Lois' death—never imagining that it would be he and his friends who would be charged with her crime.

Michael waited as Sergeant Harley pulled out his camera

and snapped photographs of the interior of the room where
William had been staying. The investigator wanted to document the condition as police had found it. Upon completion
of the search of the one-bedroom cottage, Michael led the
investigators along the stone patio past the shaded area
where Alex and one of the police inspectors were still talking. A tepid breeze rustled the brilliant red flowers of the
bougainvillea bushes that trimmed the house just beside the
double glass sliding doors that led to the living room.

Michael waited outside as Sergeant Harley photographed
the exterior of the two structures, the small wood guesthouse, and the concrete main building painted in a light
shade of tan. He watched the sergeant slowly circling the
pool, stopping and focusing his lens on two small mounds of
sand that he observed. The first was on the stonework on the
southern side of the pool, where Inspector George had found
the sneakers during his earlier visit. The second was in the
trap of the outdoor shower, also on the southern side of the
guest cottage.

Inside, the police were systematically lifting pillows
from the couches, and scanning the tops of the small end
tables as they made their way around the sun-filled salon
and formal dining area. When Michael joined the officers in
the living room, he again noted how professional they
appeared. He was growing upset at how they were tearing
his place apart, but he still wanted to believe that somehow
all of this would assist him and his friends in proving their
innocence. Yet, it was slowly dawning on him that the police
really had no idea who had killed Lois. He wondered if the
fact that they were searching Zebra House meant that they
had found no leads at the crime scene. For a moment, he
contemplated an ugly scenario: that police might try to
frame him and his friends, and make them patsies for the
murder.

The officers showed no emotion when it became clear that
Michael and Evan shared the second bedroom—and that they
were lovers. Tortola had only recently annulled a law making
homosexuality a crime. It was not apparent if the revelation

that at least two of the men staying at Zebra House were gay took the investigators by surprise. The police revealed nothing as they continued with their examination.

The spare bedroom was furnished in the same natural wicker that dominated the house, and was accented with pretty wood pieces that Michael's parents had purchased on their whirlwind trips. The room's two single beds had matching wicker headboards. Identical orange-and-yellow-striped bedspreads and furry throw pillows gave the room its finished look. In the closet, Michael kept a full island wardrobe that included several more pairs of the K-Swiss sneakers he so loved. When he had arrived on the island, he had only a carry-on bag in tow. It was the way he always traveled when he visited Tortola, where he kept a closet full of garments at the ready.

After inspecting the closet, the investigators folded back the bright coverlets from the beds and mindfully collected the gray topsheets from the mattresses. Next, they removed the plastic trash liner from the brown waste bin in between the beds. Inside the garbage bag, investigators found a piece of white paper with some writing on it, and the metal screw portion of a broken light bulb. What caught their attention was that this bag, too, contained fingernail clippings.

Crossing the hall to the master bedroom, the investigators were met with protestations from the room's current occupant, Alex Benedetto. Up until that point, Alex had been cooperative, openly sharing with Inspector Charles the details of his brief and intimate romance with Lois, and trying to assist him in understanding the way in which she saw the world. But according to Michael, his demeanor changed when he learned that investigators intended to search the bedroom suite where he had been staying since his arrival at Zebra House. Suddenly, he became argumentative, insisting that the exploration was an infringement of his rights.

"Why do you want to search my room?" Alex grew upset; his tone was one of concern and aggravation. Racing inside the house, he positioned himself in the doorway to the master bedroom and continued to carry on. "I didn't do anything wrong. This is an infringement of my rights. . . . Do you guys have a warrant to be doing this?"

The room where Alex was staying was located at the end of a short hallway that was just off the spacious living room and dining area. The wide, airy corridor to the back of the house led to two bedrooms, and a small powder room. The master bedroom was the larger of the two sleeping quarters, and had an en suite bath. Both bedrooms had sliding glass doors that opened to a tiled terrace finished with a simple iron railing. The veranda ran the length of the house and boasted unparalleled views of the ocean, and the sandy crescent-shaped Smuggler's Cove beach below. In spite of his protests, the team of investigators pushed Alex aside and began a meticulous search for clues. Meanwhile, Michael stood in the sun-drenched hallway, where black-and-white sketches of zebras decorated the white walls. The Tortola vacation house was one of several homes owned by the Spicer family.

Michael listened in stunned amazement as Alex continued to carry on about his civil rights. His ranting did not really surprise Michael. He had witnessed Alex's histrionics countless times over the past three years, stating that his friend had a tendency toward dramatic outbursts of emotion. Michael believed that his melodrama was more a function of his wacky personality than an attempt to prevent the investigators from searching his room. But the officers were suspicious. They interpreted his objections as an indication that he had something to hide.

Alex seemed oblivious to how his behavior might be viewed by police and offered little in the way of an explanation. He would later say that his difficult family history was to blame. He pointed to his mother and her continuous accusations that he had done something wrong. The allegations upset him. They left him feeling a moral obligation to protest when he was being falsely accused, and caused him to react with indignation when he felt that he was being unfairly singled out.

"Can you tell us what you were wearing last night, sir?" One of the investigators directed his question at Alex.

His query was met with an incredulous stare.

Michael was unaware of his friend's emotional baggage, and smiled nervously, trying to ignore Alex's boisterous protests before finally pulling him into the bedroom and admonishing him to hand police the clothing he was wearing the previous evening. In a low voice, he advised Alex it seemed an inappropriate time for such an indignant display.

"Here, take the sheets, take everything. . . ." Alex bellowed as the latex-gloved investigators pushed past him and proceeded to collect items from the master suite. He watched as they carefully removed the green-and-yellow topsheet from the queen-size bed, following standard evidence collection procedures to ensure that any material on top of the sheet was not lost as it was removed from the bed. The officers began at the bottom end of the sheet, slowly removing it from the mattress, lifting it and bringing the bottom corners toward the middle of the bed. Next, they went to the top of the bed and repeated the process. Then the officers stood on one side of the bed and folded the long side of the sheet inward. They repeated the process on the other side as well and continued folding until the sheet was small enough to be placed in an exhibit bag. Next, they removed the pillowcases from the pillows and put them in evidence collection bags. The bedding was then tagged with Alex's full name. In a corner of the room sat a wood loveseat with delicate carvings; more pictures of zebras graced the walls.

Alex's complaining provided a bizarre backdrop to the rumbling sounds of the police officers moving about the room, pulling open the closet doors, and poking their heads under the bed for clues. They even brushed the windowsill looking for hair and other evidence. His griping continued when a plainclothesman in white latex gloves emerged from the bathroom with the shiny white plastic garbage bag that lined the waste pail. Inside were eight pieces of clipped fingernails, eight stained tissues, and three tampons.

"This is crazy," he ranted.

It was well after three p.m. when the team of officers packed up their equipment and readied themselves to return to police headquarters. They had seized more than sixty items from Zebra House. Among them were a camcorder and a Fuji pocket camera with film in it. The camera and the images on the film inside would become key as the men tried to prove their innocence.

Police were especially interested in the articles of damp clothing, and the fingernail clippings that belonged to all four men. Even more interesting to the investigators were the tampons found in the wastebasket in the master bedroom, where Alex Benedetto had been staying. In the days to follow, investigators would learn they were the same brand as the one found in Lois McMillen's purse.

CHAPTER NINE
Suspicion of Murder

It was nearing four o'clock when Alex, Michael, and William returned to the West End police headquarters, reuniting with Evan, who had been detained there while police executed their search of Zebra House. The nearly hysterical Benedetto had calmed down and willingly agreed to accompany Inspector George and his team to the West End substation. All but Alex had already been to the tiny headquarters that afternoon, but none of them had been officially interviewed. Less than six hours had passed since police discovered Lois' body on the shoreline, and already it seemed that investigators were starting to focus their attention on the four men. The group was escorted to small separate but adjoining offices where they were told to wait to be interviewed.

Not long after they arrived at the substation, Sergeant Julian Harley approached Alex Benedetto.

"Mr. Benedetto?" Harley introduced himself to the man with the golden highlights.

"Yes?" Alex responded, and turned his attention to the graying investigator who was calling his name. Rising from his chair, he followed the reed-thin detective to a back office.

"I am Sergeant Julian Harley," he said with a nod of his head. "I am assisting in the investigation of a report where the body of Lois Livingston McMillen was found along the shoreline leading to the West End Jetty. Your fingernail scrapings and fingerprints are required in connection with this investigation. Do you have any objections, sir?"

"Why?" Alex was incredulous.

Michael could hear him from his room around the corner from Alex, and listened as his friend complained that police should be focusing their attention elsewhere. But after several minutes, he relented and agreed to cooperate with Harley's request.

"May I see your hands, sir?"

Alex extended his arms and spread his fingers with his palms facing downward toward the floor. He watched as Harley pulled a small tool from his bag, and then attempted to collect some matter from beneath his fingernails.

"Does this mean I am a prime suspect in this?" Alex asked, growing increasingly alarmed.

"This is just standard procedure, sir," the sergeant responded dryly. "We have to do this kind of stuff."

Harley was taken aback by how low the man's nails had been trimmed as he worked to scrape the residue from beneath each one, dropping it in a plastic bag for evidence. Next, he attempted to cut samples of Alex's nails, but soon realized that they had been cut too short for him to be able to retrieve an adequate specimen.

"I don't believe this. This is insane," Alex grumbled, watching as the sergeant attempted to snip bits of his nail with the stainless-steel clipper. "Can I help?"

"Yes, that would be okay." The sergeant stood by as the man with the neatly combed streaks of silky yellow hair clipped tiny pieces of his fingernails, dropping them into the separate plastic bags that the sergeant was holding. As Harley stood watching Alex nip at his nails, his attention was drawn to several abrasions on the man's right arm and his right leg.

"Sir, I would like to take photographs to show these markings," Harley announced, pointing to the thin scratches above the man's right ankle and the ones on the inside of his right arm. "Do you have any objections?"

"No," Alex answered, and then compliantly posed for the camera.

Harley next sought out William Labrador, who was seated in a cramped office with chalky-colored walls. "Sir, my name is Julian Harley," he nodded his head at the olive-skinned man. "It's my intention to take photographs showing the bruise on your nose. Do you have any objections?"

Labrador shook his head and quickly rose to his feet. He stood motionless as the sergeant focused the camera lens on the small cut on the bridge of the man's nose, and snapped two frames. He was then told to wait in the room that was directly across the hall from the one where they had placed Michael.

As they waited, Michael and William exchanged glances. They were sharing a silent chuckle over the strange, overly sweet beverage that police had served to them with their lunch of fish and hamburgers. Michael would liken it to the sort of watery "bug juice" that he'd had at summer camp as a kid. As he waited to speak with officers, Michael wondered about Evan. Since he was not able to see Evan from where he was sitting, he assumed that police were talking with him in another part of the headquarters.

The police's interest in the men's whereabouts over the past several days had them concerned. Yet none of the men, including Michael, a law school graduate, had asked for an attorney. Alex was the only one who had raised any objection to the investigators' actions and even he relented after his boisterous protestations at Zebra House and let the police continue their work. Michael would later recall that they all found the evidence-collection process more a nuisance than a cause for worry. All were convinced that the evidence that police were gathering at the crime scene on the beach would surely point them to whoever had harmed Lois McMillen.

The afternoon dragged on and there was still no indication from police that they were going to release the men anytime soon. Police had told Michael that he and his friends were

being taken to the West End substation as a pro forma matter
to describe their evening with Lois. At first, Michael assumed
that officers were taking statements one at a time, and that
they had started with Evan because he was the only one who
was not interviewed back at the house. He could not see the
room where Evan had been taken, but figured that the
twenty-two-year-old was in there speaking with detectives.
As time passed, and nobody came to see him, he began to
wonder what was going on. He wanted to get to the beach
and he was hoping that someone would get to him soon.

Spicer had no way of knowing that detectives and top brass
were seated around a conference table twenty minutes away
in Road Town discussing the men's possible involvement in
the case, and slowly coming toward the conclusion that they
may have played a role in Lois McMillen's death. The white
cement headquarters with the Mediterranean archways faced
a small courtyard on the city's bustling shorefront main road.
A large blue-and-white sign marks the two-story complex,
although several of its letters have faded from exposure to the
intense tropical sun. A small fountain, complete with native
plantings and seating areas, graces the public space in front of
the stationhouse. Businesspeople often gathered there at
lunchtime, as did tourists visiting nearby shops. In odd contrast to the official-looking headquarters were the flocks of
wild brown chickens roaming the courtyard and squawking as
they combed the blue-colored stones for food.

When Harley and the others stepped into the meeting,
Johnston was already briefing Commissioner Vernon Malone
on what his teams had learned since the grisly early morning
discovery. Malone had worked every murder that had
occurred in the BVI since he joined the police force thirty
years before—including the still-unsolved shooting death of
the young athlete in Sea Cow Bay several months earlier. A
photograph of Lois McMillen was passed around for the
investigators to view. In attendance were Chief Inspector
Jacob George, the lead investigator in the case, and the heads
of the other units, among them Sergeants Julian Harley and
Anderson Blackman, and Acting Supervisor Roy Stoutt.

From this point forward, Commissioner Malone would take over the investigation, with Deputy Commissioner Johnston playing an administrative role in the case. Johnston would continue to attend meetings in relation to the investigation and to offer suggestions and guidance to investigating officers. Yet, further actions taken by police would need to be authorized by Malone—which, at times, would cause frustration and even confusion for investigators.

It was already late in the day when Inspector George related the details of his search of Zebra House, and of his suspicions of the four men he was now detaining at the West End substation. Harley, the forensics expert, recounted the evidence he had collected at various locations throughout the day, and the observation he made when he'd tried to collect fingernail samples from Alex Benedetto. Harley had been instructed by Inspector George to take the samples from the man who had admitted to an affair with the dead woman.

During the hour-long meeting, Malone named Stoutt, a lifelong resident of Tortola, to act as senior investigating officer. In that role, he was to oversee the entire inquiry. All the unit heads were to report to him and he, in turn, was to report to Johnston. Stoutt would be responsible for all decisions on matters of policy and strategy, and his appointment effectively placed him at the helm of the day-to-day management of the investigation. He would be required to provide the deputy commissioner with detailed briefings on a daily basis, and to seek his advice on matters of policy and strategy.

Stoutt's deep voice cut the noiselessness that permeated the large room, where empty coffee cups and crumbs of pastry littered the table. A strapping man standing at well over six feet in height, he commanded immediate respect. It was learned that his initial canvass of the West End area had yielded no witnesses. It was still unclear if Lois had left her rental vehicle parked at the ferry terminal and taken a ride with someone else, or if someone had purposely dumped the SUV there after a deadly fight with her.

The discussion next turned to the issue of how to find a pathologist. The commissioner grew frustrated when he learned that his men were still having trouble finding a medical examiner to conduct an autopsy on Lois McMillen's body. The officers still had not made contact with Dr. Landron at his house on Puerto Rico, nor had they been able to find another M.E. on any of the neighboring islands. There was little the officers could do to advance their investigation until they had the results of a post-mortem exam.

Johnston was uncomfortable that his department was detaining four men in connection with the case even though they had no confirmation that Lois' death was the result of foul play. The investigative team wanted to hold the four Americans until they knew for sure if Lois McMillen had in fact been murdered as they all suspected. The team also feared that the foursome might try to flee the Territory if they were released from police custody.

For reasons that remain unclear, Spicer and the others said that investigators at the West End station never interrogated them that afternoon. In fact, police never asked them any additional questions during the hours that they sat waiting in the small adjacent offices. Spicer later recalled that he and his friends had no idea that investigators intended to hold them overnight—while they conducted an investigation into Lois' mysterious death.

By nightfall, Spicer and the others were growing anxious. They did not realize that the fact that they were among the last people known to associate with Lois McMillen in the days before her death made them suspects.

There were other issues the officers considered red flags: the men's initial reaction to police when they first came to Zebra House, Alex's outburst when officers tried to search his room, the one-inch stain on Michael Spicer's shirt that police suspected was blood, the wet and sandy sneakers by the pool, and the fact that Michael had not answered the McMillens' repeated phone calls earlier in the day.

Even more suspicious in the minds of police was that all of the men had recently trimmed their fingernails very short—so short, in fact, that the officers needed the men's assistance to obtain adequate samples for evidence testing. And then there were the scrapes on Alex Benedetto's arm and leg, and the fresh cut on William Labrador's nose.

When an officer finally came to see Michael Spicer in the small rear office where he had been waiting for much of the afternoon, it was not to release him or to take his statement, but to inform him that he was being detained on suspicion of murder. Inspector Jacob George reported that when he delivered the news to each of the four suspects individually, none of them offered a response.

It was not unusual for police in the British Virgin Islands to hold people for days, sometimes weeks, before charging them with a crime. But for William, Michael, Alex, and Evan, the idea of being detained with no formal charges was truly foreign in concept. They were accustomed to the US system of justice in which suspects are often brought before a judge for arraignment and charged with a crime within twenty-four hours of being detained.

Following police protocol, the officers at West End next seized personal items such as wallets and papers from the men's pockets. The rules of law required that they catalogue the items in a record book before taking the men into Her Majesty's custody. That's when police made a curious discovery. Inside Alex Benedetto's wallet, investigators found a receipt from the Barclays Bank ATM machine in Soper's Hole, West End, located less than one mile from the Jolly Roger, where McMillen was last seen on Friday night. It was a record of a three-hundred-dollar withdrawal made from Alex's personal checking account, and it was dated 1/14/00 and time-stamped 23:15—11:15 p.m.

Officers immediately alerted Inspector George to the find. It seemed strange that none of the men had told police about their trip to the West End that night. Could it be because they knew it would put all four of them in the area where Lois McMillen was last seen alive—and near where her body was recovered on the rocky southern shoreline? Inspector George mused.

Deputy Commissioner John Johnston would later recall
that during the investigators' initial questioning of the men
that Saturday afternoon, none of the four had mentioned the
ATM stop on the island's south coast. It was only later in the
day, after police confronted them with the receipt from
Alex's wallet, that they recalled their detour to Soper's Hole
that Friday evening.

"Their initial story is that they went to Quito's and spent
the night there," Johnston later explained. "They told us,
'We were picked up by a taxi driver and taken there.'

"Now we have to find the taxi driver, and all of this pro-
gresses through a period of time," the commander continued. "In the meantime, the investigators bring these people
in. And having brought them to the police station, they are
searched, and lo and behold, in the wallet of Alex Benedetto
we find an ATM machine receipt, which is from the ATM at
Pusser's Landing, West End, which is not far from the place
Lois is last seen alive. And it is time-dated at or about the
time she was last seen alive. We've now got them in the area
where she was last seen alive at or about the time she was
last seen alive.

"All four of them had omitted when they were first asked
about their movements the previous night, to mention that
they had ever been anywhere near the West End," the commander continued. "And it was only after they were presented with the physical evidence of the ATM machine
receipt that they said 'Oh yeah, that's right. We stopped off
to pick up some money.'

"You can say to yourself, one guy might have forgotten,
but all four of them?" Johnston had his doubts about their
truthfulness.

Michael and Evan were ordered to accompany detectives to
the Road Town police station. In a back area of the main headquarters was a small jail. The detention area was cramped and
unclean. Inside the solitary cell was a wooden bunk with a
thin foam mattress and a filthy commode. It was there that

Michael was told he would spend the night. Evan's accommodation was even more squalid. He was ordered to sleep on a small wooden bench in a filthy waiting room of the secured section out of sight of Michael's cell. It was an area where the overhead fluorescent lights were never turned off, and where people were constantly walking through on their way to other areas of the building. The arrangement stirred anxiety in the twenty-two-year-old, who had never before traveled outside the United States, much less stayed in a foreign jail. He could not even see Michael. Yet, he could hear his friend yelling out, "Evan, are you okay? Evan, don't worry, everything is going to be fine."

Detectives had driven William Labrador to the East End substation on the opposite end of the island, where he was also confined to a small cell. The only one to remain at the West End headquarters was Alex Benedetto, who was placed in the holding pen in the rear of the cement substation on Drake's Highway. Police found him the most interesting suspect of the four, since he had once dated the McMillen girl.

Holding the men overnight in diverse locations was a tactical decision on the part of the investigators. Inspector George realized that the West End substation was not the proper place to interview all four men, in part because of its small size and its layout with tiny adjoining offices. He wanted to ensure that the four were unable to confer on the stories they would tell police. He was also hoping that one of them would break and confess to the crime.

CHAPTER TEN

Death of an Angel

Russell and Josephine McMillen dined in near silence, staring blankly across the kitchen table at each other as they struggled to come to grips with the fact that their daughter was really gone.

Lois was only seven years old when she first visited Tortola in 1972. It took just one visit to the island and the McMillens were sold. In 1979, the family purchased the semi-attached residence in Belmont Grove, a small villa complex in the Belmont Estates section of the island. They had been looking for a place in the Caribbean and were directed to the largest of the British Virgin Islands by friends from their hometown. The neighborhood where they bought their villa was on the western tip of the island's north coast, and was reached by a dizzying dirt road that wound around steep hills. It was where the wealthy snowbirds had built expensive vacation homes, and was full of well-to-doers from the East Coast and Canada who had discovered the sleepy island paradise more than two decades before. The insular group of foreigners socialized at afternoon cocktail parties that were attended by other members of their "set," and rarely mixed with the local folk.

The place was magical to Lois. She looked forward to family vacations so she could swim, sail, and scuba dive to her heart's content. Much of her high school artwork depicted scenes of the dreamy island locale, bold blue backdrops with drawings of sailing ships and palm trees outlined in metallic gold paint.

Even as a young child, Lois expressed a love of painting. Her parents marveled at her ability to concentrate for hours, working on a picture that she would proudly present for their critique. It seemed to be the only time that Lois was ever able to stay focused.

As Josephine made her way to the bedroom, Lois' latest and still unfinished painting leaning against a wall by the kitchen caught her gaze. A whirlwind of thoughts began flashing through her mind. She kept remembering the surprise dinner party that Lois had thrown for her parents back home in Connecticut on December 10, just weeks earlier.

While she and Russell were busy opening the villa on Tortola for the winter season, Lois had stayed home in Middlebury to decorate their house for the holidays in a fashion that only she could dream up. She purchased two towering artificial trees with feathery white branches and placed them at opposite sides of the sage-green living room. Lois artistically trimmed them with treasured family ornaments and some she had painstakingly made by hand.

In the formal dining room, she set a dramatic table of linen and silver. There were eight place settings, each one adorned with items that had once belonged to relatives who had died. Her maternal grandmother's antique napkin rings and a favorite aunt's silver teapot were among the heirlooms. On either end of the table were candelabrums with tapered candles, their flames casting magical shadows on the original signed art that graced all four walls.

Her parents were surprised when they returned home on December 10 to find every inch of the house dripping in Christmas décor and the dining room table set for dinner. It was not unusual for Lois to decorate the house, and in fact, it was often a bone of contention between her and her mother, who did not share her daughter's penchant for ostentatious displays. When Lois' mother entered the first-floor dining room, she counted the eight place settings, and then inquired about the guest list.

"Lois, who's coming to dinner?"

"Everybody!" Lois answered with excitement. She was dressed elegantly for the occasion in a sweeping gown and fashionable high-heels.

"I don't understand," her mother said, confused.

"I've set the table for all of our relatives." Lois smiled, then explained that she had set a place for each beloved family member—living and dead. There was a seat for her deceased grandmother, another for her great aunt, and so on.

"Lois, this is nonsensical," her mother announced. She implored her daughter to stop her silliness and admonished her to remove all but the three settings they would need from the table. Looking back on that evening, Josephine now regretted being so short with her daughter about the dinner party, and wondered if maybe it was not some sort of premonition. Did Lois have some sense she would be joining her deceased relatives?

It was hard for Josephine to believe that her only child had died on a family vacation when she had lived away from home in so many dangerous and risky places over the years.

Born in New York City on May 23, 1965, Lois' arrival marked the beginning of the family's life in the suburbs of Connecticut. Russell and Josephine had met on a blind date set up by a mutual friend who acted as chaperon at their dinner at chic Café Nicholson on East 58th Street.

At the time, Jo Portong was the director of development for the Wood Tobé-Coburn School of Fashion Merchandising. She traveled the country lecturing high school girls on manners, etiquette, and style, and recruited students from every state to attend the school. Russell McMillen lived in Connecticut with his son Jeffrey, one of three children from his first marriage. His two daughters Stephanie and Meridee resided in Colorado with their mother.

Even after they married, for a time, the couple kept separate residences. It was a perfect way for the new bride to continue to work at the fashion school, and for Russell to be close to his job at a manufacturing company in Connecticut. Once Lois arrived, Jo gave up her apartment and the couple bought their first house, a small, but tastefully decorated residence in Woodbury, Connecticut. They soon traded up for a roomier place with a sprawling backyard in the adjacent town of Middlebury. The elegant residence was set on five rambling acres off a quiet country lane.

At first, young Lois was lonely, since none of the families nearby had small children. The age difference between Lois and her siblings was great. By the time she was of school age, the three were married or busy forging careers. They had all settled far from Connecticut, with Jeffrey in Seattle, Stephanie in Denver, and Meridee in Kentucky. Nevertheless, Lois looked forward to visits at holiday time. She was thrilled when she discovered that a young couple from Norway had moved into a house on a nearby street and had a daughter, Inger Imset, her age.

At age six, Lois began riding with the local pony club. When it became clear to her parents that she was a natural horsewoman, they leased her a pony of her own. Lois spent hours caring for her prized pet, named Carley.

When Lois was nine, her parents sent her to an all-girls' sleep-away camp in pastoral Bristol, New Hampshire. Next, it was boarding school in Switzerland for Lois, whose academic performance at the nearby Catholic school had been less than stellar. Over the years, school officials had periodically called home to say that Lois was having difficulty paying attention to her studies. Her parents hoped she would do better at the Swiss school on Lake Geneva, in the cosmopolitan city of Lausanne. But their hopes were dashed when they learned that Lois was not keeping up with her studies there, which included classes in French etiquette. Once again, she exhibited difficulty with the structured educational environment.

"She just did not do the work," her mother said, recalling that Lois was more interested in a young Swiss man named Christof than her schoolwork.

Lois then attended another exclusive boarding school, the Chapel Hill–Chauncy Hall School in Waltham, Massachusetts. The rambling campus was about ten miles from Boston in an upscale residential suburb. Lois liked being

near the bustling New England city, but was not thrilled with
the academics and again, did not fare well. Upon graduation,
she began to look toward college.

She enrolled at the College of Boca Raton, now Lynn University, in Southern Florida, where she completed two semesters. But she decided she preferred Boston, and set her sights
on the College of Fine Arts at Boston University. When she
learned that she would need to submit a portfolio of her best
work, Lois did not have any art that she deemed suitable for
consideration. In only thirty days, she produced enough
impressive drawings to gain admission for the fall of 1984.

College life at BU was congenial. Her accommodation
was in a quiet cluster of historic brownstones, just a short
walk away from the main campus and the expansive brick
building where she attended art classes.

Early in the semester, Christof joined her in Boston. Lois'
parents were not thrilled when they learned that their daughter was focusing more on her boyfriend from Lausanne than
on her studies. He was a constant distraction. "It was more
Christof than college," her mother complained. Lois even
incorporated the tattoo he had on his arm into one of her
paintings with a UFO theme. The McMillens breathed a sigh
of relief when Christof returned to Europe.

But Lois soon became disillusioned with the art program
at Boston University, complaining to her mother that she
was bored. She was uninterested in sketching vases and
flower arrangements, and she said she wanted to be somewhere more creative.

Lois dropped out of BU after completing the fall 1985
semester and returned home. She took a course for poise in
Middlebury, then enrolled in modeling classes at the John
Casablancas Modeling school in nearby New Haven. She
also signed up for voice lessons and acting classes at The
American Academy of Dramatic Arts in New York City.

Lois' dazzling looks won her spots as a finalist in model
competitions in New York, Connecticut, and Massachusetts.
She even appeared in a music video that aired on MTV.
Spurred on by her success, and scornful of her parents'

objections, Lois moved to Los Angeles in December of 1988 in search of stardom.

The McMillens worried about their daughter, feeling that while she was mature in her attitude, she was naïve in the ways of the world. Upon arriving in Hollywood, Lois took the stage name Lois Livingston, using her middle name, which was her maternal grandmother's maiden name. She was proud to be a direct descendant of a signer of the Declaration of Independence—Philip Livingston of New York.

Lois rented a small apartment in Studio City, just outside the Los Angeles city limits. In addition to a jungle of plants, she created a funky piece of art: a decorative birdcage that she strung with sparkly lights and called "Captured Light." Within weeks of her arrival, she found an agent. She even introduced him to her mother when she came to visit several months later. But Jo McMillen wasn't impressed by the agent or his office, which was cramped and littered with papers, and she urged Lois to move on.

In LA, Lois made a few new friends. She even landed some bit parts in movies and was a stand-in for Sharon Stone. She appeared as a dancer in *Teen Witch,* and had a small part in Walt Disney's *Who Framed Roger Rabbit.* But overall, her time in "Tinsel Town" was a disaster. The five-foot, seven-inch knockout with the flowing blond hair and dazzling green eyes quickly learned that the business was full of unsavory characters, including directors looking to trade sex for roles in feature films. It did not take long for her to figure out that it was best to steer clear of directors who asked her to come to their apartments to audition. For a time, a male friend she had made in California, Jim Morris, escorted her to casting calls. Morris, a documentary film-maker, was very protective of Lois, and referred to himself as her "bodyguard." Lois, in turn, was always there to lend a sympathetic ear when things did not go his way, both personally and professionally.

Ultimately, Lois did not win the starring roles she had dreamed of. Instead, she worked sporadically, and supplemented her meager income as an actress with unrelated side jobs as a front-desk clerk at the posh Beverly Hills Hotel, an assistant real estate broker, and a sales rep in a dealership specializing in classic and European cars. She also worked hosting benefits and parties at trendy LA nightclubs.

When Lois finally decided that things were not working out in California, she announced that she intended to return to Florida where she had spent one year in college. She believed that Florida was the new and upcoming location for wannabe actresses and models, and she told her parents that she was certain she would do better there. The McMillens were not thrilled, but felt Florida was safer than Hollywood.

In Florida, Lois met a movie producer at the hotel where her parents stayed while visiting her. At first, the handsome older man seemed interested in Lois' career goals. He handed her his card and told her she should come by his office for an interview. But when Lois went to see him, he was more interested in her than her talent. He had recently separated from his wife, and the two began a romantic affair that continued even after Lois returned to the Northeast.

Eventually, Lois decided that acting was not for her and in the early 90s enrolled at the Parsons School of Design in New York City. At first, she was pleased with the way her studies were going. One instructor even told Lois that one of her paintings was the "most striking" piece of work that she had ever seen in a class. But a break-in in the art department changed her view of the school. Among the things that were stolen was a painting that Lois had worked on for weeks— one she was particularly pleased with. She told her mother that the painting was spiritual in nature.

"It has something to do with you, Mother," she had told Jo McMillen.

Lois became infuriated when she found out that the college was focusing its attention on the missing computers and not on the "priceless" artwork. Yet, she continued to attend classes at the downtown campus, as well as at the New School for Social Research on Fifth Avenue. She studied everything from advertising to film production. She even took a course in UFO research. On St. Patrick's Day, she came to class wearing green shamrocks and tulle, and on Bastille Day she donned a tattered, vintage ensemble similar to a French officer's uniform.

Everything about Lois McMillen was a contradiction. Although she presented herself in a manner that demanded attention—her flashy clothes, her drive to be onstage and famous—friends and family say she was actually subdued and shy. Many mistook her reserve for snobbishness, and were overwhelmed by her continuous conversations about world peace and UFOs and other mystical topics. In reality, there was nothing stuck-up about Lois. She was accepting of all people and held no prejudices.

"She is beautiful inside," said her mother, Josephine, who after Lois' death continued to speak of her daughter in the present tense. "She is absolutely wonderful. But she is also very naïve."

Lois volunteered her time for a variety of causes and organizations, including the Make-A-Wish Foundation, Greenpeace, the Womens Action Coalition, ACT UP, and The Humane Society. She was also a Daughter of the American Revolution.

One of her professors at Parsons, an artist named Dustin Spear, interested her in Women in Black, an international group that protests violence against women. After attending one of Spear's courses, Lois became increasingly sensitive to the treatment of women around the world, and continued to express her contempt for injustice in many of her paintings. Her mother saved pictures of Lois marching on the United Nations dressed in shrouds. She was proud of her daughter's willingness to take a stand, as was her father. "It's too bad more people don't stand up for what they believe," Russell McMillen said.

Lois continued to date the older man she met in Florida. He divorced his wife, and the two spent long weekends together whenever he visited Manhattan. Her parents were not happy about their relationship, and let their feelings be known, even though it was clear that Lois was smitten, and she was devastated when the relationship ended.

Lois was celebrating her thirty-first birthday when she graduated from Parsons in 1996. She had already had some success as an artist. A month-long exhibit she put on at a gallery near her home had yielded $10,000. With her parents' financial help, she rented a small apartment in a doorman building on Manhattan's East Side between 44th and 45th Streets. She immediately started to look for a job. She was hoping to land a creative position that would augment the stipend she was receiving from her parents and give her time to paint. Her résumé detailed her many numerous passions:

OBJECTIVE MONEY—Travel Internationally

To create Avant Garde Art, design and visual effects. To continue Experimental & Underground animation for Video and Motion Pictures. To work with a Motion Picture Studio in the areas of Art, Direction, Entertainment, and Documentary Works that are unique and inventive. To learn and work more with Multimedia, To Write Creatively and Poetically. To climb on board with a company that deals with unique materials. To continue higher education. To research and investigate Science versus religion, and exploration of the Universe, the unknown, and theories of the Supernatural and the Occult, To find more spiritual projects. To create Visions. To be kind to all creatures and animals, uncover truth.

On the same résumé, she listed her hobbies as: "Sailboat racing, will work as a crew member to race or transport large boats, the dream to sail and race to Europe and through exotic islands worldwide. Horseback riding, Scuba Diving, Swimming, Dancing and Magic."

She got few responses, and the only offers she received were for internships at art galleries.

"How's that going to buy you breakfast?" Russell McMillen asked when she told him about the unpaid apprenticeships.

Lois' father was a pragmatist. He had grown up during the Great Depression in Bridgefield, a small steel town in northern Pennsylvania about ten miles from Pittsburgh. A self-made man, he had little understanding of the creative field that interested Lois. To him, a day's work should be rewarded with a day's pay. He saw a non-paying internship as free labor. He had worked his way through college, paying his tuition with a summer job in a local steel mill. He'd attended Carnegie Institute of Technology, now Carnegie Mellon, where he studied metallurgic engineering.

Russ was determined to make something of his life after seeing that his classmates with no college degrees ended up in blue-collar jobs at the steel mill. He graduated from Carnegie Tech and landed his first job as a metallurgist for Aluminum Company of America (Alcoa) in Cleveland, Ohio.

Eventually, he returned to the East Coast, where he held several prestigious positions. His career ended on a high note, as the chairman and CEO of the Eastern Company, a manufacturing firm in Naugatuck, Connecticut. He was pleased by the prospect of spending his retirement years with "Joie," the pet name he had for his wife.

And while Russell earned a fine living, he was not one to flaunt his material wealth. When Lois was living on her own, he agreed to help pay her bills, but made it clear that she needed to supplement the funds he was providing. Still, she was always overdrawn on her bank account, and routinely went to her parents for help.

While living in New York, Lois landed a series of unfulfilling jobs, as receptionist for Fiction Records and sales girl at the Stendhal Gallery in Soho, according to her résumé. Even Lois' career as an artist did not go as she had hoped. As hard as she tried, she could not match her early success at the Stairway Gallery in New Milford, Connecticut.

She was also grappling with personal issues. In her early thirties, she was hoping for marriage and a family of her own. Yet she had grown increasingly paranoid about men and had pulled herself out of the dating scene. She had even started carrying Mace after being mugged twice. She began collecting dolls—her mother speculated that her new interest might be in preparation for the children she longed to have.

Life in the Big Apple was lonely for Lois, and she missed the security of home. She decided to move back to Connecticut where she could concentrate on her artwork without the pressures of paying bills, and split her time between Middlebury and Tortola.

Back in her childhood home, she found comfort in gardening and became a virtual recluse, spending hours in a small studio in her parents' finished basement. Her parents continued to supplement her with a weekly allowance. She supplemented the stipend by selling hand-made items such as ornate Christmas wreaths for $200 apiece.

Her continued efforts to curate an art show on Tortola were all for naught. She needed a government license to run the show and bureaucrats never responded to her application for a license.

In Tortola, she sat in the kitchen area working on what would be her final piece of art, a project she would never complete. She told her father that the painting, with stars and crescent-shaped moons, and the Queen of Hearts playing card glued to its canvas, "has something to do with death."

Her father did not quite understand what she meant.

CHAPTER ELEVEN

Day Two

As many Tortolan residents were heading off to church on Sunday-morning, police were working their sources in the community. One tipster pointed a finger at a local man named Alvin Martin. The unidentified source told police that he had seen Martin on Friday night in the company of a white woman who fit the description of Lois McMillen. Martin and the woman were in a vehicle similar to what Lois had been driving that night, the informant said.

When police found the slim, five-foot, eleven-inch–tall black man, he willingly accompanied them to the West End headquarters. They learned that he was not a "Belonger" on Tortola, but hailed from a neighboring island. During the interview, Martin identified the woman he had been with on Friday evening as his fiancée, a white woman with blond hair. He had no objection when police asked him for finger-nail clippings and a sample of his hair, thick dreadlocks that fell down past his shoulders. Investigators followed up on the information provided by Martin, and confirmed his story. He was never a suspect in the minds of police.

Another name came up in the investigation, too—Luigi Lungarini. Jo McMillen had given police a short list of Lois' friends and associates on Tortola. Lungarini was among them. He had dated Lois during the family's visit to the island in the summer of 1998. Mrs. McMillen remembered that he had just moved to Tortola from Montreal in Canada, when the two started dating. "He was starting a new life," she recalled. "I wasn't too keen on him. But I believe that you have to let your children do their own thing, and let them know what you think."

At first, Lois was quite taken with the strapping man with the light Italian accent. Lungarini was born in Rome, Italy, and had moved to Canada some time later. On Tortola, he lived in an apartment he rented in Josiah's Bay on the island's East End. He had earned a reputation as a skilled craftsman and was best known for his expert tile work at a restaurant and catering hall just outside Road Town.

When Lois invited him to the villa at Belmont Grove for cocktails and to meet her parents, Lungarini brought his portfolio along to show her parents.

"He tried to do things in the proper way," the mature woman recounted. "When he came for cocktails, he brought photos of the work he had done. He tried quite hard to have us like him." But Lois' mother did not think Luigi a suitable match for her daughter.

"He seemed to be quite a bit older," she went on. "He was too old for Lois. He had a nine-year-old son, and he was starting out all over again. Too many red flags."

At the time, Luigi was thirty-five years old, but the fact that he had already been married and started a family had made him seem much older to the McMillens.

In spite of her mother's wariness, Lois carried on a relationship with the dark-haired Canadian man that lasted for eight weeks. Lois even confided details of her relationship with Luigi in e-mails she sent to her friend Jim Morris in Los Angeles. According to Morris, Lois was taken with Lungarini, and was even thinking about marriage. Jim would later recall that Lois was interested in settling down and starting a family, and was searching for a proper mate. But, as time passed, Jim claimed the e-mails she wrote to him talked about Luigi's temper and other personal information that Morris declined to reveal.

Toward the end of the summer, Lois was cooling off on the darkly handsome Canadian man and was even trying to break away from him. Her mother recalled that her attempts to quell the relationship were met with resistance. Luigi was persistent and did not want to let Lois go. Jo McMillen said she stepped in when she learned that Luigi had borrowed the family's rental car, and had been involved in an accident. He then tried to cover up the collision, taking the car to a mechanic friend who did a poor job of patching up the wreckage. Hours after the McMillens returned the car, a representative from the rental company called to alert them to the damage. The agent told Mrs. McMillen that he intended to charge her husband's credit card in the amount of $800 to cover the cost of the repairs.

To make up for the incident, Luigi invited the McMillens out to dinner at a local restaurant and subsequently prepared several meals for them at their villa in Belmont Grove. But Lois' mother was not impressed. She told her daughter that what Luigi had done after the car crash spoke volumes about his character. She then informed Lois that the family was leaving the island that Saturday, and if she wished to remain on Tortola she would have to find another place to stay. She also politely asked Luigi for the $800 that had been charged to her husband's credit card, suspecting that he probably didn't have the money to pay the bill. "He was very upset that we left so abruptly," Jo McMillen recalled. "Luigi came and took Lois to the ferry, and that was the end of it."

Mrs. McMillen remembered being surprised when a letter from Luigi that was addressed to Lois arrived at the family's home in Connecticut some months later. Inside was a check in the amount of $500. She said that she really never expected to recover any of the money and was pleased that Luigi had accepted responsibility for his actions by sending Lois what he could.

By then Lois had all but forgotten about Luigi and had moved on to other things, said her mother. "She wasn't focused on anybody at that point," Mrs. McMillen recalled. "Once she got home, she started to think about things in a more clear fashion, and she realized that it was not right for him to borrow that car and then not pay for the damage."

Police were anxious to speak with Lungarini about his whereabouts on the night of January 14. Neighbors told investigators who went to his residence in Josiah's Bay that he had not been home in the last forty-eight hours.

At Road Town police headquarters, Sergeant Julian Harley was taking a closer look at the evidence the investigative team had collected the previous day. The forensics expert began by examining the men's wet sneakers that Inspector George had found by the pool at Zebra House, and the delicate ladies' sandals that police discovered at the crime scene. He noticed what appeared to be blood on the tongue of one of the Adidas sneakers taken from William Labrador. He also observed what appeared to be blood on the two back straps of Lois' Pierre Dumas sandals. When his examination was complete, the sergeant placed the Adidas sneakers and the Kastels that belonged to Evan George in a locked exhibit room to dry.

Later that day, he examined Lois McMillen's vehicle, which had been hauled to Road Town headquarters on a flatbed truck. Constable Mason had already turned over to him the key police found in the ignition, along with other items of evidence that had been collected in connection with the investigation. Lab tests would later reveal the presence of DNA on the key, but its origin would never be traced— prosecutors said it was because a number of officers had handled the key, contaminating potential evidence.

As Harley sifted through the items, cataloguing them in police record books, young Evan George was in a first-floor office of the Road Town headquarters talking with two uniformed officers. The twenty-two-year-old man had been in the small office with the investigators since ten a.m. that morning. He had spent a near sleepless night, tossing and turning on the wood bench that he had been ordered to use as a bed. Under the glare of the ever-glowing fluorescent lights of the jail's locked waiting room, he had struggled to settle down and get some rest. But with no pillow or blanket to ease the discomfort of the hard bleacher-like bed, and people walking in and out of the area all night long, he had slept barely five minutes.

Evan was hopeful that once he gave his statement to the officers, he would be released from custody. He believed the investigators' often-repeated reassurances that "It won't be too much longer,"—the stock response they gave to Michael and Evan every time they entered the secured holding area.

"Good morning." An officer in a pale gray uniform had greeted Evan that morning. Chief Inspector Jacob George had instructed Police Constable Adrian Kartic to visit the youthful, sandy-haired man for the purpose of obtaining an official statement from him.

"Yes, hello," Evan responded politely.

"Please follow me, sir." Kartic and another officer led the lithe young man to the small, sparsely furnished incident unit room, where he introduced himself to Evan.

"I am Adrian Kartic. And this is Constable Johnny," the lean, uniformed officer gestured to the man standing by his side. "The police are conducting an investigation into the death of Lois McMillen and are of the view that you can assist."

Evan nodded. "I will try to assist you as much as I can. I only met her a few times."

"I intend to make a written statement of what you have to say. You can write it yourself, or have someone write it for you."

"You guys do the writing," Evan announced. "I'm on vacation."

"Fine. Let's begin," said Kartic, pulling a standard police statement form from a desk drawer. He handed the page over to Evan, and asked him to read it and then sign his name in the blank space provided.

"Did you read it, sir?" Kartic was referring to the cautionary preamble typewritten on the form.

"Yes."

"Do you understand what you have read?"

"Yes." Evan nodded.

"Okay, let's begin. What is your full name, sir?"

"Evan Steven George."

"What is your occupation?"

"Construction."

"Date of birth?"

"June first, 1977."

Officers Kartic and Johnny would spend the next five hours with Evan George. The constables found the man's recollection of his time on Tortola so detailed that they asked him to repeat his story a second time—hoping the twenty-two-year-old would slip up and reveal information they could use in their investigation. Officer Kartic took notes as Evan, in between bites of a candy bar, began by recalling the snafu with immigration authorities that he encountered en route to Tortola.

Below is an excerpt from Evan's signed statement to police. The passage begins with recollections of his movements on Wednesday, January 12, and pertains to his personal interactions with Lois McMillen. It continues through Friday, January 14, the day of Lois' disappearance.

On Wednesday, 12th January 2000 . . . Sometime around 8 p.m., Michael, Alex and I left the Zebra House and walked over to Bomba Shack, as far as I can recall William remained at home. At Bomba Shack, we had more drinks and Michael and I shared a plate of food. Alex spoke to a Taxi-man named "Salo" about getting us a ride back to the house when we were ready to go home. Salo is a friend of Alex.

Whilst we were still at Bomba's, Alex was talking to a woman. He then introduced Michael and I to join him and the woman. We went over to where they were and I introduced myself to the woman who told me her name was Lois. Sometime previously, Alex had mentioned Lois to me. He had said that he was at the Zebra House about three years ago and he had met her and slept with her a few times and that one reason he is here right now is because she is also on the island.

After I met Lois, we all got one beer each. Lois had a Carib Beer with a lime stuck in the top of the bottle. She requested this lime so that no one could put anything in her drink. Lois was wearing a very dressy outfit. She was wearing black and gold pants, black shirt with a fish net with beads draped around her. She had on very large earrings shaped like hearts and sailboats. She also had glitter on her face.

Lois drank about three beers with us. She had mentioned earlier that she only intended to have one beer with us. After we met Lois, Alex told Salo that he would not need a ride from him again since Lois would take us home to the Zebra House in her vehicle.

Lois does not like anyone to smoke around her. She dropped Alex, Michael and I off at the driveway of Zebra House and she left. She did not come out of her jeep when she dropped us off.

Evan recalled that later that day, Michael called Lois to invite her to hang out:

She said that she had to take her dad first and then she will check with us. Sometime around 5 p.m., Lois drove up to our driveway in her jeep. William, Michael and I boarded the jeep and we went to Pusser's Restaurant at West End. We left Alex at the Zebra House. He was sleeping. As far as I can recall, Lois did not ask for or about Alex when she picked us up.

At Pusser's, Lois, William, Michael and I ordered some beers and forty chicken wings. Lois and William were sitting at the bar and Michael and I sat with two girls named Cathy and Catherine and their family at a table next to the bar where William and Lois were.

We sat at the table until the chicken wings we had ordered arrived, at which time we joined Lois and William at the bar. Lois was wearing a gold colored shirt with paisley designs; gold colored pants and gold high heel shoes that had glitter on them. Her shirt was long sleeved and it had a big gold colored button on it. We remained at the restaurant until some time around 6:30 p.m. We then left this restaurant with the intention of going to the Pusser's Restaurant in Road Town. However, William did not want to go to Pusser's Restaurant in Road Town, so we dropped him off in the area of Sebastian's.

After dropping off William at Sebastian's, I moved into the front passenger car seat. Lois drove Michael and I to the Pusser's at Road Town. There she parked at the Pusser's parking lot and she, Michael and I went into the restaurant. There were very many people at this restaurant. We ordered some drinks along with a bacon cheeseburger and sat outside. We had a few drinks and some people who were sitting at the table next to ours were complimenting Lois for being Miss Tambourine Equinox some years ago. She said that she was and that she was in the newspaper for it.

Whilst at Pusser's, I left Lois and Michael and went across the road to the pay phone and I telephoned Alex and asked him if he would like to join us. He declined.

I returned to Pusser's and then we started making jokes about Alex. By the end of the evening, it came out that Alex and William are lovers. This was a joke. I assume that they aren't.

While we were also at Pusser's, a black guy who looked to be about 17 yrs old with short locks on his head, about 5'6" or 5'7" tall, of medium build and wearing a blue shirt was trying to get Lois undivided attention. He made comments like "I know you," "You are beautiful." "What are you doing?" He was also trying to get her telephone number. His friend then came and got him and he went into the restaurant. He had said to her before going into the restaurant that she must check with him before she left. Sometime around 10 p.m., we said goodbye to the people who were sitting at the table next to us and we left. Lois drove us home. When she dropped off Michael and I, we invited her to come into the Zebra House for a drink; she refused saying that she will come over for lunch the next day instead. Alex, Michael and I smoked a little pot and had a few more drinks and then we went to sleep.

On Friday 14th of January, 2000 I awoke sometime around 11:30 a.m. . . . Then Michael, Alex and I went for a hike and rock climbing. While we were rock climbing, Alex fell and scraped his right arm and left leg I think. I twisted my right knee. Michael and William were not injured as far as I know . . . At the Zebra House, William started to fix dinner and I took forty dollars from Michael's wallet and I went to the commissary at Long Bay. There I purchased some wine, Long Bay rum, coconut mix, pineapple, cigarettes, and candies. I returned to Zebra House and Michael, William and Alex and I smoked some cigarettes, drank some Red Stripe beers and ate some crepes and chatted. Sometime around 8 p.m., we had pasta for dinner. After dinner, we had Piña Coladas made by William. In the mean time, Alex had contacted "Salo" and made arrangements for him to pick us up at 10:30 p.m. Sometime around 8:45 p.m. Clifford telephoned and said he is bringing a friend by the Zebra House from the Equinox House.

At 8:50 p.m., Clifford arrived over with a guy named Jeffrey. He is about 27 years-old, blond hair, blue eyes, slim, about 5'9". He said he was high on mushrooms. Jeffrey is from the coast guard boat. Clifford said he found Jeffrey at the beach. Some time around 10:30 p.m., Clifford left with Jeffrey. Salo arrived around 10:40 p.m. for us. Alex and I boarded "Salo's" car while William and Michael were getting dressed. About five minutes later, they joined us.

From Zebra House, "Salo" drove to Pusser's West End. There, Michael and Alex went to the ATM machine. William and I remained in the car and "Salo" went into Pusser's for a drink.

We then left Pusser's West End, and dropped off William in the area of Sebastian's because he did not want to go with us. "Salo" then dropped Michael and I off at Quito's, and he and Alex went to run an errand. There was live music at Quito's. I think that it was sometime like 11:45 p.m. when we arrived at Quito's. Michael and I had about two or three drinks before Alex and "Salo" returned.

At Quito, I met a pretty girl named LaDonna who works at the plastic surgery hospital in Tortola. She sat at the same table with me, Alex and Michael. There were other persons at this table also. We did a lot of drinking at Quito's. Michael and I then went for a walk on the beach. Alex then joined us but left to go roll a joint for us. "Salo" then joined Michael and I and asked us where was Alex. We then returned to the club and met Alex standing next to the bathroom speaking with his friend named Steven. Michael, Alex and I boarded "Salo's" car and "Salo" collected a Rasta friend of his named "Moon."

From Quito's, "Salo" drove us up to the bottom of Belmont Hill and dropped us off. This was sometime around 2:30 a.m. on Saturday 15th January 2000. For the whole of that day and night I did not see Lois. Personally, I would say that we called "Salo" instead of Lois on Friday because of convenience.

. . . During the night, we met Lois at Bomba Shack she had invited me and Alex to go sailing with her some time, once we packed our own lunch basket. She said that she has a captain friend. I don't know if she was serious or not.

Evan George signed the account at 3:00 p.m. that Sunday afternoon, after having it read back to him by Constable B. Johnny. Police were fascinated by the detail that he provided, particularly about the men's use of marijuana during their stay on the island.

But giving his statement did not win Evan his freedom as he had hoped.

CHAPTER TWELVE

The Case Against the Four Men

It was Michael Spicer's turn to speak to police. At ten minutes after three on Sunday, January 16, Sergeant Duncan Williams found the seemingly unflappable Spicer seated on the bunk bed in the cell where he had spent the night. The conditions at the Road Town jail were horrific. The unit itself was filthy, as was the tiny bathroom area. The units were initially used as "drunk tanks" where people picked up for disorderly conduct and such would be put to sober up overnight. The island's prison facility had been located in Road Town, not far from the police station, but its doors had been closed for good several years earlier when work on the new facility at Balsam Ghut was completed. It has been reported that the prison complex in Road Town was considered among the worst in the Caribbean. It was so filthy and dilapidated that it had to be shut down.

Unlocking the heavy bars of the cell, Sergeant Williams directed Michael to a small conference room.

"Mr. Spicer," Sergeant Williams introduced himself. He had been instructed by Chief Inspector George to take a statement from the resident of Zebra House. "I would like to speak with you about your whereabouts for the past few days."

Michael was agreeable.

"Can you please state your full name and address for the record, sir?"

"Michael Graves Spicer. I reside at Zebra House in Belmont Estate."

"What is your occupation, sir?"

"I am a law student," Michael responded in a calm voice. Williams would later learn that the information was simply not true. While Michael had attended Georgetown University Law School in Washington, DC, he failed to reveal that he had graduated from the prestigious institution in 1990. More than nine years had passed since he had completed the rigorous program, yet he was telling police that he was still a law student.

Michael later stated he was embarrased to admit that he was unemployed and had never passed the bar.

"Date of birth?" Sergeant Williams continued.

"January first, 1964."

"Place of birth?"

"Watertown, New York." The Upstate New York town was where Michael had grown up, and where his father had run a successful law practice. It was also where Michael's sister, Chrysta "Chris" Lynne, lived with her husband and son, and near where his older brother Lewis "Casey" Spicer III resided with his wife and five children. Michael's brother worked as an educator at one of the schools in the area.

"Mr. Spicer, I intend to make a written record of what you say. You can write it or have someone write it for you," the sergeant announced.

"You can write it," Michael replied. He began his story with details of his arrival by ferry, and then described his two evenings with Lois McMillen.

On Wednesday 12th of January, 2000, sometime during the night, I think it was about 11:00 p.m., we saw Lois McMillen at Bomba Shack. It was Alex who had already spoken to Lois who said that she'll give us a ride home. William was not with us, he had stopped off at Sebastian's. Lois spoke to us at Bomba's, she complained about a local guy who was drunk and stumbling over everybody. Alex told us that he knew Lois in New York and he had dated her there. However, he was avoiding her down here since he felt that she was a little "nutty" crazy and not his type.

When it was time to go home, I offered her a beer, she had two, then she drove us home. We did not go any other place. On arrival home, Alex lingered in the car with her [Lois] for about two minutes then he came inside. The rest of us were already inside. Shortly thereafter, we went to bed.

On Thursday 13th January 2000 around 4:00 p.m., I called Lois and I invited her to come over to have a drink or to swim. She told me that her father was not doing well and that she was going to take him to the beach. At about 5:00 p.m., I called her back and spoke to her mother. I told her to inform Lois that since it's already late, we shall go to Pusser's instead. She said that will be okay and she'll tell Lois.

Lois came about 6:30 p.m. picked up Evan, William and I and we drove to Pussers at Frenchman's Cay. Alex stayed behind for some reason. At Pusser's, we had a bottle of wine and some chicken wings. We then drove to Sebastian's to drop off William and then Lois, Evan and myself went to Pussers Road Town. There Lois and I had a drink and Evan had a hamburger. We stayed there for about forty minutes. We left Pusser's and drove straight home to Belmont. We arrived home about 11:20 p.m. On our arrival home, Alex was at home but William wasn't.

On Friday 14th January 2000, we got up at about 10:00 am, we hung around the house until about 1:00–1:20 p.m., then came down the hill to go walking around the point. When we got to the bottom of the driveway, we saw a strange man walking a dog at the entrance to the driveway. We then went back up and secured the house. Alex was kind of upset about the guy being around. The guy was tall, over six feet, brown skin, slim build, nothing unusual about his facial features. After securing the house, we went walking around Gunn Point and Belmont Point. Then we went for a swim at Long Bay Beach, that is Alex and I. William and Evan walked ahead of us. Evan came back down the hill to go to the commissary at Long Bay Hotel to buy something for dinner.

We arrived home about 6:00 p.m. that evening. We prepared dinner, then we invited a neighbor Clifford and Jeffery who are both visitors to the island, to join us for dinner and a drink. After dinner, we called "Salo" our cab driver to give us a pick up. He came about 11:00 p.m., picked us up and drove to the ATM machine at Soper's Hole, where I made a withdrawal. We then left for Quito's in Cane Garden Bay. On our way to Quito's, William was dropped off at Sebastian's. We then continued straight to Quito's that is Alex and Evan and I. We remained at Quito's until the music stopped and the place closed down.

I never saw Lois anytime on Friday 14th January, 2000. The last time I saw her was when she dropped me at home on Thursday night. "Salo" drove us home from Quito's, while at Quito's, we didn't hang together, that is "Salo" however, when the business closed, he was there to take us home. We went straight home from Quito's, "Salo" picked up a friend at Quito's and dropped him off at Carrot Bay. I do not know his name. I think it's someone who Salo knew.

It was 4:23 p.m. when Michael Spicer signed the above statement in front of Sergeant Duncan Williams—almost the exact same time that William Labrador was signing the statement he had just given to Sergeant Dennis Jones.

Jones had been instructed by Inspector George to visit

Labrador at the East End police station where the olive-skinned man had spent the night in a small, sparsely furnished cell.

Like his three friends, William Labrador had chosen to let someone else write down his statement. Oddly, his official deposition to police listed his name in separate locations on the document with two different middle initials. The first read: William J. Labrador. The second: William B. Labrador. Court records show that his real name is William Benjamin Labrador.

"What is your address, Mr. Labrador?"

"Southampton, New York." William gave police the address of his mother's residence on the East End of Long Island, and not the one for the spacious Soho apartment that he told Michael he had once rented in the old Police Building in downtown Manhattan. It is unclear where William was living at the time that he traveled to Tortola for his Millennium holiday.

"What is your occupation, sir?"

"Businessman, model, and talent agent." Mr. Labrador had initially told police that he was an investment banker. But investigators contend that that statement was misleading, and maintain that he is not qualified to work in that field.

"Date of birth?"

"November fourteenth, 1963. I am thirty-six years old."

"Okay, sir. You may begin."

William Labrador detailed his first visit to Tortola in 1989, and then moved into the details of his current visit to the island and his interaction with Lois McMillen.

> I first met with a friend of Michael's, namely Evan George, who according to Michael had been friends for the past two years. I met him on Tuesday, the 11th day of January 2000, when he arrived into the island. For this Christmas season vacation, I arrived on Tortola on Friday the 31st of December, 1999 along with Alexander. Alexander and I stayed

at the Jolly Roger from that time until the 3rd of
January 2000. On that same date, Michael arrived
from Virginia and was picked up at the West End
ferry by myself and Alexander. I also picked up
Charles Bailey aka "OB". I drove Michael and OB
to the Zebra House and Equinox House respectively.

The Zebra House is owned by Michael's parents. The Equinox House is owned by Mr. Bailey
and it is located at the base of Michael's driveway.
While driving to Belmont that, [sic] I had seen
Ms. Livingston driving out of Belmont in a blue
jeep, which I believe is owned by her parents. I had
met Ms. Livingston for the first time in 1997 at the
Bomba Shack. On that particular night at the end of
the evening she had driven Alexander and myself
back to the Zebra House. Of the two of us, during
that night, Ms. Livingston spent most of the night
with Alexander.

On the 3rd of January, 2000 after the arrival of
Michael, myself and Alexander moved to the Zebra
House. Alexander stayed in the main house and
Mrs. Spicer's bedroom while I stayed/slept in the
guest house adjacent to the main house. For our
stay, we enjoyed biking, hanging out and socializ-
ing. Evan George from Washington, D.C. arrived
on Tortola on the 11th of January 2000. According
to Michael, Evan was a friend of his whom he had
met about two years ago. Evan he says stays in one
of his houses at Washington, D.C. Evan stayed in
the main house. In a conversation with Michael, he
had told me that on Wednesday the 12th of January
2000.

Alexander, Evan and himself had met Livingston
at the Bomba Shack during the night and she had
given them a ride home. There was no conversation
about Ms. Livingston apart from the fact that they
had met her. The next time I saw Ms. Livingston
[was] on Thursday the 13th of January, 2000.

Myself and the Guys [sic] had spoke and based on the fact that she had given the three guys a ride the night before that it would be appropriate to ask her to come up for a drink. Michael had the Livingston telephone number. After we had spoken, Michael called Lois and invited her as planned. Then after he had spoken to Lois, we all decided that we will go to Pussers in Soper's Hole. Lois came to pick us up at approximately 5:30–5:45 pm. She was driving a small four-door vehicle, a rental. It was not a jeep, more like a standard mini van. We arrived at Pussers approximately 6:00 pm. It was myself, Evan, and Michael along with Lois. Alexander stayed at home, he said he was feeling under the weather, tired and wanted to clean the kitchen. We spent about one hour at Pussers because we left about 7:00–7:15 p.m. Evan and Michael wanted to go into Road Town. I had decided that I wasn't going into Road Town and Lois was not sure. Eventually, we drove back over Zion Hill. I walked over to the Sugar Mill Hotel and had dinner at the restaurant on the seaside. I left the Sugar Mill around 10:00–10:15 p.m. and stopped at Bomba Shack. There, I stayed for about 15 minutes in conversation with a heavy-set bartender. A white, blonde lady. I eventually returned home around 11:00–11:15 p.m. When I had gotten home all of the lights were out in the main house which is an indication that everyone was already in bed. I went to bed shortly after I arrived home.

On Friday the 14th of January 2000, I woke up at about 7:45–8:00 a.m. and proceeded to hike over Belmont hill. When I left, everyone was asleep. My hike took me down to the post office at the ferry dock where I sent off two post cards, one to my sister, and one to my mother. I returned from hike approximately 9:15–9:30 am. I proceeded to make coffee. Then everybody got up no later than 12:00

midday. Then we all decided that after coffee, we will go hiking over Gunpoint and Belmont Point. We stopped at Smuggler's first. We left at around 1:00 p.m., so Smugglers stop would have been about 1:30 p.m. From there, we hiked around Gunpoint at which point we had found a blue bumper guard for a yacht which all presented to Mr. Dennison's son on our return. Then from Smuggler's we proceeded to hike around Belmont Point. Upon completion, Michael and Alexander went swimming and Evan and I proceeded to the Zebra House. That would have been around 5:30 pm. I showered and started cooking thereafter. Everybody was back at the house by 6:30 pm. We all had dinner which was over by 9:00 p.m. After dinner around 9:30 p.m., Michael contacted Clifford at the Equinox House and invited Clifford and Jeffrey up to Zebra House for a drink. Clifford had left a message on Michael's answering machine at 4:06 pm stating that he would like to come by with a gentleman he met at the beach whose name was Jeffrey. Clifford I know as a friend of Mr. Bailey who has been visiting for some years now. Jeffrey and Clifford arrived at the Equinox House [sic] around 10:00 p.m. We all had a few drinks except Jeffrey who had water in recuperation from Bomba Punch that afternoon. That night we had to go to Cane Garden Bay and we arranged for Salo the taxi driver to pick us up around 11:00 pm.

Upon Salo's arrival around 11:00 p.m., Clifford and Jeffrey left. Prior to this, Jeffrey mentioned that he was a petty officer onboard the Coast Guard vessel which was in front at Road Town. Jeffrey had circled over from Road Town and had planned to spend the night on the beach in Long Bay. Alexander, Michael, Evan and myself left to go to the Barclay's ATM in Soper's Hole to get money for Cane Garden Bay. Michael and Alexander were the ones who went to get money while Evan and I stayed in the car. While in the car, I said to Evan that I was too tired and I would go home instead. After leaving, we drove back over Zion Hill and I got off at the junction opposite Sebastian's. I proceeded to walk home, which was about 11:20 p.m. I arrived home at 11:50 p.m. I watched the rest of NFL Tonight on ESPN and then at midnight I watched Area 51 on the Learning Channel and proceeded to go to bed around 12:15 am. I was awakened by voices around 2:15 am–2:30 am. I recognized Michael's voice and there were other voices. Then, I went back to bed. During the time I was at the house, and when the guys came I did not receive any call or any visitors. In the morning around 7:45 a.m., I woke up and walked over to the Sugar Mill for breakfast.

Upon my return from Sugar Mill, I stopped at Sebastian's to pick up provisions at 9:30 a.m. I returned home by 10:00, put the groceries away, at which point Alexander had awakened.

Around 11:00 am, Alexander left to go into the main house around 11:15 am. I sat by the pool for about forty full minutes and read. At 12:15 p.m., the police arrived for the first time and wanted to speak to Michael to inform us of what had taken place in West End. That was, that Ms. Livingston was found dead. Shortly afterwards, the police left, I was in shock when I heard the news. We sat there stunned basically did nothing. Then Michael was contemplating if we should contact Clifford or the Livingstons but I told Michael not to interfere because it was a criminal investigation. Then the police returned again at 1:45 p.m. To my knowledge, none of the guys had or was having an intimate relationship with Ms. Livingston.

It was 5:25 p.m. when William Labrador completed his recounting to Sergeant Dennis Jones. Jones had been among the seven investigators to search the Drake's Highway location the previous morning.

Another member of that same search team, Sergeant Anderson Blackman, had been dispatched to the West End police substation to take the statement of William's longtime friend, Alexander Benedetto. When Blackman reported to the Road Town police headquarters for duty earlier in the day, he had been called into a meeting with Chief Inspector Jacob George. He was already convinced that all four of the men from Zebra House were lying to police. In fact, it was his initial distrust of their responses to the questions he posed when he first visited Zebra House that had prompted police to focus on the foursome so early in the investigation.

Blackman had already convinced the inspector that the men had been acting suspiciously when he first went to see them that Saturday morning, and by nightfall on Saturday evening his superior officer had come around to his way of thinking.

But Deputy Commissioner Johnston remained cautious. Johnston had instructed his officers to continue their line of inquiry, yet took steps to insure that they followed up on all leads. While he was not convinced that his investigators had sufficient evidence to charge the men with a crime, he, too, believed that there was cause for suspicion. A veteran of law enforcement, he knew all too well that a "policeman's hunch" was never enough to win a case in a court of law. He was waiting to hear something that would prove to him the men's involvement in the McMillen girl's death.

As Blackman steered the brawny Mitsubishi Montero along the Sir Francis Drake Highway en route to the West End substation, a team of plainclothesmen was conducting interviews with employees at the Jolly Roger Inn, which sat at the end of the two-lane main road. The two-story bar/restaurant was a tenth of a mile past the West End ferry terminal at the end of the Drake's Highway. It was the last known destination of Lois McMillen that past Friday night, and the first stop for two of the four men police were now detaining.

Employees at the waterside restaurant were surprised by the sight of the plainclothes investigators, who were there to conduct interviews into the possible murder of one of their regular patrons. Several of the workers recalled seeing Lois at the bar that night. One was Omar Hurst. Omar, a strapping man with curly, close-cropped hair and piercing brown eyes, told police that he was one of the bartenders manning the small upstairs lounge that night. The upstairs dining area has a casual feel to it, with big wood tables, each with a map of the British Virgin Islands laminated onto the top. Colorful nautical flags flap from the rafters, and the clank of sailboat riggings from the harbor is all but drowned out by the music that plays from the stereo tucked in a corner of the L-shaped bar. Above it, a television set connected to a satellite dish broadcasts American programming. One of the more unusual aspects of this bar/restaurant is a small lending library tucked into a corner where patrons could pick up a book to read or drop one off for others to enjoy.

Omar told the investigators that Lois McMillen was by herself when she arrived at the restaurant on Friday evening, and recalled that when he saw her leave the bar that night, she was still alone. He remembered watching her pull away in her SUV from his perch behind the upstairs bar.

Two other bartenders told police they, too, had seen Lois there that night. They both said that she was alone when she left the Jolly Roger sometime after ten p.m.

The bar's owner, Louis Schwartz, spent several hours talking with plainclothesmen about the striking blond woman he had known for nearly ten years. He was a friend of the McMillen family. He and his wife, Kay, lived in the same Belmont Estates complex as the older couple, and had many of the same friends. Both families were members of the regular cocktail party circuit, and often saw each other at the unending string of get-togethers and dinners hosted by neighbors in the private community.

Schwartz, a fortyish man with thinning locks of wavy

brown hair, was visibly disturbed by news of Lois' death. He recalled the previous evening's conversation with the sweet-natured woman who, over the years, had been a regular at the restaurant. "When Lois first arrived that evening, I spoke with her at the upstairs drink rail for about twenty minutes," he recounted, referring to the long wood bar that rimmed two walls of the restaurant and boasted views of the wharf of Soper's Hole across the harbor. He told police that he and Lois talked about superficial things, her parents, his kids, the BVI, local happenings, and New York. Schwartz said that she was in good spirits, and seemed happy when she went downstairs to the patio area, where she sat at the bar. He was not sure if she was drinking, but he thought it most unlikely.

"Lois never had more than one or two drinks," he smiled. "She never got drunk."

When he saw Lois again, she was seated at a table talking to a man he did not immediately recognize. It was only later that he realized it was Chris Crawford, the American from Massachusetts whom he had also known for close to ten years. Shortly after, Schwartz, too, watched Lois pull away in her car. He said he was standing on the ground level of the restaurant, under the towering palms that shade the parking lot, when she climbed into her vehicle and drove off. "It was around nine to nine forty-five or so," he recounted. "I saw her drive out by herself with no car following her, and no evidence of anyone else in the car."

"Lois was often alone," Schwartz recalled in a throaty voice. "Sometimes she came and met friends, but more often she was alone. It was difficult to miss Lois. She always wore very bold and colorful clothes, like a bright red bustier with a black cardigan and ruby-red lipstick.

"She wore a modicum of makeup, and her hair was dyed bright blond," he said with a broad smile. "She was always making a statement. But she wouldn't hurt a fly. If there was an ant on the ground, Lois would walk around it."

Louis Schwartz also knew three of the men police were now holding at the West End substation. William Labrador and Alexander Benedetto had rented rooms from him earlier in the month, as they had done on previous trips to the island.

"They'd rent rooms from me off and on over the years," he recalled of the two New Yorkers. "They'd call from the States and say, 'Lou, do you have any rooms for these dates?' They'd reserve one or two rooms. William and Alex would stay for two or three or four nights until they met their friends who owned homes."

Michael Spicer was also a familiar face at the restaurant, and his mother's house was not far from the Schwartzes' in Belmont Estates.

"Alex, William, and Michael were like a bunch of college guys," Schwartz said of the three men. "They all hung out together and partied. They were rowdy, and they had a reputation for drinking and partying.

"They would hike the trails of Belmont Estate for exercise and perhaps once a week, they would come in to get soda or beer and their legs and arms would be all scratched up from getting caught in the thorny bushes," Schwartz recounted.

He was referring to the rugged terrain on the western tip of the island between Belmont Estates and the area by the Jolly Roger. The area is criss-crossed by a mix of dirt roads and hiking paths and two sugar loaves, or points, called Belmont Point and Steel Point. Local residents often used the back road that runs between the Belmont Estates and the vicinity of the West End ferry terminal. Hiking the road with its steep ascents and descents can take as long as forty-five minutes. Driving it takes about ten minutes.

"They were loud and boisterous, both at my place and at Bomba's," the owner of the Jolly Roger said of Michael, William, and Alex. "But I've never seen them violent."

Three miles up the road from the Jolly Roger Inn at the West End substation, Sergeant Blackman was greeting the constable on desk duty. "Good day, Mr. Bobb," Blackman respectfully addressed the officer in uniform standing in the lobby. "Can you accompany me to the holding cell? I need to speak with Mr. Benedetto." Kendolph Bobb was the constable who had found Lois' rental car at the ferry terminal the day before.

"Mr. Benedetto, my name is Anderson Blackman. Can you please follow me?"

Alex was immediately mistrustful of the two investigators who had come to see him. Yet he managed to stay composed and was agreeable to their request. An ominous feeling overcame him as he followed the constables to the small office that belonged to Blackman.

"Mr. Benedetto, I am carrying out an investigation into the death of Lois McMillen of Belmont Estate," the sergeant began, motioning for the man with the light, even tan to have a seat.

"I will assist you in any way that I can," Alex responded. "I will tell you what I know and you can record it."

For the next hour and forty-five minutes, Alex would tell the officers the following details of his initial contact with Lois McMillen at Bomba's Shack at eleven p.m. on Wednesday night and of his whereabouts on the night of her death:

. . . We had a very peaceful, kind and sympathetic conversation. She was alone at the time and I was with Michael and Evan. When we were ready to leave Bomba's Shack Lois gave us a ride to the driveway of Zebra House at our request. This was about 1:00 a.m. on Thursday 13th 2000 when she dropped us off. I gave her a hug and wished her well with her father and that was the last time I saw Lois McMillen.

On that said Thursday none of us left the Zebra House that I can recall. On Friday 14th January 2000 we walked the trail from Belmont to Steel Point to Soper's Hole and Smuggler's Cove, jumped in the sea at Smuggler's Cove. We then walked home and William fixed lunch. We reached home sometime in the afternoon and remained for the rest of the day. On Friday evening around 7 or 8 o'clock an elderly gentleman named Clifford Lefebvre residing at Equinox House came up to Zebra House with a guest for some wine. Michael, Evan, William and myself were at home at the time. In a conversation at the house, Clifford told us that he had just had lunch with Lois McMillen. While Clifford and his guest were at the Zebra House I showed some scrapes and cuts which I had sustained while the four of us were climbing around Belmont Point on that said day. At 10:00 p.m. a cab driver by the name of David Blyden came to the Zebra House and picked us up intending to take us to Quito's. Upon reaching Sebastian's Hotel, William decided that he did not want to go and got out of the cab. The three of us then continued to Quito's where we remained until 03:00 a.m. until the band finished.

On our return home, William was at home in the guesthouse asleep. I saw his feet through the sliding glass door on the bed. Michael, Evan, and myself watched a movie for about an hour and then went to sleep. I woke up about 10:00 a.m. on Saturday 15 January 2000 and saw that everyone was still asleep so I went down to the end of Long Bay Beach and jumped into the ocean as well as got a burger at the restaurant.

On that morning I heard the telephone rang twice before I left home. When I returned from the beach, I did not see anyone at home so I took up a book went on the porch and started reading until someone came home. Quite surprisingly when Michael came he was accompanied by police officers. I then asked him what happened and he told me that something very bad had happened to Lois McMillen. Inspector Charles then pulled me aside and I spoke with him for about an hour telling him

everything I knew about, quote "what's going on in
Lois McMillen's head," to which I tried to help.
[The quote is from Inspector Charles.]

"Sir, can you please read the statement you have just
made to me?" Sergeant Blackman put his pen down and
looked up at Alex. "You may correct, alter, or add anything
you wish. Once you are comfortable, please sign it in the
designated space."

Later that evening, Sergeant Julian Harley went to see
Evan George. He identified himself to the young man, and
then informed him that his fingernail clippings and fingerprints were needed in connection with the investigation into
Lois' death.

"Do you have any objections?"

"No," George responded in a soft voice.

"May I see your fingernails, Mr. George?" Harley
examined all ten of Evan's nails and noted that, like Alex
Benedetto, his had recently been trimmed very low. After
scraping some residue from beneath each of them, he then
accepted help from the accused man in cutting samples of
the nails, which he placed in separate exhibit bags and
labeled with Evan's name. Next, he recorded his fingerprints
and palm prints on three separate forms before asking him to
sign his name to the papers.

Harley next went to see William Labrador at the East End
substation. He identified himself to the man with the thick,
slicked-back hair. "I am assisting in the investigation into a
report where the body of Lois Livingston McMillen was
found along the shoreline leading to the West End Jetty," he
began. "Your fingerprints, fingernail scrapings, and fingernail clippings are required in connection with the investigation. Do you have any objections, sir?"

"I am not submitting any of this without the advice of my
lawyer," William announced. The Southampton man would
later explain why he did not agree to provide police with the
samples. "I refused as no reason for my detention was given

nor was one given when I asked," William wrote in a sworn affidavit. "I also refused to label and give any other items of clothing at that time."

His refusal to cooperate was reported to Deputy Commissioner John Johnston.

"Is this the act of an innocent man?" the commander questioned.

Until this point, Johnston had remained impartial. He was aware that two of his officers, Anderson Blackman and Jacob George, had already concluded that the men from Zebra House were lying to police. But Labrador's refusal to submit to forensic tests had him raising his eyebrows.

Yet he continued to reserve judgment until he heard something definitive, something that would convince him that his investigators had the right people in custody. The fact that all four men had initially failed to mention their stop at the ATM near Pusser's on Friday night until officers discovered the cash machine receipt in Benedetto's wallet had his attention, but he wanted more solid evidence.

Ironically, that bit of evidence about the ATM stop never made it into the trial proceedings against the men because officers failed to relate it to the prosecutor, Crown Counsel Terrence Williams. It was only after the case was closed that Prosecutor Williams learned of the circumstances surrounding the stop at the ATM from one of the investigators. Intrigued, he went back and reviewed each of the men's official police statements and found that all but Alex had included the West End excursion in the signed affidavits taken by police the following day, Sunday, January 16.

Alex's omission struck Williams as "odd."

Meanwhile, Michael, Alex, William, and Evan were growing increasingly concerned after the statements they gave police did not win their release. As Sunday drew to a close, the four men were still in separate holding areas at police facilities around the island, and they saw no indication that they were going to be discharged and permitted to return to Zebra House.

Instead, investigators continued to assure the four that "It shouldn't be too much longer" and "You'll soon be free to go." Even Michael was beginning to worry. Up until this point, he had been confident that the information police gleaned from their investigation, and from the crime scene, would surely clear the four of all suspicion. But it was growing increasingly clear that the officers had not found anything to lead them in another direction, and it appeared the police were intensifying their focus on Michael and his friends.

Michael recounted that during the investigators' search of Zebra House the day before, he had briefly pondered their actions as he watched them systematically search his home. He recalled that even as the officers tore apart the bedrooms, he had continued to believe that their efforts were all part of a thorough and methodical murder investigation, and not aimed at him and his guests. Yet as he sat on the cot in the small holding cell, it was slowly dawning on him that his ongoing custody might mean that police really had no other leads in the case. Panicking was normally out of character for the perpetually tanned and unruffled son of a millionaire. But Michael's equanimity quickly shifted to concern and fear of a possible "frame-up" when he learned that police intended to keep him and his friends locked in cells for a second night. He winced when he heard that Evan was again being ordered to sleep on the wood bench in the locked area of the Road Town police headquarters where he had spent the previous night.

The news had both men suspecting that police were targeting Evan—trying to break him by keeping him in the most squalid of conditions. They decided that it was no mistake that Evan was being relegated to the busy waiting area, which was dirty and reeked of urine. They believed that the investigators had singled Evan out as the weakest of the foursome, and were hoping to wear him down by forcing him to sleep under the glare of the overhead fluorescent lights in an accommodation that provided absolutely no privacy. Michael and Evan also had no idea that officers had moved William Labrador from the East End substation to the same jail they were currently occupying.

Michael, Alex, William, and Evan had no way of knowing that the investigators intended to keep them in custody
until they were able to check out all of their alibis. The
investigators would begin bright and early Monday morning
with a visit to Quito's in Cane Garden Bay on the island's
northern shore.

CHAPTER THIRTEEN

Focusing In

Deputy Commissioner John Johnston was alerted by telephone that a canvass of Cane Garden Bay had not produced a single witness to verify that three of the four men from Zebra House had been to the lively beachfront restaurant that Friday night as they had claimed. The officers did, however, find a man named Octave Williams, a marina worker in Soper's Hole, who attested to seeing Lois McMillen on the dance floor at Quito's at one point that past Friday evening. A reed-thin man with thick locks of frizzy dark hair tucked beneath a colorful knitted cap, Moon, as he liked to be called, told investigators that he was certain Lois was at the club that night because she had asked him to dance. He recounted how she approached him on the dance floor at Quito's, and said he had declined her invitation because he was there on a date. The Rastafarian man went on to say that he later saw Lois walking down the beach, sometime after eleven p.m., with three figures trailing in the shadows behind her.

"Can you please view these photographs and see if you recognize anybody?" the investigator asked, pulling several mug shots of the men from his patrol car.

Moon studied the mug shots, but said he did not recognize the men in the pictures. The fortyish man from the island's north coast explained that he would probably not be able to make an identification. He had not been able to

see the guys who were walking on the beach well enough to
offer any solid description because they had their backs to
him as they kept pace with the girl.

It was not at all unusual to see people taking late-night
strolls along the sandy seashore behind Quito's. The lively
bar/restaurant drew some of its clientele from the adjacent
beachfront bungalows and cottages, and the other bars that
lined the soft stretches of sand that dotted the island's north
coast. It was also popular with boaters, who would anchor
their crafts right off the beach and use dinghies to row to
shore to enjoy dinner and live music.

As investigators continued to scour the area around
Quito's in a vain search for witnesses to back up the men's
story, other officers were in the field looking for the cab
driver the men said they had hired to take them to Cane Garden Bay on Friday evening.

A few miles west on the North Coast Road at the Sugar
Mill Hotel in Apple Bay, detectives were querying restaurant workers about the story William Labrador had told
them. They were anxious to find the credit card receipt that
would show he had been to the hotel's restaurant for breakfast that Saturday morning—the morning they found Lois'
body on the beach. William had told police that he had
woken at his usual time—7:45 a.m.—and walked to the
quaint hotel, where he had eaten breakfast. But a look at
restaurant receipts produced no such evidence.

The restaurant at the Sugar Mill Hotel was William's
favorite dining spot on the island, and many of the wait staff
knew him by first name. According to the staff, William was
a creature of habit; he always sat at the same table, ordered
the same meal, and paid in the same fashion. He always
selected Table No. 9 in the lower part of the main dining
room where breakfast is served. He liked that table for two
because of its unparalleled views of the beach and the sea.

Restaurant employees recalled that not only did William
have a "usual" table, but he also had a "usual" breakfast.
Every visit he ordered the same thing: the Beach Breakfast, an
omelet brimming with beans, and a second plate of fresh fruit.

He was known among the wait staff as a friendly, quiet person, although some of the employees regarded him as a cheapskate, saying he never left more than one or two dollars on the table as a tip. One employee remembered seeing him with a pretty dark-haired girl on his arm one day. But for the most part, he came alone.

An employee of the hotel said a search of the restaurant's receipts for the Saturday turned up no sales slip for William Labrador. While he might have paid the bill in cash, hotel personnel who had hosted him dozens of times in the past reported that he always paid with American Express. Additionally, their search of the register tape turned up two charges that William had made at the restaurant on Thursday evening—the night before Lois' murder. He had come by himself for dinner, which he billed to his American Express card, and then went to the upstairs gazebo bar for a cocktail—which employees of the hotel said he never did—and asked if he could charge the drinks to the same card.

Interestingly, one employee, a waitress at the restaurant, later said that she remembered seeing William Labrador there that Saturday morning. She recalled that a man she believed to be Labrador was seated at Table No. 9, and that he had a surfboard that he had leaned up against the wall near to the restaurant's entrance. But police could never confirm William's visit to the restaurant that day, because they said they had no receipt to show that he was there. William would later testify to having a receipt for his breakfast that morning.

As officers continued their work in the field, the administrative team at police headquarters in Road Town was continuing its search for a pathologist. The three officers assigned to the administrative task force had not yet made contact with Dr. Landron, and were now resigning themselves to the reality that they would probably have to wait until his office reopened on Tuesday—nearly four days after Lois' body had been found on the beach. And while police had still not confirmed that Lois' death was a result of foul play, they were carrying out their investigation as if they had a murder case to solve.

That same day, Sergeant Julian Harley returned to the Road Town police headquarters. He had collected fingernail samples and fingerprints from all but Michael Spicer. The forensics expert found the bespectacled man with the chestnut brown hair and deep tan seated on the small cot in the secured holding area where he had spent the two previous nights.

"I am Sergeant Julian Harley," he said politely.

Michael looked up at the lofty investigator with the wiry gray-and-black sideburns and nodded. A heavy smoker, he was longing for a cigarette.

"I am assisting in the investigation of a report where the body of Lois Livingston McMillen was found along the shoreline leading to the West End Jetty." Harley was direct. "Your fingerprints, fingernail clippings and scrapings are required in connection with this investigation. Do you have any objections, sir?"

"No," Michael replied flatly.

"Can you follow me, please?"

Michael walked shoulder to shoulder with the long-legged sergeant, keeping pace as he and the officer strode the sterile-looking hallway to a small office area.

"When will we be free to go?" Michael was imperturbable.

"It shouldn't be too much longer, sir. May I see your fingernails, please?" The sergeant's dark eyes scanned the man's long, slender fingers. Focusing his attention on the man's fingernails, he observed that, like his three friends, Spicer had recently trimmed his nails to the nub.

News that his team had not turned up a single witness to confirm that Alex, William, and Evan had been at Quito's on Friday night was the final nugget of information that swayed Commissioner Johnston, and confirmed for him that his officer's initial hunch was on the money.

"We'd already established, of course, when they were brought in that the men weren't averse to telling lies," the commander explained. "Because when they were brought in they were asked questions such as 'What's your full name? Date of birth? Occupation?' William Labrador claimed he was an investment banker. William Labrador never was and never will be an investment banker. Mr. Spicer claimed that he was a law student.

"Simple things like that, just telling lies. Once they were confronted with the ATM receipt, a more advanced [detailed] story of what they'd done and where they'd been emerged. Young Evan George went much further, telling us about the drugs.

"So now we've got guys that are lying and omit to tell us exactly where they'd been. We've got bloodstained shoes. We've got bloodstained shirts. We've got wet clothes. We've got a whole range of things. We've got them in the area where Lois McMillen was last seen alive at the time she was last seen alive. So we've got a line of inquiry which is pointing fairly strongly to these guys being more involved than they were admitting to be. And they were reaching a point where they were getting beyond the mere suspect stage," he continued. "We then asked them if they were willing to provide specimens of their blood and saliva, and they totally refused.*

"From that point on, they refused to cooperate with anything that we wanted that might have helped with the inquiry. Is this the action of innocent men?

"They've lied openly, they've lied by omission. They're found in a house that has all sorts of potentially damning evidence lying there against them. They're known to have been in Lois' company for the three or four previous days. They were always together. And now they are saying, 'No, we weren't with her.' "

Johnston was not buying the men's story.

---

*Michael Spicer later said that he did offer to submit to blood and other tests, but his offer was ignored by police.

CHAPTER FOURTEEN

The Autopsy

Four days after police discovered Lois McMillen's body on the boulder-strewn shore just off Drake's Highway in West End, investigators and her family would finally learn how she died. Getting the medical examiner to the island to conduct the autopsy was just the first of many obstacles police would face as they moved ahead with the investigation.

It was Tuesday, January 18, 2000, when members of the department's administrative team finally made contact with Dr. Francisco Jose Landron at his office on St. Thomas. The veteran pathologist agreed to come to Tortola that day to conduct the autopsy. Since Saturday, police had been operating on the assumption that Lois had been murdered, but now they would know definitively.

Sergeant Anderson Blackman was among the team of detectives waiting at the Davis Funeral Home in Road Town where Lois' body was being stored. While all of the officers there were curious to hear what the doctor's examination would uncover, it was Blackman who was most curious of all. It was he who believed that the men at Zebra House were somehow involved in Lois' death. And it was his initial suspicions that had prompted police to look closely at the four American men, take them into custody, and hold them on "suspicion of murder."

Blackman and the other officers were assembled in the sparsely furnished entrance foyer when Dr. Landron arrived at the funeral home, which was in the rear of the bustling Rite-way supermarket. After formal introductions and a brief overview of the particulars of the pending case, the investigators escorted the US-trained pathologist to the room in which he would conduct his post-mortem examination.

For the last six years, Dr. Landron had been Chief of Pathology and Medical Examiner at the Roy Lester Schneider Hospital in St. Thomas. He had also served as the forensic pathologist in the BVI. Upon graduation from medical school in Puerto Rico, he spent four years at St. Vincent Hospital and Medical Center of New York, where he specialized in combined anatomic and clinical pathology. He had also served a fellowship in forensic pathology at the office of the chief medical examiner and coroner in Los Angeles, California, and worked for four years as a forensic pathologist at the Institute of Forensic Sciences at San Juan, Puerto Rico.

Dr. Landron had been to the Davis Funeral Home a number of times in the past to conduct other autopsies. But the one he was about to undertake would be the highest-profile examination he had ever participated in. He waited as Lois' mother stepped forward to again identify her daughter's body. The McMillens had been told that verification by a next of kin was required before officials could begin the autopsy. Jo McMillen knew the task would be difficult, but she agreed to come into Road Town to spare her ailing husband the tiring trip.

"Yes, that's my daughter." The clearly shaken woman lowered her head and turned to leave the room.

Uniformed officers and plainclothesmen stood in silence along the perimeter of the room as the man in the surgical scrubs once again pulled back the sheet that was covering the once-vibrant Lois Livingston McMillen. One of the first things Dr. Landron observed was that sand, seaweed, and twigs were scattered across her still-wet clothing and skin. Strands of her shoulder-length blond hair fell onto the table. Her once-glistening green eyes were slightly collapsed. The doctor observed tiny hemorrhages in both of Lois' eyes, but noted that the bleeding was more prominent in the right one.

"Excluding trauma, this is a well-nourished, well-developed white female, appearing the stated age of thirty-four years," Dr. Landron remarked. "She measures sixty-five inches in height, and weighs an estimated one hundred and thirty pounds.

"Rigor mortis is generalized and livor mortis is fixed on the posterior dependent portions of the body," he continued aloud, referring to the stiffening of the body that takes place after death when muscles contract.

For the next several hours, Dr. Landron would painstakingly conduct an examination of the young woman's body and its internal organs. He noted everything from the color of the polish used on Lois' finger- and toenails to the size and shape of her heart.

"I would say that the cause of death was compatible with drowning," he announced to the roomful of investigators, pulling the thick latex gloves from his hands. "The mechanism of death in drowning is a lack of oxygen. The brain can't be without oxygen for more than several minutes."

In his report to police, Dr. Landron concluded that Lois McMillen had drowned, possibly after a struggle that ended in water. One of the key findings of Dr. Landron's autopsy was the discovery of sand particles in McMillen's upper and lower airways, suggesting that she was struggling to breathe while under water and in close proximity to a sandy bottom.

"The significance of finding sand particles in the lower airways would be suggestive of breathing while under water," he explained to the officers looking on in the small back room where the autopsy was being conducted.

To further support his findings of drowning, the doctor pointed to the fact that he had observed pulmonary edema, increased water content in the lungs; bilateral hydrothorax, a watery fluid in the chest cavities; and cerebral edema, increased water content in the brain.

During the examination, the doctor also discovered that the woman had sustained several injuries consistent with a struggle. He observed "incision-like" wounds on the palms of her hands, one below her right index finger and three more below her left index and middle fingers. All of them appeared to have been caused by some sort of instrument with a sharp edge, such as a knife. "In my opinion, an instrument, any instrument with a sharp edge would have caused those wounds," Dr. Landron said in response to questions from the investigators. "A knife may have caused it."

In addition to the tiny cuts on the palms of her hands, Dr. Landron found multiple abrasions (scrapes) and contusions (bruises) on her body and face. "The superficial layer of the skin is scraped away by the friction of rubbing against a rough surface," he noted. "Dragging someone on a rough surface could cause an abrasion. Holding someone down against a rough surface could cause an abrasion."

The doctor told the investigators that he could determine when Lois sustained the scratches based upon the color of her wounds. A reddish-brown color meant that the injury was sustained while she was alive, while those that were yellow in color indicated that she had sustained them after her death—and after her blood had stopped circulating.

Dr. Landron found the reddish-colored abrasions—the ones Lois sustained while she was still alive—on her face, left hip, left arm and shoulder, both knees, and on her left ankle.

More significant still were the three contusions he observed. One was at the base of her neck, another was on her chest below the left clavicle, and the third was in the middle of her chest. The doctor pointed to the front right-hand side of Lois' neck to show the investigators a light blue bruise that was one-and-a-half inches in diameter. He noted that the contusion on the upper chest, just below the left clavicle, was also light blue in color and measured half an inch in diameter. The third bruise was dark red and about one inch in diameter. The color of the bruises indicated that Lois had also sustained these three injuries while she was still alive.

Dr. Landron noted that there were a number of other wounds on Lois' body. He called the officers' attention to the numerous circular puncture-type wounds on her chest, hip, thigh, legs, and shoulders. The bruises were bluish-purple in color, and appeared to be consistent with sea urchin stings. With its long black spines, the black sea urchin is commonly found in the warm sapphire waters off the British Virgin Islands. It is not an aggressive animal, but can be risky to swimmers and divers who get too close to its pointy spines, which can cause painful puncture wounds. A number of the bites were found on areas of her body that should have been covered by her clothing—an indication to police that her blouse was most likely pulled up before she died.

Dr. Landron also observed "multiple linear and irregular yellow abrasions" that he determined to have occurred after Lois' death. The bruises were on her back, shoulder, chest, abdomen, arms, left hand, knees, and feet and could have resulted from wave action moving her body to and fro against the rocks.

An internal examination of her head revealed "multiple hemorrhages" in the frontal, parietal, and temporal areas, in other words, the tissue beneath the forehead, the top of the skull, and the areas above the ears. The doctor theorized that Lois may have been struck one or more times in the head with enough severity as to potentially cause the loss of consciousness. In theory, that kind of head trauma could be caused by a person slipping and falling on rocks. But the doctor cautioned that in order to cause that type of injury the fall would have to be against a very flat and smooth type of rock—and not the sort of smaller, jagged stones found at the beach where Lois' body was discovered.

An examination of the contents of Lois McMillen's stomach showed that she had ingested a small- to medium-sized meal. He estimated that the stomach contained 250 cubic centimeters of residual food, including pieces of vegetables, potatoes, and beans. Judging by the contents of her stomach, police were able to approximate that she died sometime between one-and-a-half and four hours after her meal at nine p.m.

The doctor found no sign of sexual assault during his lengthy examination, and noted that Lois McMillen had been wearing a tampon at the time of her death.

Upon completion of the autopsy, Dr. Landron would turn over a number of items to forensics expert Julian Harley. Among them were articles of Lois' clothing, including the Versace blouse she had purchased on St. John, the white capri pants, which were now stained with blood, and a delicate white brassiere and matching white panties. Harley was also given samples of Lois' blood and urine, as well as the contents of her stomach and the "rape kit," which included the oral, vaginal, and rectal swabs the doctor had collected.

Police had already determined that robbery was not a motive for the former model's death. They had recovered her purse and its contents from her rental vehicle, and the pretty diamond ring that her mother had given her was still on her finger when they discovered her body along the shoreline.

About one week after the autopsy, Dr. Landron visited the Drake's Highway crime scene where police had found Lois McMillen's body, to determine if there was anything there that could possibly have caused the tiny razor-like incisions found on the palms of her hands. He concluded that there was nothing at the scene that could have caused those injuries. Landron also pointed out that there were no similar sorts of cuts on any other part of her body, leading him to believe that she did not get the deep, incision-like wounds by brushing up against or striking something in the water.

Investigators theorized that one or more people may have been lunging at Lois with a knife and that she had raised her hands in front of her in a classic defense posture.

As the autopsy was being conducted at the funeral home in Road Town, investigators were canvassing the West End. Officers going house-to-house along Drake's Highway found their first solid witness—Beulah Romney.

She was alarmed at the sight of uniformed police officers knocking at the front door of her house in Freshwater Pond. Like many residents of the British Virgin Islands, Beulah was fearful, even suspicious of police. Part of her uneasiness was that she was aware that at least sixty percent of the

force's nearly two hundred officers were not born on Tortola
or any of the smaller British Virgin Islands. Instead, many
had joined the department after training at the police academy on Barbados and had come to the BVI from various
other islands in the Caribbean. "Belongers" like Beulah
worried that the foreign officers did not have the same community interest as those born and raised locally.

The female taxi driver and part-time cook told police
about the car that had come to a screeching halt on the roadway just below her house, and the screams that followed.
She watched through plastic-rimmed glasses as one of the
constables took notes on an official police "minute sheet."
She was able to fix the time of the incident—11:45 p.m.—
recalling that the screaming had begun soon after she arrived
home from dropping off her last fare of the night, a couple
she had picked up at the Frenchman's Cay Hotel. Her statement provided police with an approximate timeline as to
when the woman may have died.

That same day, police spoke to an American man named
Christopher Crawford. Crawford was a sailor and marine
surveyor who split his time between Tortola and Martha's
Vineyard in Massachusetts. He had been coming to the
British Virgin Islands since the 1970s, and had owned a
home in Soper's Hole since 1987.

A gangly man with untamed salt-and-pepper hair, Crawford told investigators that he had known Lois McMillen for
more than a decade. He remembered seeing her at the Jolly
Roger on Friday night. He recounted that Lois was sitting at
the restaurant's patio bar on the ground level near the parking lot when he sat down next to her. Nothing seemed amiss,
he said, although he did remember that she appeared a bit
under the weather, and told him that she was just getting
over the flu.

"I went down to the Jolly Roger at about nine p.m.,"
Crawford recalled, watching as the officer in front of him
took notes on a small pad. "A woman named Sheryl Harris,
I'm not certain of her [last] name—I believe it is Harris, she

was a guest in my house, and accompanied me to the Jolly
Roger.

"I met friends of mine from the States there. They were
staying at Sebastian's. There was a dinner crowd at the Jolly
Roger. A band was playing. I did speak to Lois that night.
She was sitting at the bar by herself. I first spoke to her at a
little after nine. She was wearing a white pullover sweater
with what I believe was a gold pattern on the back, and
white capri pants. They weren't full length; they covered
just below the knee.

"I left the Jolly Roger at about ten thirty," Crawford continued. "When I left, Lois was sitting at the bar downstairs
by the patio. When I left, she was by herself. I believe she
may have had a drink close to her. There were drinks all over
the bar. It was crowded.

"She certainly didn't appear intoxicated. I knew her in
social settings. I never saw her drunk or impaired by alcohol. I didn't know her to be a heavy drinker or much of a
drinker at all."

After the Jolly Roger, Crawford said he went to the
Bomba Shack in Apple Bay, but later returned to the Jolly
Roger to retrieve the purse his friend had mistakenly left on
the table. "We went back to Jolly Roger some time between
eleven fifteen and eleven thirty. When we returned, Lois was
not there."

In the course of conversation, Crawford told the investigators that around ten p.m., he observed Lois talking to a
black man. He said the two were chatting for about ten or
fifteen minutes, but he did not recognize the tall, heavy-set
fellow as someone he knew. Crawford provided police with
a brief description of the man, who, he said, had short hair,
and was dressed casually in a black T-shirt. He told the
detective that he could furnish few other details because the
gentleman was facing away from him and he did not get a
good look at his face.

Next, police went to Belmont Estates. They wanted to
speak with a man named Clifford Lefebvre. His name

had come up in all four of the accused men's statements, and investigators were anxious to hear what the older American gentleman would have to say about his social call to Zebra House that past Friday night.

According to Johnston, police found the seventy-one-year-old retired lawyer with the pencil-thin moustache, and wavy hair dyed a deep shade of black, at the Equinox House. The stucco-and-wood residence was located at the base of the driveway to Zebra House, and on the same side of the street as the McMillens' villa.

Police found the diminutive man gracious. He told the team that he had been coming to Tortola for close to two decades, although he did not own property in the Caribbean. Instead, whenever he visited the wind-swept island, he stayed at Equinox House, the vacation residence of his good friend Charles Bailey. Bailey was a tall, white-haired man in his early seventies, and was known to his friends as Obie.

Clifford appeared relaxed, and in between sips of a cool beverage, told officers that he had known Michael Spicer for about fifteen years. He recalled being introduced to Alex and William in the BVI during previous visits. Clifford said that he had met Evan George when Michael brought him to spend the night at his summer house in Southampton the previous year. He explained that he resided on Manhattan's Upper East Side, and that he owned a vacation home on the East End of Long Island in the same town as William's mother, Barbara Labrador.

The officers found Clifford responsive to their questions, although he seemed hesitant at moments, as if thinking through his answers before speaking them aloud. One of the investigators was taking notes as Lefebvre recounted his phone calls to Michael at Zebra House earlier that Friday. He said that he was calling to ask if it would be all right for him to come up to Zebra House with a friend he had met at Smuggler's Cove beach that afternoon.

Investigators, at that point, were surprised when Clifford said that he did not recall seeing any scratches on Alex

Benedetto's arm or leg, nor did he remember a bruise on William Labrador's nose. His failure to recollect the two men's injuries raised eyebrows among the team, and contradicted the story that Alex had told police. The officers thanked Clifford for his time and hospitality and advised him that they might be back to speak with him at some future date.

CHAPTER FIFTEEN

"Known to Us"

In the days to follow, police would broaden their investigation to look at other suspects and conduct interviews with involved parties around the island. They would also place a call to the Federal Bureau of Investigation in Washington, DC, to find out if the four men from Zebra House had criminal records.

"Yes, they are all known to us," was the clipped response of the federal agent who took the call from the investigator on Tortola. But the FBI agent who punched the men's names into the national crime database did not offer any further details. If the Royal Virgin Islands Police Force wanted more information, they would have to follow official procedures to obtain it.

It would turn out that none of the four were strangers to the law. All of the men had been arrested before, charged with offenses ranging from drug possession to DWI.

On June 29, 1990, Alexander Benedetto had been stopped by police in Suffolk County, Long Island, and charged with driving while under the influence of drugs or alcohol. He pleaded guilty to the lesser charge of driving while ability impaired. He was ordered to pay a $250 fine and his license was temporarily suspended.

His boyhood friend, William Labrador, was also picked up by police in his hometown of Southampton on February

4, 1996, and charged with drunk driving. An article in *The Southampton Press* reported:

> *NY City resident William Labrador, 32, was charged with driving while intoxicated at the corner of County Road 39 and Wiltshire Street on February 4. Police said he had failed to keep right of markings and to stay in the designated traffic lane.*

On March 5, 1996, William, too, pleaded guilty to a reduced charge, driving while ability impaired, and paid a fine of $400.

Michael Spicer also had a minor brush with the law, but no details were reported in the press.

Yet Evan George had the most serious police record. The young man from the West Coast had a number of arrests and convictions in Multnomah County, Oregon, for theft, criminal trespass, and other petty crimes, according to an article published in *The Sunday Oregonian*. The paper reported that in January 1999, Evan was arrested for felony possession of a controlled substance. He then violated the conditions of his parole on the drug charge when he moved to San Francisco, and then to Washington, DC, to be with Michael. Subsequent articles about the McMillen case that appeared in other US newspapers portrayed Evan as once being "homeless" and a "heroin addict." While the information about the men's pasts raised a few eyebrows, it did not figure prominently in the investigators' work. Under the laws governing the British Territory, police are not allowed to introduce prior criminal activity, or what they refer to as "Prior Bad Acts," unless that activity is of direct relevance to the case at hand. And in this case there were no links.

The strict rules of the British legal system also barred police from revealing any details about their investigation—even to the McMillens. Already four days had passed since their daughter's murder, yet Russell and Josephine knew little about what police were turning up. Learning the information about the men's prior arrests convinced the couple that the four Americans in police custody for their daughter's murder were not the upstanding citizens they were purporting to be.

In the days after police recovered Lois' body, the commander assigned one of his officers to act as family liaison to her parents. He handpicked Inspector Reena Rivera for the job. She was actually the head of the police department's traffic division, but as a member of a small community police force, she and the other officers were expected to wear several hats. Rivera was a widow and had raised three children on her own. Johnston had selected her because of her warm, gentle personality, and her experience as a mother and someone who had lost a loved one. He was certain that she would be most sympathetic to the couple's loss.

Rivera's role was to report to the McMillens' villa in Belmont Estates on a daily basis to answer questions that Russell and Josephine might have about the police's ongoing inquiry into their daughter's death and to help them with any special needs. The couple took an instant liking to Rivera. They came to expect the visit from the pretty officer with the warm smile and gentle voice, and had a pot of coffee on the stove ready when she arrived at their front door each morning. But the breadth of what the officer could reveal to the grieving couple was severely limited by the laws governing the British Territory.

"I really can't tell you much," she would explain apologetically.

Her responses were frustrating to the couple, yet her regular visits to the villa provided Russell and Jo McMillen with a sense of inclusion and participation. So far, all that Lois' parents had been able to glean from police was that Lois had been severely beaten about the face and head, and left on the rocks near the police substation where she died. They were also told that she was not sexually assaulted and that robbery did not appear to be a motive in her murder.

Most disturbing to the McMillens was that police had

taken their neighbor and his houseguests into custody, and were detaining them in connection with Lois' death.

Michael was just one of the names the couple had mentioned to Sergeant Anderson Blackman when he came to their villa that past Saturday. Also on the short list of Lois' island acquaintances was her former boyfriend, Luigi Lungarini.

Police had been looking for Lungarini since Sunday. It was already mid-week when a tip led officers across the Sir Francis Drake Channel to the exclusive palm-lined island of Virgin Gorda. They had learned that he was involved in a construction project in a remote corner of the fashionable British Virgin Island, and that he had a boat that he used to go back and forth between Tortola and Virgin Gorda on a regular basis. In good weather, it would take less than thirty minutes to dash across the Sir Francis Drake Channel by vessel—a ride that could easily be made without detection. Police said that when they located the stocky, well-spoken man at his home at just after nine a.m. on January 18, he was "cooperative."

"Lois' mother broke us up," he reportedly told police when they asked him about the pretty blond American woman whom he had dated in the summer of 1998. Then he related the incident with the rental car and the conflict over money with Lois' mother that led to their breakup. In response to questioning, he detailed his whereabouts on Friday, January 14, and provided police with an official statement.

Anderson Blackman was the officer who took the report.

Luigi Lungarini states: I was born in Rome, Italy on May 19, 1963. I am now a Citizen of Canada presently residing at Josiah's Bay . . . I knew the deceased Lois McMillen. I first met her about (2) years ago at the Pub in Road Town. We started a relationship then which lasted for about four to five months. Our relationship started in 1998 and ended the said year. The last time I saw Lois was in 1998 in Tortola. The last time I spoke with her was in 1998 via telephone. She was at her mother and father's house in the New York area. We spoke about money for the repairs of a vehicle, which was rented by her father that got into an accident while I was driving. At the time, I sent her five hundred dollars ($500.00) U.S.C. to cover the cost of the repairs. At that point, I asked her not to call me back again because the relationship was over. During the time that the deceased and I spent together in Tortola we had a dispute because I wanted to leave her. At that time, she became very annoyed and started to break things in my apartment and from the balcony. She also tore one of my shirts and at that point, I called the police at East End and made a report. On arrival of the police, they spoke with me but she had already left the apartment. The following day, she came back to my apartment crying and apologizing. I accepted her apology and we continued to see each other until her mother came to Tortola that said year and took her back to her home town. I have not seen her since. During the time that we were together, I noticed that she had a drinking disorder. She was not necessarily a heavy drinker, but if she drank a few, she would do things out of the ordinary. During our short relationship, I never threatened to beat or strangle her. I did not beat her, but had to push her away from me on the occasion when she tore my shirt. I have never seen her using drugs during the time we were together . . . On Thursday 13th January 2000, I caught the North Sound Express Ferry from Beef Island around 4:00 p.m. and went to Virgin Gorda. On arrival at Virgin Gorda, I was picked up by Victor. I do not know his last name but he owns Paradise Beach Resort in Mango Bay. I stayed at that resort with my girlfriend, Alexia Malo, until

Monday 17th January 2000. On Friday 14th January 2000, my girlfriend and I went to Anegada with Victor and a guest of Paradise Resort and we returned that said day. I was on Virgin Gorda all day on Saturday 1/15/2000. On Sunday 16th February [sic] 2000, my wife, Ben, Vincent O'Neal and I had lunch together at the Paradise Resort and that is when I heard that a girl had died. Mr. O'Neal was not certain about the name, but when he mentioned Belmont, I thought it could have been Lois.

— Luigi Lungarini

The alibi that Luigi provided for the day that Lois was murdered was that he was sailing with friends from Virgin Gorda to Anegada, a quaint sandy paradise about twenty-two nautical miles northeast of Tortola, about a ninety-minute powerboat ride, and double that time by sailboat.

In his conversation with Sergeant Blackman, Lungarini had provided names of witnesses to his whereabouts, and said that they were aboard the boat with him when he returned to Virgin Gorda that same day.

Over the next several days, investigators would follow up, interviewing people at various sites around the two islands that Lungarini said he had come into contact with the previous Friday night into Saturday morning. Police would later confirm that those individuals had corroborated his story. Yet investigators continued to explore the possibility that Lungarini had used his boat for a late-night excursion to Tortola.

Anegada, the outermost of the main islands of the BVI, has a flat landscape and is fringed by miles of powdery white-sand beaches. But the waters around the island are difficult to navigate and require the wherewithal of an experienced captain. It was for that reason that police initially believed it unlikely that Lungarini could have made his way to Tortola on the night of Lois' murder, but they still wanted to check out his alibi.

In the weeks that followed, they painstakingly re-created his movements—to be certain that there was no span of time unaccounted for—until they were satisfied that he was in the clear.

Nevertheless, the defense would continue to bring up his name in the months ahead.

CHAPTER SIXTEEN

Habeas Corpus

As Lois' parents struggled to come to grips with the death of their daughter, the four men suspected of her murder remained in police custody for a fourth night. It was becoming increasingly clear that the "boys" (as they referred to themselves) from Zebra House were in trouble when continued questions to police about their detention were answered with the same pat response, "It shouldn't be too much longer."

By Wednesday, January 19, Michael Spicer and the others were quietly getting ready to go before a judge with legal counsel and ask the court that they be released. That past Sunday, Michael had been allowed to place a local telephone call from jail. He dialed Kay Carpenter Doyle, his longtime neighbor from Belmont Estates.

Kay and her sister were co-owners of Villa No. 6 in the Belmont Grove complex. Their place was several doors away from the McMillens, and just downhill from the Spicers. Like many of the residents of Belmont Estates, Kay, too, was eccentric. She was often sporting colorful outfits and wide-brimmed hats, and liked to gossip with neighbors about the latest goings-on in the private West End neighborhood. She was particularly friendly with Obie Bailey, owner of the Equinox House.

Kay had known Michael for a number of years, and was always eager to come up to Zebra House to join him for cocktails and a swim in the pool with the unparalleled views of the sea. The two had grown close over the years, and had even traveled to St. Bart's one year with Michael's mother.

When Michael reached Kay at home, she told him that their friend, Persia Stoutt, a member of a prominent local family, had given her the names of several good attorneys in Road Town. She suggested that Michael contact one of them for help. She then called Michael's mother in Charlottesville, Virginia, to alert her to her son's situation.

At seventy-six years old, Teena Spicer was often forgetful. At other times, she just put unpleasant things out of her mind, hoping that if she did not think about them, they would go away. It is unclear what prompted her to wait a full twenty-four hours before calling Michael's older sister, Chris Matthews, in Upstate New York, where she lived with her husband and two children.

"A girl has died, and they have taken Michael away," is about all that Chris could decipher from her mother's scattered thoughts.

The news was heart-stopping for Chris, who had always taken special care of her youngest brother, fourteen years her junior. In fact, when Michael was a toddler, Chris and her best girlfriend liked to occupy their days by dressing him up and playing with him as if he were a living doll. They even taught him his very first words—"bird shit."

Without hesitation, Chris ended the conversation with her mother and dialed Tortola. When she finally reached the Road Town police headquarters, the officer who answered the line told her that Michael was locked in a cell and could not get to the phone.

"I must talk to my brother," Chris insisted. "Please take the phone to him."

Chris Matthews was an interesting contrast to her younger brother. She had traveled the world, yet in many ways she had led a sheltered life. It was not unusual for Michael's sister to spend weeks at a time traveling through Europe with the family, or a month at a clip at her friend's home on the West Coast of Florida, or in Tortola at the family's vacation residence. Yet, at the same time she retained a certain naïveté.

Upon graduation from Russell Sage College, a small liberal arts school for women in Albany, New York, she immediately found a job at Troy High School, where she worked as an English teacher. Like her older brother Lewis, Chris chose to remain in the Upstate region where she was born and raised. In her early thirties, she met and married a man who was some years her senior. In many ways, marrying Tom Matthews was like marrying the boy next door. Although he was older and had a young daughter from a previous marriage, he was handsome and kind, and best of all, was a local man from the neighboring town of Clayton. Everyone in the Spicer household liked the bright businessman and avid outdoorsman who treated Chris with the utmost respect. Soon after their nuptials, Chris gave birth to the couple's only son, Spicer Thomas Matthews. Chris then chose to remain a traditional housewife, limiting her realm to home and family.

"Hello?" Michael spoke into the cordless phone that police had brought to his cell.

Chris was surprised and relieved to hear her brother talking in such a calm manner. It was the first time she had ever really known him to be in a crisis situation, and she was proud of how well he appeared to be handling it. Chris listened as Michael related the unbelievable events of the past weekend—the search of Zebra House and the men's detention in separate jail cells around the island, where they were being held on suspicion of murdering the young woman who lived down the hill.

Chris had never met Lois McMillen or her parents. She and her husband usually visited Tortola in May, well after the winter season, when many of the snowbirds of Belmont Estates had already returned to their homes for the summer. Chris was dumbfounded by her brother's situation. She stumbled over her words as she tried to assure Michael that she would do everything she could to get him out of jail.

But Michael did not sound all that worried. His tone was relaxed, and he seemed surprisingly calm. To him, the whole situation was just a big misunderstanding, and he was certain that it would be only a matter of days before he and his friends would be released from custody and sent on their way. But Michael could hear the anguish in his sister's voice, and before they hung up, he consoled her, telling her not to worry, and that everything was going to be fine.

Chris wasted no time. As soon as she said goodbye to her brother, she quickly dialed one of the attorneys who had been recommended to Michael by the family's longtime friend. When Chris reached Mary Lou Creque on her cell phone, the energetic young attorney was eager to help. A member of the Road Town firm Price Findlay & Co, Creque was frank, telling Chris that her expertise in criminal affairs was limited. There was not much criminal activity on Tortola, and for that reason, not many criminal attorneys on the island.

"When I get in over my head, I will let you know," the lawyer said.

Chris was pleased with her responses, and asked the young attorney to go at once to see her brother at the jail in Road Town where he was being detained.

During their conference at the Road Town jail, Ms. Creque informed Michael that in the British Virgin Islands, it is unlawful to hold a person for more than seventy-two hours without bringing formal charges against them. She suggested the men seek a writ of habeas corpus. The motion would force police to bring the men before the court and tell the judge why they were being detained.

For Michael, the legal petition seemed an appropriate next step. He was growing tired of hearing "You'll be leaving shortly," or "Oh, you're still here?" from investigators each time they passed, and when he was led down the hall to provide fingernail samples and other such related matters. His patience was turning to fear with every hour that passed. He was now envisioning a "set-up" with him and his friends at its center.

He was worried that the island's dependence on tourism dollars might lead police to charge him and his friends with the crime—in what he regarded as an attempt to cover up the possibility that the real killer was a local from the island, and was still at large.

Michael told the attorney that he needed to confer with his friends. He had not seen any of his pals since the four men had been separated and jailed that past Saturday night. He asked Creque to visit Alex, William, and Evan at the various locations where they were being detained to solicit their thoughts on the habeas corpus action. He also instructed her to ask them if they would like to contact anyone, and to make phone calls on their behalf. Unlike Michael, none of the other men had been permitted to place phone calls. Instead, they had remained locked away in cold, dank cells with wooden benches and thin foam mattresses to sleep on.

When the lawyer went to see Evan in the waiting area where he was being held, he handed her a list of names of people to contact. One was his good friend Ed, whom he'd met while working construction in San Francisco. Another was his cousin Jake, a police officer in San Francisco. Alex asked that she contact his dad in New York. William told her that there was no one he wished to contact as yet.

The three men thought it wise that Michael had hired the local attorney to represent them. They were even more relieved to hear that their wealthy friend was willing to foot the lawyer's bill on behalf of all four of them. They knew the legal maneuver they were planning would push police to either charge them with a crime or set them free for lack of evidence to hold them. To Michael, who was a law school graduate, the petition seemed apropos for the situation. He was certain that police had no evidence against him and his friends. With the others' consent, he had given the nod for the attorney to file the application with the High Court, and believed it would only be a matter of days before the men were released.

But in the end, the strategy would prove a big mistake.

It would not be easy for the lawyer to pull the motion together in a timely fashion. She required lengthy affidavits from each of the four. The men contended that police delayed her by making Alex, William, and Evan unavailable when she came calling at their respective jail cells.

In the signed affidavit that was to be presented at the Thursday morning hearing, Michael made a number of declarations, among them was that he had not been cautioned prior to giving his statement to police. Another was that he had not been charged with an offense, or received any warrant, nor had any reason been given for his detention. He also swore that he fully cooperated with police and wrote that he offered to give them "tissue and blood samples and to take a lie detector test."

Additionally, he pointed to three witnesses who could attest to his being at Quito's at the time of the murder that past Friday night. Michael even named the threesome, who, he claimed, had shared a table with him and his friends at the beachside eatery that evening.

Yet as he waited for the opportunity to go before a judge with the petition, hoping to gain freedom through legal channels, the investigators in the field continued to build a case against the foursome. Much of what the police had thus far stemmed from their search of Zebra House and statements from people they had interviewed during their canvasses of the island. There was Moon Williams, the marina worker who attested to seeing Lois at Quito's on Friday night, and who remembered watching three males following behind her as she walked the beach that evening. There was Spicer's friend from Equinox House, Clifford Lefebvre, who said he did not recall seeing any scratches on Alex or William when he visited Zebra House in the early evening of January 14—the night that Lois was murdered.

Alvin Martin, the man seen driving with a blond woman that Friday night, had been quickly eliminated as a suspect, as was Lois' former boyfriend, Luigi Lungarini, who had witnesses to attest to his whereabouts on the night Lois was killed. Further canvasses of the lush tropical paradise produced no other suspects, and no witnesses to back up the men's claims that they had been to Quito's that night. Even the circumstantial evidence found at Zebra House—the damp clothing, the shirt with the quarter-size stain that appeared to be blood, the wet, sandy sneakers, and the tampons in Alex's garbage pail—was pointing police to the four men.

Yet police had no confessions, and no analysis had been performed on the forensic evidence they had collected to link the men to Lois.

In fact, forensics expert Julian Harley had been spending much of Wednesday afternoon in a second-floor office of the Road Town police headquarters, cataloguing the items that he and his team had collected during their search of the Spicer residence. He was readying them for transport to a lab off the island. At one point during the afternoon, he received a visit from Constable Mason and other members of the Scenes of Crimes division, who brought over twenty plastic exhibit bags of fingernail scrapings and clippings, and fingerprint forms all belonging to William Labrador. After initially denying their request, William Labrador had consented to the collection of the material. The constable also turned over fingerprint forms he had taken earlier in the day from Alexander Benedetto.

Once the items were properly sealed and labeled, Harley photographed the four pairs of shoes he had in custody. He focused in on the tongue of the Adidas sneaker owned by William Labrador, carefully capturing the dark-colored splotch that he believed to be a bloodstain. He also snapped a picture of the seemingly bloody strap of Lois' gold-accented sandal. In a small darkroom, he then developed the film into negatives and printed 4×6 photographic enlargements that he would arrange in an official album to be presented as evidence if the case should go to trial. Harley was creating an index for the ninety-three photos, describing each of the pictures he had taken before pasting the manifest to the inner front cover of the album, when he was suddenly interrupted.

In another part of the stationhouse, investigators were learning of the legal maneuver being planned by the four men they were holding in custody. Inspector Jacob George had received a telephone call the night before from the AG's office, during which he was told that there "were rumors on the street" that the men were planning some sort of legal maneuver. It was learned that Michael Spicer and the boys from Zebra House had retained a local attorney who was preparing a writ of habeas corpus to present to the court at a hearing scheduled for the following morning at ten a.m. Rumors of the men's intention to go before a judge with the petition prompted investigators to take immediate steps to block the legal maneuver.

That afternoon, Inspector Jacob George went into an emergency meeting with members of the attorney general's office.

It was six thirty p.m. on Wednesday, January 19, when the inspector returned to the Road Town police headquarters, and went to see "the boys" from Zebra House, who were now all in the secure holding area at the rear of the building. Michael and Evan were still unaware that William had been brought to Road Town from the East End substation several days earlier and was being housed in the same area where they were being held. Alex had remained at the West End substation until now. The long-legged inspector with the threadlike moustache admonished the men one at a time, reading aloud each of the warrants he had in his possession, and advising them that they were under arrest for the "murder" of Lois McMillen.

Michael could overhear the inspector talking to Alex from just outside the small interrogation room where he was now standing. When he was finally brought in to the area, he saw that his three friends were already there.

". . . whatever you say will be taken down in writing, may be given as evidence at your trial," the officer cautioned furtively.

"Murder?" each of the four repeated the inspector's words in voices low as a whisper. A murder conviction in the BVI carries a sentence of life imprisonment with no chance of parole.

"You guys are going to make yourselves pariahs in the Western Hemisphere, and be poster rogues on CNN for framing four innocent Americans," Alex reportedly announced to the officers who were processing him and his friends into custody. It appeared he had a need always to say what was on his mind.

For Michael, it was the single worst moment of his life. To be suspected of committing an act of violence, and then to be charged with the heinous crime, was unthinkable.

Before he and his friends could even compose themselves, the now-frightened foursome were being rushed to the Magistrate's Court in the center of Road Town behind the police headquarters for a nighttime arraignment on a charge of "murder." Even the normally even-tempered Evan George was in a tailspin. He could not believe that his first international holiday was turning into a Kafka-esque nightmare that now included an allegation of murder.

There were no family members at the eight p.m. session. There on the men's behalf was their Road Town attorney, Mary Lou Creque. Creque had spent the last four days feverishly preparing for the writ of habeas corpus that was supposed to have taken place the next morning. All she could do was stand by and watch as police paraded the men in front of the magistrate, and then listen as her clients were formally charged in the murder of Lois McMillen.

"Michael Spicer between the fourteenth and fifteenth day of January in the West End in the Island of Tortola in the Territory of the British Virgin Islands did murder Lois Livingston McMillen. Contrary to Section 1-4-8 of the Criminal Code 1997 (Act No. 1 of 1997) of the Laws of the Virgin Islands," the court clerk read the charge aloud.

At that moment, Creque knew that her work thus far had been in vain.

It was already dark outside when the four Americans were remanded into police custody and then taken back to their cells at the Road Town headquarters. It turned out that Her Majesty's Prison at Balsam Ghut would not process incoming prisoners at that late hour, and police would have to wait until the following day to turn the men over to the warden at the sprawling hilltop facility.

CHAPTER SEVENTEEN
Her Majesty's Prison

Brilliant rays of afternoon sun illuminated the near-treeless courtyard of the Royal Virgin Islands Police Force in Road Town where Michael Spicer, Alex Benedetto, William Labrador, and Evan George were being held. They had already entered "not guilty" pleas to the court, and had been ordered to wait in front of the two-story headquarters with the peeling white paint for the official police vehicle that would take them to the high-security prison at Balsam Ghut.

It was just before two o'clock on Thursday, January 20, when Chief Inspector Jacob George strode over to where the men were standing on the stonework, catching the tail end of their conversation as he neared.

"You see that place in there they call the lab?" Inspector George reported overhearing William Labrador say as he pointed a finger at the police department's tiny makeshift laboratory. "You think those guys could solve anything from in there?"

The inspector said nothing as he herded the four Americans, who were now in handcuffs, into the official SUV that would transport them to Her Majesty's Prison at Balsam Ghut. Michael's attention was immediately drawn to the old machete that lay on the floor in the rear of the vehicle. To him, it was yet another sign of an inept police force. The men sat in near silence for much of the twenty-minute ride, passing through a busy East End neighborhood of simple white

houses where children on bicycles dotted the streets, and
then up the steep road that winds its way to "the Ghut," as
the prison is known. A warm breeze blew in through the
vehicle's open windows as it rounded the twisty bends of the
narrow two-lane route, which was planted with cacti and
tamarind bushes. The men watched from the rear seat as the
residential houses and the clamor of activity gave way to a
quiet barren stretch of bumpy dirt road. It seemed that where
they were going was an all-but-uninhabited section of the
tiny twenty-one-square-mile island, one with breathtaking
views of the deep blue waters of the Atlantic Ocean.

Alex kept his sense of humor even as the constable
steered the four-wheel-drive vehicle toward the looming
prison. "There will be no one ugly enough in Hollywood to
play your part in the movie," he giggled, directing his comment at the uniformed officer driving the Montero.

The officer chuckled, taking the remark in good fun. They
were pleasant enough, he thought. He even told the men they
were in for a real treat—the food was good at the prison.

The four men sensed the jerky movement of the Montero
as the officer shifted the vehicle into second and prepared to
stop. Broken-down junk cars lined one side of the dusty road
that led to the gravel parking area just outside the prison
gates. A cluster of low-slung buildings with bright green
roofs hugged the mountainside. From a distance, the rambling tan-and-green structures shaded by palm trees resem-
bled an apartment complex, save for the scrolling barbed
wire fence and towering overhead lights that surrounded
the property. A large sign posted at the gated entrance to the
house of detention reads: *Her Majesty's Prison Service
serves the public by keeping in custody those committed by
the courts. Our duty is to look after them with humanity and
to help them lead law-abiding and useful lives in custody
and after release.*

Michael could feel the lump in the base of his throat
growing as the police vehicle paused at the guard booth to
check in. He watched from the window as prison guards in
crisp uniforms and matching caps motioned for the white

van to pass through the heavy olive-green iron gates and into
the prison courtyard. Once inside, the warden, a menacing
figure in official attire, received the boys from Zebra House.
He was direct; yet there was gentleness in his tone as he
explained that it was his duty to make their stay at the
island's prison as comfortable as possible while they
awaited trial. Scenes from the movie *Midnight Express*
raced through Michael's mind as he and his three friends
were shown to a confined area where they were searched
and "processed" before being led to their quarters in the
"remand" wing, which was located in the newer of the
prison's two buildings. Since they had not yet been convicted of a crime, they were to stay in cells in a section of the
complex that was separate from the areas where the convicted felons and other guilty prisoners were housed. All
told, there were about ninety to one hundred prisoners
locked away at the facility.

Michael and Evan were ordered into the cramped cell
directly across the way from the one where William and
Alex had been placed. The units were small, and each had a
single "window" with heavy bars. There was no glass on the
openings, which provided the men with a constant source of
fresh outside air. The view from Michael and Evan's cell
was of the cool waters of the Eastern Caribbean, while the
one that William and Alex looked at was the grassy hillside
behind the prison. The buildings were not air-conditioned,
but a constant trade wind blew in from the windows, and
kept the climate in the units at a bearable temperature.

The sprawling prison facility at Balsam Ghut had
recently undergone renovations, and was considered to be
cleaner and better run than the other jails in the Caribbean—
yet inmates complained of a terrible odor that never seemed
to go away. The four American men were being housed in
the newer wing, which had a fresh coat of paint and more
modern conveniences. The accommodations at Her
Majesty's Prison were a marked improvement over the
squalid jail cells where the men had spent the previous five
nights.

Waiting to greet the foursome in the remand wing was the only other white person in the lock-up. An American named Jeffrey Plante shouted "Hello!" from the corner cell just down the corridor, where he had been jailed for nearly three months.

The terms of the four men's imprisonment would be harsh, with twenty-three-hour-a-day lockdown in the nine-by-twelve-foot cell units. Each had a working toilet and a sink. They were permitted just sixty minutes a day for exercise and shower time. The one-hour free period soon became a bargaining point between the men and the prison guards on duty. Some were kinder than others, and would let the guys have the full sixty minutes in the prison yard, while others would make it clear that the free hour included their time in the shower.

Their meals were served to them on their cots, mostly Spam, Vienna sausage, and dishes prepared with Caribbean spices and local vegetables. They were permitted just one ten-minute phone call per week, although guards would send faxes for the men upon request.

Nearly immediately upon their arrival, Alex Benedetto became excitable, screaming through the bars of the cell every time a guard would enter the remand area, which was no bigger than twenty-five square feet. "We're innocent," the blond-haired Benedetto ranted, pressing his face against the metal barrier as he shouted at the men in uniform. "You call this justice? Is this how you treat visitors to your country?"

When he wasn't targeting the prison guards, Alex was siding with William in his fight with Michael over their imprisonment. He and Labrador had decided that it was all Michael's fault that the four men had been jailed, and spent much of the first few days blaming him for their predicament. Like Alex, William was angry that the slender, perpetually tanned Spicer had allowed police to search Zebra House, and felt that as their host on the island, it was Michael's responsibility to make the situation right.

Evan George said little. The young man was frightened, and hung close to Michael for comfort.

• • •

The following morning, Michael's sister Chris and her husband arrived on Tortola. The attorney she had hired, Mary
Lou Creque, was already hard at work trying to help
Michael and his friends gain their freedom. The lawyer was
outraged by the men's sudden arrest, which appeared conve-
niently orchestrated to thwart her attempt to present a writ of
habeas corpus to the court the very next day.

In a meeting at the jail, she told her clients that she was
not surprised by the maneuver, and alluded to having had
similar experiences in the past with the island's officers. The
sneak attack on the part of police made her even more eager
to take on the men's cause, and she told the foursome that
she was confident she could win their release for a fee of one
hundred thousand dollars.

"Do you think the police are trying to frame us?" Alex
and Michael asked collectively.

"It's possible," Creque responded with an air of cynicism.
"But not likely."

Michael implored her to continue her search for three
people he said had seen him, Evan, and Alex at Quito's on
the night of Lois' murder. He was also anxious for her to
find David "Salo" Blyden, the taxi driver Alex had hired to
drive them around the island that night.

Alex had first met Salo at Bomba's Shack during his initial trip to Tortola in 1997, and had taken an instant liking to
the Tortolan man. Alex told Michael that he felt safe in his
company, especially after learning that Salo's mother moon-
lighted at a local church. Alex liked using the same driver
for all his excursions. Many of the roads on Tortola had serpentine curves and rugged stretches of terrain, and he preferred to have someone who was familiar with the routes
driving him around. It was customary for repeat visitors to
use the services of a single taxi driver. Most of the island's
cabbies distributed business cards with their cell numbers
for quick service. Alex told Michael he was pleased when he
spotted Salo at the West End ferry terminal the day that he

and William returned to Tortola for their Millennium holiday on December 30, 1999.

Michael recalled that he, too, had met Salo in 1997, when he had gone out one evening with Alex and William. But he had never actually arranged for a ride with him, and did not even know him by name. He was not one to use taxis, preferring to stay close to home and walk to nearby destinations for provisions and meals.

It would turn out that Salo was not really a full-time cab driver, and that the vehicle he was using that Friday night was actually his mother's cab. Police said that he was borrowing it on off-hours to pick up extra cash.

It took police six days to locate Salo, a.k.a. David Blyden. When they finally found him on Friday, January 21, he was in the backyard of his mother's house in West End skinning a goat. He didn't even look up, or stop what he was doing when the investigators began their questioning. The tall, forbidding man was no stranger to the police. He had a reputation as a small-time dealer who sold marijuana to tourists.

Clutching a bloodstained knife in one hand, Salo continued to butcher the goat carcass as he answered the officers' inquiries. He made it clear to the investigators that he did not have much to say. The information that he did provide was very brief. It confirmed for police that he had picked up the four men at Zebra House around eleven p.m.—the time they had said in their statements. He detailed their stop at the Barclays bank ATM machine, which was located adjacent to Pusser's on the side of a building that was painted in bright tangerine.

It was three-forty in the afternoon on Friday, January 21, when Alwin James recorded the official statement that David Blyden gave to police. The meeting between the investigators and Salo lasted just thirty-five minutes and is excerpted below:

> I know a white guy called Alexis [sic] from the
> United States. He resides at the Zebra House in

Belmont Estate. I first met him about two (2) years ago through taxiing. Since I first met him, he uses me as his taxi driver. He is in possession of a business card to call me. He first called me this year sometime earlier this month. I do not recall the date. I have taxi them [sic] several times since, but I can't recall exactly where I took them. Alexis [sic] have three (3) friends with him. I do not recall their names. Sometime on Friday 14th January, 2000, Alexis [sic] called for me to take them to Quito's. I do not recall what time it was when they called. However, I went to pick them up at about 11:00 p.m. They walk down to the bottom of the entrance to Zebra House. I was driving my mother's car. It was Alexis [sic] and his three (3) friends. I took them to the ATM machine at Soper's Hole. From what I recall, only Alexis went to the machine. During that time, I went to the bar and got a drink. I then left for Cane Garden Bay via the Zion Hill Public Road. When I reached Sebastian Hotel, one of them got off. I do not know which one. I then proceeded to Quito's. On arrival at Quito's, all of us went inside. When we got there, the band was playing. Alexis [sic] and I then left to smoke a joint (marijuana). We stayed about fifteen (15) minutes. I went to dance, I do not know who they associated with while there. I did not walk the beach with them, but there is a beach, I believe they went on the beach. When Alexis and I came back inside, the other two (2) guys was [sic] at the bar. The band finish playing sometime about 2:00 a.m. I did not see them with any woman while we were there. I also did not see the woman I was shown in the picture. I did not know the deceased. When the band was finished, I left Cane Garden Bay with the three (3) guys and Moon for home. I took them to their gap, they paid me and I went to West End with Moon. Moon sat in the back seat of the car with the

other two (2) guys. Alexis [sic] sat in the front passenger seat. Moon was very intoxicated. We were
all nice. We had a few drinks. There was [sic] a lot
of people at Quito's that night.

—David Blyden

Salo was not responsive to further questions, and police
did not feel satisfied at the completion of the interview. Officers would later tell their superiors that they had found Salo
less than forthcoming in his replies, and sensed that he was
not telling them everything he knew. They were also suspicious at his early attempts to evade police.

Johnston was suspicious of the fact that it took so many
days to trace Salo, and that he was reluctant to come in to
headquarters to sit down with police.

To complicate matters, when investigators returned to
Soper's Hole to question Moon about his taxi ride with
Salo on Friday night, they were stunned by his response.
Contrary to Michael's and Evan's accounts, Moon told
officers that he was certain that there was no one else in
the taxi with him when Salo gave him a lift home. His
pronouncement was not consistent with information provided to police by the two men, who had each, without the
other knowing, recounted being in the car with Moon that
night.

Later, the significance of these observations would be
discounted.

In Salo's statement, he, too, had told police that Moon
was sitting in the back seat with Michael and Evan, and that
he had dropped the three Americans off first, and then proceeded to West End with Moon in the car.

With Michael and his friends now under lock and key—
charged on "suspicion" for the murder of Lois McMillen—
it seemed clear that the men were going to need a top-notch
lawyer. Mary Lou Creque had offered to take the case, but she
had already made it clear that she was a general practitioner,

and not a criminal attorney. Michael realized he'd have to make a change.

Spicer's sister Chris had already done some preliminary research on her brother's behalf, talking to people on the island, and phoning the American consulate in the States for a list of attorneys in Tortola. She selected a man named Joseph S. Archibald of J. S. Archibald & Co, and arranged to see him the day after her arrival on Tortola. Archibald was one of two Queen's Counsels on Tortola, a distinguished title that permitted attorneys to be seated at the lead defense table when arguing a case before the court. He had earned a reputation as the top criminal defense attorney in the Territory. He had represented a number of high-profile, high-paying clients, with good results.

Diminutive and impeccably dressed, Archibald was the president of the Bar of the Organization of Eastern Caribbean States, and was well regarded by his peers. He had passed the Bar in December of 1959, and had been admitted as a Barrister at Law of Lincoln's Inn in London the following year. Lincoln's Inn is the oldest law school in London, having been established in 1344, and many of its graduates have gone on to become world-renowned attorneys. Among Archibald's distinguished accomplishments were the Inns of Court Special Certificate in Public International Law, and an appointment of Queen's Counsel in 1980. On two occasions he had acted as a High Court judge and, after the McMillen case was completed, he would sit twice as one of three justices on the Court of Appeals in the Eastern Caribbean district.

Archibald operated his practice from an elegant suite that spanned the entire second floor of a building on a side street directly behind St. Williams Catholic Church in Road Town. His offices were decorated with hardwood antique furnishings, some with intricate carvings. Expensive artworks that had been gifted to him by previous clients covered the soft white walls.

Among the small team of attorneys who worked alongside Archibald was one named Oscar Ramjeet. Like Archibald, Ramjeet had an impressive list of credentials that included a two-year stint as a magistrate in Montserrat, and six years as solicitor general of St. Vincent and the Grenadines. He had also served as assistant attorney general in the US Virgin Islands for two years and was a citizen of the United States. In his spare time, he worked as a freelance journalist for several regional and international media outlets. A slight man with thick wavy graying hair, Ramjeet was also an avid cricket player.

Ramjeet accompanied his boss to Zebra House that Saturday to meet with Michael's sister at the family's residence. From the moment Chris Matthews shook hands with Joseph Archibald, she knew that he was the right man for the job. He was smart and straightforward, and he impressed the woman with the platinum shoulder-length hair with his expansive knowledge and glowing credentials.

Meanwhile, the attorney who was currently representing Spicer and his friends was meeting with the foursome at Her Majesty's Prison. It was midday Saturday when Mary Lou Creque arrived at the hilltop facility with the three patrons from Quito's: Nadia Pecinski, a nurse from Sweden; Johnny Tattersall, the son of a prominent doctor; and Johnny's girlfriend, Cordelia. They had agreed to come up to the prison to determine if the men in custody were the ones who had shared their table at Quito's on the night of Lois' murder.

William had already told police that he had opted not to join them at the beachfront restaurant in Cane Garden Bay, choosing instead to turn in early for bed.

Upon her arrival, Creque informed Michael that she had reached out to Salo, their taxi driver, but had been told that he was unwilling to give a statement. He had just spoken to police and would say nothing more for the remainder of the case.

Michael later reported that all three of the patrons from Quito's recognized him, Evan, and Alex, and that they willingly gave his lawyer a statement on their behalf. But there was never an occasion for their affirmations to be entered. Instead, they would be held by the men's respective attorneys for use at a future time, if need be.

Deputy Commissioner Johnston would later say that police did locate and speak with Pecinski, the nurse from the Bougainvillea Clinic. Yet he could not recall if his investigators were able to determine whether Nadia and her friends had actually seen the men at Quito's on the night of Lois' murder—or whether they were confused and basing their recollections on a meeting they'd had on a previous night.

"I am not sure if we were ever able to put that one to bed," said Johnston. "It is common practice for people who try to construct alibis to take the events of a previous occasion and relate them as their actual movements on the night of the crime. If nothing else, it causes confusion, and many witnesses then become unsure of the actual date or time being referred to." At that time, Johnston was "pretty convinced that their supposed alibis were more fiction than fact."

It has been reported that Nadia Pecinski corroborated the men's story and that, soon after providing Michael's lawyer with a supporting statement, she returned home to Europe.

The bad feelings between the four men intensified when William learned that Michael intended to retain the services of the island's top criminal attorney, and was no longer going to foot the bill for William's or Alex's defense.

Michael was introduced to the man who would become his new lawyer—Joseph S. Archibald—at his next court appearance on Monday, January 24. This time, he and his friends were brought before a magistrate for what would become a weekly activity, the Monday morning remand hearing. It was at these hearings that prisoners awaiting trial were informed of the status of their case, and could relate any problems or complaints about the terms of their incarceration.

Archibald spoke with Michael and Evan in a rear office of the Magistrate's Court directly following the hearing that Monday. Michael later recalled that he found the lawyer with the thin moustache and round wire eyeglasses dignified and intelligent, and was immediately impressed by his breadth of knowledge. But he did not like what Archibald had to say about his situation.

"I will win you acquittal at trial," the five-foot-tall attorney told Michael.

"At trial?" Michael was perplexed. "No, no, I want to get out of jail right now. I didn't do anything wrong."

Michael would soon learn that that was not how things worked on this tiny Caribbean island.

Archibald had brought along his law associate, Oscar Ramjeet, to the meeting with Michael and Evan at the Magistrate's Court. In addition to his government posts, Ramjeet had worked in private practice doing criminal and civil litigation.

"At the first meeting at the Magistrate's Court, I chatted with Michael and Evan and they told me they were innocent and I believed them," Ramjeet later recalled. He said he based his opinion on the men's demeanor and their responses to his questions.

Later that same week, all four men were brought before the court for the habeas corpus hearing. Michael later recalled that the presiding judge seemed disappointed when the foursome told him they did not intend to go forward with the application. Mary Lou Creque had already advised them that the habeas corpus petition was no longer appropriate and that it would be best to adopt a new tack. They had now been formally charged with murder, which she said made the filing of the application moot.

J. S. Archibald agreed with Creque on that point. Later, he would advise his clients that he regarded Creque's decision to file the writ of habeas corpus as a tactical error—forcing police to file charges before they were ready to do so. Michael would only later learn that it is not uncommon in the Caribbean Territory for people to be detained for weeks at a time before being formally charged with a crime, if at all. Police work in the BVI can proceed at a much slower pace than in the United States, and delays in off-island forensic testing and examinations are often to blame for the lag. Michael would later realize that he and his friends might have been better advised to wait it out, and let the police complete their investigation before forcing their hand with a habeas corpus application.

In spite of his sister's insistence that he retain Archibald, Michael reported that he first queried Alex and William about their ability to pay for their own lawyers. He later said that he and Evan only separated from the others when he was assured that they could both afford legal counsel. But Alex and William viewed the move as a betrayal and bristled at Michael's attempts to explain his logic. Alex was upset because he believed that it was strategically better for the men to remain unified. He spent much of the first week in a hysterical state, and his behavior even alarmed the guards. They found it disconcerting when the fair-haired man dropped to the ground, curled up in a ball on the prison grounds during exercise hour, and began rolling from side to side as he ranted in German.

William was upset for other reasons, according to his friends. He was angry that Michael had secured the best lawyer on the island. But what really disturbed him most was that as the host, Michael was not taking responsibility, financially or otherwise, for his houseguests. Michael reported that William said little to him during their first week at the prison, and in fact, stopped talking to him altogether soon after the men's incarceration.

William was already moving to separate himself from the group, reasoning that police had a circumstantial case against his friends, but had nothing of substance to connect him with the crime. He understood that there was an eyewitness who'd told police that he had seen three guys trailing behind Lois as she walked the beach behind Quito's that Friday night, and felt that his own alibi—that he had gone home and gone to bed—made him safe from suspicion. He also knew that police had taken from Zebra House a shirt belonging to Michael that allegedly had a bloodstain on the chest.

The men were insisting the stain was not blood, but

barbecue sauce but their explanation did not much matter to Labrador. With little to connect him to the case, Labrador thought it best to pull away from the others. He showed little allegiance to his friends, and made it clear that in their current situation, it was every man for himself.

As the days of the first week passed, the infighting intensified. Alex continued his attack on Michael, snarling angrily at his friend in the cell across the way. William meanwhile said barely a word, but continued to fume in hushed tones. At one point, William even tried to get Alex to calm down and admonished him to lay off Michael.

Michael knew that at times Alex could be high-strung. And William's silent fury also did not surprise him. For as long as Michael had known him, Michael felt that William had exhibited an air of arrogance and an odd sense of entitlement that was way out of line with his monetary means. It seemed to Michael and others who knew William that he often expected others to pay his way. Already, Alex's dad had footed the bill for the two men to go into the modeling business together, and Michael had graciously invited William to stay with him at Zebra House to avoid a hefty hotel bill for his vacation. Yet, in each instance there appeared to be no acknowledgment by William that his friends had picked up the tab.

It appeared that little had changed since Michael first met the wavy-haired Labrador in 1989 at a dinner party in Cane Garden Bay that was thrown by a minor member of British nobility. At the time, William was staying with his girlfriend, Alida "Bucky" Albright, and her family at the villa they rented in the popular beach area on the island's north coast. After their introduction, the two men remained in touch, checking in just before the winter season each year and seeing if their winter vacations would coincide.

One year, William joined Michael at the Gold Cup races in Middlebury, Virginia. Another time, Michael was staying at the East End home of Obie Bailey, his friend from Equinox House, and attended the annual AIDS fundraiser in

Southampton with William. Subsequent to being introduced
to Alex on Tortola in 1997, Michael joined the men on
St. Bart's, and then met up with them again in Miami's
South Beach one winter. On that trip, William and Alex were
staying with a German nobleman, whom William had met
through his connections. Michael understood he owned a
house on exclusive Fisher Island, a secluded residential
resort community off the East Coast of Florida that is only
accessible by boat or plane.

During their travels, Michael had observed that William
had a kind of haughtiness that could repel some people. At
times he could be mysterious, and he had a tendency toward
long-winded stories that went off point and touched on a
number of topics both current and past. Oftentimes, by the
end of the conversation the initial point of his narrative was
unclear. But Michael liked to hang with him because, like
Alex, he enjoyed some of the benefits of being one of
William's friends. It was exciting to gain access to all the
right parties, and to meet the jet-setters who traveled in those
circles.

William would soon call on some of those contacts to
assist him in his current predicament. Meanwhile, his partner in the modeling business was growing increasingly
unnerved.

Imprisonment seemed too much for Alex Benedetto to
bear. Soon after his arrival at "the Ghut," he was taken to the
hospital in Road Town. Alex had thrown himself into a
panic, worrying that the scratches on his arm and leg would
become infected. He also feared that bites from the swarms
of mosquitoes entering through the open windows would
transmit malaria or HIV through the blood of a diseased
inmate.

Police, who wondered if he was trying to cover up his
wounds in some way, viewed Alex's hysterical visit to the
hospital with suspicion. They soon learned that doctors at
Peebles Hospital had prescribed an anti-anxiety medication
for the fair-haired American that he was to take on a daily
basis. In light of his hysterical state, prison officials decided

that it would be best to move the emotionally-charged man to the single cell in the corner of the wing where he would have more privacy, and a window with a serene view of the ocean.

Upon his return to Her Majesty's Prison, Alex was given his own cell—the one that American Jeffrey Plante was now occupying. With no other free cells available in the small remand wing, officials moved Plante to the cell with William Labrador.

The switch would prove disastrous to Labrador, who would befriend the middle-aged American and, in an attempt to separate from the others, cut contact with Alex, Michael, and Evan.

CHAPTER EIGHTEEN

Phoning Home

Word that William had been arrested, and was being held on charges of murder on the tiny Caribbean paradise where he had gone to spend his winter holiday, sent Barbara Labrador into a frenzy. Worse, he had let nine days pass without alerting his mother to his plight.

Since his arrest on January 15, the thirty-six-year-old Southampton man had said very little. After his initial fit of anger, William Labrador had kept to himself. He was subdued and introspective, and remained in a state of disbelief. In his usual businesslike fashion, he reasoned that police would soon see their error, and was certain that it would not be long before the situation would sort itself out on its own.

The tall man with the inky-black hair had turned down repeated offers from Michael's sister to contact his mother at her home on Long Island. When Chris Matthews had asked William if he had called home to alert Barbara, he told her that he had tried but had been unsuccessful. He said that he had attempted to fax her, but that his faxes had not gone through. William had avoided phoning his mother directly, saying that he did not want to worry her unnecessarily. To Chris, he seemed almost like a little boy who was afraid of the consequences of calling home to say that he was in trouble.

It would turn out that William did not want to burden his mother with news of his latest fiasco. Since his father had left the family when he was just a small boy, William had always been protective of her, and it appeared that delaying his call was his way of shielding her from unnecessary anguish.

Mrs. Labrador was already aware that her son had missed his scheduled flight back to New York several days earlier. But she had not been immediately concerned. William was a grown man, she reasoned, and she believed that he could take care of himself. She chalked up her son's failure to return to New York on his scheduled day to a decision on his part to extend his holiday, and maybe even to travel to another island locale.

As she went about her life in the trendy resort town of Southampton—blissfully void of summer tourists and still strung with Christmas lights—she was unaware that William was under arrest on charges of murder and sitting in Cell 404 of Her Majesty's Prison at Balsam Ghut. Winter in the Hamptons was a special time. It was when year-round residents could enjoy the beauty of their idyllic villages without the throng of thrill-seeking Manhattanites in shiny Porsches and Mercedes Benzes backing up traffic en route to their summer mansions and weekend share houses.

William delighted in life in the tony East End town where he was considered a charmer. Officials at the high school remember a reserved young man whose exotic good looks and sheepish demeanor made him popular with the girls. In the tenth grade, William transferred from a school in Newark, Delaware, to Southampton High School on Narrow Lane, a meandering country road that dead-ends at the Atlantic Ocean. Before that, he had been living with his aunt and uncle, who had agreed to care for him and his two sisters while his mother pursued a career with the Republican National Committee. In 1976, Barbara Labrador had been charged with coordinating Gerald Ford's presidential campaign in the state of Florida, and her duties required that she be on the road, stumping the state for the Republican incumbent. When she returned to Long Island, and reunited with her children, Mrs. Labrador was appointed to Southampton's zoning board of appeals, a part-time position that held a lot of clout in a community where multi-million-dollar projects were often considered by the board. She also worked as a receptionist in an attorney's office to help pay the bills.

The Labradors owned a modest home in the quiet Southampton enclave of North Sea, and it was from there that William rode the school bus to Southampton High each day.

His guidance counselor, Bernard Barboza, recalled that when the quiet, darkly handsome Labrador enrolled in his sophomore year at Southampton High, there was a potato field filled with Canadian geese across the street from the school grounds. Back then, students could see the ocean over the fertile field, which is now dotted with multi-million-dollar summer homes.

"It's sometimes difficult for kids to make the adjustment," said Barboza, who advised William and other students as they prepared to go on to college. "But William did just fine. He came and fit in. He seemed well adjusted. He was happy here."

There were about nine hundred students at the school when William graduated in 1981, just before the big downturn in enrollment as some middle-income families, no longer able to afford the jump in the Hamptons' prices, left the area, and newcomers opted to send their kids to private schools.

While at the high school, William, a tall, strapping teen with lots of confidence, showed an interest in sports, and played basketball and tennis, and went out for the track team. He was an honor society member, having maintained an 85 average, and was voted "local boy of the month" by the Rotary Club in his senior year. He wrote for the school newspaper, and was also a member of the Southampton Youth Association. There, he played floor hockey and coached youngsters in the Bird League, a basketball league for kids.

His athletic abilities made him sought after by the elementary school's principal, Dan Burns, who played paddleball with other school administrators on the weekends, and was constantly seeking a fourth to join the group. Barboza was one of the weekend regulars, and recalled that as soon as he and the other guys saw Labrador's power on the court, he became one of the people on the "call" list. That meant that Burns would dial his home before eight a.m. on Sunday mornings, in an attempt to talk him into coming out to join them on the paddleball court, or to be a member of a pick-up basketball game.

The calls would inevitably wake up William's mom, who was gracious and willingly roused her son from bed. Barboza recalled that William was "good-spirited" and often obliged, throwing on shorts and sneakers and running over to the courts just beside the high school.

Barboza, a native of Massachusetts who joined the school staff in the late 70s, said he also remembered Barbara Labrador as an involved parent. Although she was a single mother, and was working full-time, Mrs. Labrador remained in touch with officials at the school where her three children were enrolled. She was on the phone interacting with her children's teachers and guidance counselors, and would call with questions when it was necessary.

William's middle sister was particularly popular at the high school. Barbara Jean Labrador was very involved with athletics and was a member of almost every club and team. Her unusual look, a striking blend of Caucasian and East Asian features, coupled with her toothy smile, won her the role of Homecoming Queen in her senior year. At school, she went by the nickname "Honey," which was given to her by her mother when she was an infant. The story goes that when Barbara Labrador first looked at her daughter, she simply exclaimed "She's a honey!" and the name stuck.

William was not as involved as his sister, but was well liked and a member of the in-crowd. His youngest sister, Lara, also partook in a number of after-school activities, but was not quite as outgoing as her elder sister. The pretty young girl with the thick locks of dark hair was soft-spoken, and did not attract the same attention.

Socially, William was remembered as "open and gregarious" by officials at the high school. He was also labeled as "kind of shy," a quality that made him appealing to the girls in his grade. He was also an avid surfer, and would spend much of his free time at the beach riding the powerful waves of the Atlantic Ocean with his best friend, Duke Thrush. William and Duke had met one summer at the private beach and tennis club in Southampton where their parents were members. He would later be introduced to Alex, and the three would continue to share a friendship into their adult years.

As his junior year at Southampton High came to a close, William expressed a desire to attend college, and was pleased when he learned that he had been accepted to Old Dominion University in Norfolk, Virginia. He was business-oriented and showed an interest in political science, said Barboza, who recalled that William was happy at the prospect of attending school in the South because he had some kind of family connection to the area.

Yet, as interested as he was to go to college, William did not complete his studies at the small, tree-lined campus. Officials at Old Dominion University confirmed that William attended classes at the campus from the fall of 1981 through the fall of 1982. He then left Virginia, and moved back to New York. It is not clear what he did from 1982 to the mid-90s.

In 1995, William teamed up with a man named Paul Rowland, owner of a modeling agency on Greene Street, in a trendy area of lower Manhattan. Records show William listed as chief operating officer of Men Women New York Model Management, at 199 Lafayette Street, of which Mr. Rowland is listed as the chairman of the board.

Records show that William and Paul Rowland were also joint directors of a Florida-based company called Woman Direct that they founded in the mid-90s. It is unclear what type of service the firm furnished, or whether it was a modeling agency like the company in New York. The home address of William Labrador's youngest sister, Lara was

A young Lois McMillen posing for her family in 1989. (courtesy of Josephine and Russell McMillen)

Lois' family placed a small cross near the spot where she was discovered by a passerby on January 15, 2000. (photo by Doug Love)

The McMillen family villa in Belmont Estates, Tortola. (photo by Doug Love)

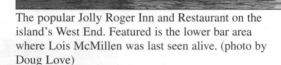

The popular Jolly Roger Inn and Restaurant on the island's West End. Featured is the lower bar area where Lois McMillen was last seen alive. (photo by Doug Love)

Bomba's Surfside Shack in Apple Bay, Tortola was a favorite hangout of Lois McMillen, and the place where she was first introduced to friends Alexander Benedetto and William Labrador during a visit in 1997. (photo by Doug Love)

Lois McMillen posing with one of her paintings. (courtesy of Josephine and Russell McMillen)

This is the last photo ever taken of Lois McMillen: in December of 1999, at the family's home in Middlebury, Connecticut. Lois is opening a special Christmas gift from a favorite aunt, Phyllis Cobb, a gold heart necklace that police found strewn across Drake's Highway on the morning her battered body was found. (courtesy of Josephine and Russell McMillen)

Alex Benedetto window shopping in Gustavia, St. Bart's in 1997, during a jaunt he made to the tiny French island with friends William Labrador and Michael Spicer. (courtesy of Michael Spicer)

William Labrador and Alex Benedetto by the pool on the terrace of the fancy Carl Gustaf Hotel in St. Bart's, where they stayed in 1997. (courtesy of Michael Spicer)

Alex is posing at Zebra House with island neighbors Obie Bailey and Clifford Lefebvre during a visit to Tortola in 1997. Obie Bailey is on the left, Alex is in the center and Clifford is on the right. (courtesy of Michael Spicer)

Michael Spicer posing in front of his posh estate in Charlottesville, Virginia. (courtesy of Michael Spicer)

Evan George and Michael Spicer reunited in San Francisco in 2002 at the Mecca Restaurant.

Michael Spicer, Alex Benedetto and William Labrador at Zebra House in 1998. (courtesy of Alex Benedetto)

A view of the guest cottage and pool at Zebra House, where William Labrador stayed. (photo by Doug Love)

Deputy Police Commissioner John Johnston climbing into his police vehicle on Tortola. (courtesy of John Johnston)

A view of Her Majesty's Prison at Balsam Ghut, where William, Alex, Michael and Evan were held. It is where William Labrador spent two years of his life sentence before being cleared of murder charges, and where he met fellow inmate Jeffrey Plante of Plano, Texas. (photo by Doug Love)

Jeffrey Plante posing on the island as he waits to testify at the murder trial of William Labrador.

William Labrador giving directions to a friend to join him at a party in Long Island to celebrate his homecoming from Tortola in April of 2003. (photo by Doug Kuntz)

Josephine McMillen's favorite photo of her daughter, Lois. (courtesy of Josephine and Russell McMillen)

listed as the headquarters for the now-defunct firm. Later, in court, William refused to testify regarding the Woman Direct operation.

William had made a number of important friends during his years in the modeling industry. One was the German nobleman, whom he and Alex had visited in Miami. Michael later recalled that the nobleman was among the first people to come to William's aid, flying down to Tortola to offer his help as soon as he heard about his friend's incarceration. Apparently, he was particularly fond of William, especially since it was William who had introduced him to the beautiful woman who was now his wife, according to Michael.

Mrs. Labrador recalled in a telephone interview that when she did not hear anything from William by Monday, January 24—nearly a week past his scheduled return date— she began to get worried, and decided to dial Tortola to find out if he was okay.

It was early evening when Michael's sister answered the phone at Zebra House. She and her husband had just returned to the cliffside house from a visit to the prison, and a short stop in Road Town for provisions. Chris listened as the woman with the raspy smoker's voice on the other end of the phone explained that she was calling to find out why William had not returned home to Long Island.

Chris drew a deep breath. Cupping her hand over the receiver, the five-foot, five-inch woman mouthed the name of the caller to her husband, who was standing nearby, and then whispered, "What should I do?"

"You're a mother and she's a mother," Tom whispered back. "You would want to know. Just tell her, mother to mother, what has happened."

"Mrs. Labrador," Chris began in a gentle tone, and then delicately presented the fifty-something woman with news of her son's arrest.

William's mother did not react as Chris had anticipated. Instead, the Long Island woman remained controlled, asking only a few details before hanging up the phone.

William was not the only one who was reluctant to contact his mother. Alex Benedetto was also skittish about notifying the matriarch of his family about his arrest. Already, he had placed a call for help to his dad in New York.

During their conversation, the two men had agreed it best not to alert Alex's mother to the situation. In fact, Karin Benedetto would not learn of her son's imprisonment until several months after Alex's arrest, when a reporter covering the case would telephone their Long Island vacation home for comment.

It took seven days, a trip to the hospital, and time in his own cell for Alex to finally settle down and realize that Michael was right—they were in trouble, and getting separate counsel was the appropriate strategy in light of the serious charges facing them.

"Did you speak to any other attorneys on Tortola?" Alex inquired of Michael, hoping to get the name of a good criminal lawyer to take his case.

Alex believed it was important for all four men to present a united defense in the case—no matter what attorney represented each of the four.

But William Labrador wanted to break away from the others and present his own defense. While he saw value in hiring his own attorney, he made it clear that he was unwilling to remain unified in the matter. Months later, he would explain his position on live television, telling a TV reporter that he could account *only* for his own whereabouts on the night of Lois' murder and was unwilling to speculate on the activities of his three friends. His position would infuriate the others—especially Alex, who was not only a childhood friend but also his business partner back in New York. Alex felt that William did not care about his hurt feelings and said William let it be known that he intended to focus on his own situation and would make decisions based solely on what was best for him.

William's mother had sent a man named Sean Murphy to Tortola as her emissary. The older half-brother of William's childhood friend, Duke Thrush, from Southampton, Murphy was an attorney with the New York law office of Clifford Chance Roger Wells, which is headquartered in London, England. Another attorney friend of William's from New York would also come to Tortola to interview local lawyers on William's behalf. It was this friend who would recommend that William hire Gerald Ferara, a Queen's Counsel, who had a law office in Road Town.

As a youth, Sean had, on occasion, chummed around with his younger brother's friend William. He remembered that Duke and William were inseparable as kids. As adults, they shared an apartment in Manhattan and even ended up working at the same modeling agency for a time.

Sean had gotten to know William better in recent years. The model handler liked to come out from Manhattan and stay with Sean and his wife at the summer house they owned on the North Fork of Long Island. William told Sean that he envied his "perfect" marriage, and even though he was a bachelor, he preferred to spend quiet weekends with the couple at their house in the country with the wrap-around porch. William enjoyed puttering around in the Murphys' garden, and sharing quiet dinners at home that he cooked up with the fresh vegetables he purchased at the nearby roadside farm stands.

Alex had already been moved from William's cell when the Southampton man consulted with Sean and another New York lawyer about his case. The attorneys advised him that seeking individual counsel was appropriate in his current situation. They believed that in a murder case, it is imperative that each defendant has his own counsel looking out for his interests.

William hired Gerald Ferara. Mr. Ferara had a fine reputation on Tortola, where he was one of only two Queen's Counsels on the island. Michael's lawyer, Mr. Archibald, was the other.

• • •

The day after Barbara Labrador learned of her son's incarceration, the BVI forensics expert working the murder was on his way to Barbados. At eight thirty on Tuesday morning, the twenty-fifth of January, Sergeant Julian Harley climbed aboard a police aircraft bound for the balmy West Indian island southeast of Tortola. In his possession were fifty-three of the more than ninety items he had methodically catalogued at the Road Town headquarters. Among them were articles taken during the search of Zebra House, as well as hairs, and fingernail clippings and scrapings from the four men and from the body of Lois McMillen. Hair samples from Alvin Martin, the man police had brought in on a tip that was ultimately discredited, were also turned over to the lab for examination. Police had deemed it unnecessary to take any specimens from Lois' former boyfriend, Luigi Lungarini, although they said he had said that he would provide them if they so desired.

The decision to take the evidence to Barbados was not made in haste. Police brass and government officials were divided on where the exhibits should be sent for forensic testing. While it was clear that the BVI had a contract with the forensic laboratory on Barbados, there was some talk of sending the exhibits directly to England to be tested at a lab there. But there were governmental considerations at stake in what they knew was going to turn into a high-profile case.

Closed-door meetings focused on the political ramifications of bypassing the lab on Barbados, an independent country, and sending the evidence directly to the UK. Officials worried that circumventing the Caribbean lab would be viewed in a negative fashion, and be frowned upon by locals who would question if justice for white Americans was different from justice for British Virgin Islanders. "If we've got a lab in the West Indies, why do we have to send it to the UK?" was the argument that Johnston and other officials feared they would hear if they opted to sidestep Barbados.

Sergeant Harley was met at the airport by Cheryl A. Corbin,

the head of the Forensics Science Centre of the Office of the Attorney General in Barbados. The 166-square-mile island is a popular tourist destination with sandy white beaches, sugar cane fields and an abundance of high-rise and low-slung hotels. Harley was familiar with the lush pear-shaped paradise and with its forensic laboratory. He had been to the subtropical tourist mecca a number of times in the past, and had attended several "Scenes of Crimes" courses there over the past eleven years. The courses were put on by the US Justice Department and held in the islands of Jamaica, Antigua, and Barbados.

The training entailed the searching of crime scenes for physical and trace evidences, and the labeling, marking, preserving, and transporting of evidence for laboratory examination. He had also attended an advanced course in latent fingerprinting at the island's Regional Police Training School in 1995. The US Department of Justice also sponsored that course.

But for all of his training, it would turn out that Harley had not been properly schooled on the preserving of evidence in a hot, humid climate such as the Caribbean. Deputy Commissioner Johnston would later admit that most of Harley's advanced instruction had been in the United Kingdom, where atmospheric conditions were markedly different from those in the British Virgin Islands. In addition, it would turn out that most of the samples collected by the medical examiner from the body of Lois McMillen had been contaminated by their prolonged exposure to the effects of seawater.

Harley remained on Barbados for two days to review the fifty-three items with Cheryl Corbin and to handle the necessary paperwork for the transfer of police evidence into Corbin's custody. On the twenty-seventh of January, the sergeant boarded the police aircraft and returned to Tortola with the signed and stamped receipt in his possession.

But the decision to send the evidence to Barbados would turn out to be a mistake, one that would further delay the criminal investigation and one that police would later regret.

CHAPTER NINETEEN

Saying Goodbye

News that police had charged Michael and his friends with the murder of their daughter stunned the McMillens. It seemed incomprehensible to the older couple that the ever-polite man who lived in the house just above theirs, the son of the woman whom Jo McMillen had befriended and even visited in Virginia, would want to harm Lois. The couple was equally perplexed over their motivation for Lois' murder.

On January 27, 2000, the McMillens held a brief and low-key memorial service for their daughter in a small chapel in the rear of the Davis Funeral Home in Road Town. Fifty-five people attended, mostly local folk who had come to say a prayer for the flamboyant American woman they recognized by face, and now knew by name. A handful of the McMillens' friends from Belmont Estates were among the mourners. The Chief Minister of the British Virgin Islands, Ralph O'Neal, traveled by boat from Virgin Gorda to pay his respects. The governor, Frank Savage, was away and could not attend.

Lois' brother-in-law, Blaine Comfort, husband to Meridee, one of Lois' older half-sisters, gave the short, moving eulogy:

Blaine remembered Lois as someone whose dress and jewelry were showy but whose personality was actually reserved. She attracted attention with her appearance but often shunned that attention because of her shyness, he said.

"She was very different and she knew it." Blaine said. "She was kind, generous, compassionate, trusting and very naive. It was both her strength and her weakness. Her strength in that she looked for the good in everyone, her weakness in that at times she saw good where none existed."

Blaine directed the room's attention to several of Lois' artworks hung on the walls; they had been brought in by family members for the occasion. He pointed to the fanciful images she dreamed up, explaining that much of what Lois portrayed was how she felt the world should be. Lois used her paintings and her other creative endeavors as a way of expressing herself and of finding consolation, he said.

"Despite growing up in a loving home, there was a hole in her life which no one or nothing could fill. Not even her parents, whom she loved more than anything else, could help her fill it, though they tried time and time again," said Blaine.

"The closest she came to serenity was right here on this island. She felt more at home here than anywhere else on earth. She loved the gentleness of the people, the simplistic lifestyle, the balmy weather. For Lois, heaven and Tortola were not very far apart."

Jo McMillen did not shed a tear. A woman of great restraint, she tended to conceal her emotions. Her husband was the more outwardly emotional of the two, and at points during the ceremony could be seen wiping tears from his face.

Less than a week later, Jo and Russell boarded a plane for Lois' final trip back to the States. There, they would lay their daughter to rest in the family plot in Port Washington, Long Island, a beautiful tree-lined suburb not far from where Lois' mother grew up.

A small group of relatives gathered at the Nassau Knolls Cemetery on February 4, to say a final goodbye to the family's beloved princess. Lois' parents had chosen to bury their daughter in the whimsical ensemble she had purchased to wear on New Year's Eve. It was a diaphanous gown, complete with a pair of glittery angel wings. A sparkly tiara graced her blond mane, and completed the "princess" look.

Eight days later, the McMillens held a second memorial service for their daughter at the Middlebury Congregational Church, a quaint wood-shingle house of worship just up the street from the family's house. The church's pastor, Reverend Dennis B. Calhoun, presided over the hour-long ceremony.

"Her death as a symbol—it is tempting to look at it that way," Reverend Calhoun told the McMillens' two hundred friends and relatives. "Maybe some of us will say to ourselves in the wake of our loss that we've had enough of the violent behavior that stalks our streets and washes up on our shores. Maybe some of us have been so profoundly shocked and disturbed by the murder of someone we knew personally that we will be inspired, as Lois was, to join the effort to bring a halt to the violence."

Josephine McMillen sat next to her husband in the front row, wearing a black suit and a single strand of pearls. As the service continued, she found herself remembering that moment at the hospital in New York City when the nurse first brought Lois into the delivery room. Her darling baby was wrapped tightly in a receiving blanket. She had a full head of silky blond hair and milky skin.

"She has no eyelashes," Jo McMillen suddenly announced, concerned.

"Don't worry," the nurse comforted her with a giggle. "They'll grow in time."

Several of Lois' childhood friends spoke during the service. Her best girlfriend from Middlebury, Inger Imset, said a few words, as did another of Lois' friends, Laura Schaeffer. Lois' half-sister, Meridee, played the guitar and sang a moving hymn about angels. Her half-brother, Jeffrey, and another half-sister, Stephanie, also took the pulpit to remember their youngest sibling. Of the three, Jeffrey knew Lois best. He had been living with the family in Connecticut when Lois was growing up, and was at home with the youngest

McMillen when he was home from boarding school on weekends and holidays. The two sisters lived in Colorado with their mother and only visited at Christmas.

Meridee's husband, Blaine, eulogized his sister-in-law again at the Connecticut service, as he had done in Tortola.

Even Lois' longtime friend from Los Angeles, Jim Morris, flew in to remember the woman who had played such a special role in his life. The two had met and dated in the late 80s when Lois was living in Studio City. The California man was heartsick at the loss of his closest confidante. He recalled that in the days before her murder, the two had been in almost daily contact by e-mail. Morris was upset that he had previously turned down Lois' invitation to come to New York to celebrate the Millennium with her in Times Square, citing business obligations. He believed that if he had come to New York to party with his favorite woman friend, she might have opted to stay in the States during the holidays, and still be alive.

After the memorial service, the McMillens stayed in Connecticut. They were anxious to be in Tortola, but they had previously leased their villa for the month of February and despite personal misgivings, agreed to stick by the terms of their rental contract.

The elderly couple rattled around the house in Middlebury during those weeks, and Mr. McMillen lamented that the sense of life that Lois had brought to their home was gone. Everywhere they turned, there were memories of Lois: a portrait of their daughter painted by her artist cousin graced the upstairs hall; her shiny yellow 2000 Volkswagen Beetle was parked in the garage under a car cover. When the wind blew, the couple could hear the musical tones of the handmade wind chime of blue ceramic spheres that Lois had hung from a tree in the middle of one of her gardens.

Weighing just one hundred and twenty pounds herself, Lois had somehow managed to drag and roll dozens of the heavy stones down a large hill in the expansive backyard to create a border around a series of flower gardens. She planted roses in one bed and then painted a sign reading "This House Protected by Angels" that she staked at its center. A small statue of an angel in a bed of yellow mums sat at the center of the one she designed outside the home's screened-in porch. And a wire sculpture of a moon, its smiling face and eyes turned up toward the sky, was placed in another.

While poking around in her daughter's childhood bedroom, Lois' mother stumbled upon a journal Lois had been keeping. In it, she expressed her frustrations and the hopes and dreams she had for herself and for the world. She wrote of her distress at not being able to accomplish her goals and asked rhetorical questions, trying to figure out her place in society. Mrs. McMillen elected to tuck the diary away out of respect for her daughter's privacy.

Amid a pile of papers, Lois' mother also came upon a six-question survey her daughter had responded to, possibly as part of a job application.

SIX QUESTIONS, it read at the top of the page. Lois' responses were handwritten on the page.

1) **What natural abilities do you have?** *Very sensitive, deep insight, "6th sense" if you will . . .*

2) **What things do you do better than most people?** *Art, poetry, dress, fashion, decorate . . . running and athletic coordination.*

3) **What are the most difficult things you have accomplished?** *. . . Staying away from drugs, drug addicts and prostitutes.*

4) **What are you proudest of?** *Becoming more moral and spiritual. Artistic insight. Being able to meet some of the world's most powerful people, and share ideas.*

5) **What about yourself would you most like to receive compliments on?** *My physical and spiritual self, art, creative ideas, environmental*

*ideas, world ideas, depth and insight, warmth,
sensitivity, love, passion and compassion.*

6) **How have you grown in the last year?** *Not
grown. Become more bitter [sic] of world, more
isolated. More disappointed in the United
States—saddened by society.*

"Lois was very disillusioned with modern life," Jo
McMillen explained. "In some ways, she didn't feel like she
belonged in this century. She didn't like the manners and
morals of young people. I couldn't get through to her that
there are evil people.

"She trusted people, maybe too much. I worry that I may
have sheltered her too much, that she was too naïve and that
is why this terrible thing happened to her," she confided,
adding that in recent months Lois had been telling her that
she and her husband needed more religion in their lives. Lois
had even started carrying a small Gideon Bible in her purse.
Oddly, she did not have it with her on the night she was
murdered, even though she had made a habit of never leaving home without it.

Her mother said she and her husband had noticed it on
the nightstand next to their daughter's bed when they
returned home from the morgue, and wondered if Lois had
left it there deliberately, maybe because of some premonition she had about her own death.

As February turned to March, the McMillens still could
not bring themselves to take down the Christmas decora-
tions that their daughter had spent hours working on. The
family dog, too, seemed to sense that something was amiss.
Sir Basil Rathbun was acting oddly, moping about the
house, refusing to eat, and avoiding Lois' room. In fact, right
up until his death in the fall of 2002, the strapping black Lab
steered clear of the frilly upstairs bedroom where he had
once snuggled with his loving mistress.

CHAPTER TWENTY

Tempers Run Hot at Her Majesty's Prison

As Russell and Josephine McMillen struggled to come to terms with the loss of their daughter in a house that suddenly seemed devastatingly empty, back on Tortola one of the men accused of killing her was busy forging a friendship with his new cellmate at Her Majesty's Prison.

Since learning that Michael had hired Joseph Archibald to represent both him and Evan, William Labrador had been making a conscious effort to dissociate himself from the other men, instead focusing his attention on Jeffrey Plante.

Plante had been moved into the cell with William on January 25, shortly after the men first arrived at the hilltop prison. Alex's fragile emotional state had been the reason given for the change in the men's living arrangements, although Plante would later testify that it was the men's constant arguments that landed them in separate units. At first, it had been Alex and William arguing with Michael, and to a lesser extent, Evan. But soon the two men began fighting with each other. Tensions were so great that at one point a bitter argument prompted police to bring Alex to headquarters to give him some time to cool down. Once he was separated and given some room to breathe, Alex seemed better equipped to deal with the challenges of confinement. He had calmed down a bit. But he continued to declare his innocence each time a guard would enter the remand area, and perhaps more disturbing, he would frequently go into weird funks in which he would lie on his cot and moan for hours.

The odd behavior worried Michael. "Alex?" Michael would yell out from his cell at the other end of the corridor. "Is everything okay?"

But there would be no response.

"Alex? Buddy? Are you okay?" Michael asked.

"Yeah," Alex would finally respond, punctuating his remark with a dramatic sigh. "I'm okay."

Most of Alex's life had been filled with ups and downs. Born on July 11, 1965, he seemed a man determined to succeed, but often found that his sensitivity and bouts of hysteria prevented him from carrying out his goals. He had enjoyed a life of privilege that included the finest private school education money could buy. But his home life was difficult, with his parents fighting often, mostly about him. Alex admitted to being willful and argumentative in his teen years, and would often spar with his mother when she would question or try to intervene in his life.

In Germany, where he had spent a good deal of his youth, it would be reported that Alex's relatives own an extensive and valuable art collection. It would also be said that he had links to royalty on his maternal or paternal side, or both. Alex was particularly proud of his Roman heritage and of the famous architects and governors that he traced through his family tree. Even more thrilling were two Benedictine Popes from the thirteenth and fourteenth centuries in his lineage.

Alex grew up in a spacious apartment on Manhattan's tony East Side, and attended Collegiate, a prestigious private school not far from his home, where John F. Kennedy, Jr., was also a student. In fact, Alex said in an interview that it was John Kennedy, who was two grades ahead of him, who actually taught him and several of his classmates to read while he was attending the school.

After graduating from Collegiate in 1982, Alex enrolled at Washington and Lee University in Lexington, Virginia, and studied Literature among other subjects. He loved to read, and often quoted from the classics in his everyday conversations. In the fall of 1984, he said he even made the dean's list. But he dropped out after completing only three semesters.

Confused and unsure of where to go next, Alex bounced around. As a child, he had had a fascination with the action figure, GI Joe, and would spend hours play-acting with his toy soldiers. He also loved scuba diving, and longed to make it part of his professional life. During several summers, he had worked as an ocean lifeguard for the town of Southampton. His post was one of the sandy beaches south of Montauk Highway, not far from where his family had a summer home in Water Mill. On a whim, he tried to turn his love of adventure and scuba diving into a full-time career with the US Navy.

He had dreamed of someday becoming a Navy SEAL. In 1987, he enrolled in a technical school, in Orlando, Florida, that offered a special "Dive Fare" program for civilians interested in becoming members of the United States Navy. The school promised a curriculum that would help candidates gain entrée into the exciting underwater unit.

Alex next traveled to Southern California where he joined the Navy and began training at a base in San Diego. But partway through the program, it became clear that the hopeful New Yorker was unable to meet the intense physical demands. The rigorous training activities were also taking an emotional toll on Alex. He was ultimately "processed out" in 1988 with a hurt knee, and advised that he was not an appropriate candidate for the prestigious SEALS. When he was arrested, press accounts inaccurately described him as a Navy SEAL, but the information was quickly corrected.

For a short time, Alex said he remained in San Diego, renting a flat on Cape May Avenue and enrolling in classes at a university there. When that did not work out, he returned to New York. In 1992, he ran into William Labrador at an East End beach. Alex was a student at New York University at the time the two rekindled their friendship. He had enrolled at the downtown campus to complete his undergraduate studies, after dropping out of Columbia University, which, Alex said, he found too academically challenging.

In 1996, Alex joined his father as an editor at Camex, the small publishing company his dad, Victor, had founded that same year. There, he could put his education and extensive literary knowledge to good use. He was extremely well read, and was fluent in Italian, French, German, and Spanish. He had picked up the languages during his childhood traveling between his father's birthplace of Rome, Italy, and his mother's native land of Germany.

Teaming up with William Labrador in the modeling business the following year had Alex dreaming of celebrity and fortune. Yet, as he sat in his cell at Her Majesty's Prison, listening to William and his new cellmate talking and laughing, he grew angered. He was furious at William's growing friendship with Jeff Plante, and of his dismissive attitude toward Alex and the money that they owed to his father. Alex did little to hide his fury at William—or his distaste for William's new cellmate.

Whenever a new prisoner would enter the remand wing, Alex would shout introductions, telling the new arrival all of their names. "I'm Alex, and that's Michael, and Evan, and William . . . And that's the elderly con man," he would yell, referring to the man sharing William's cell.

"Watch it, Alex!" Jeff Plante would snicker, his deep voice reverberating through the four-foot-wide corridor.

Evan George was particularly leery of the middle-aged gentleman and cautioned William that he should not get too close to him.

But William Labrador dismissed all three of his friends' warnings, telling them that Jeff Plante was not really an evildoer, but simply a white-collar businessman, whose only real crime was "stealing from himself." He even aligned himself with the fifty-eight-year-old American, and stopped speaking to his three friends in the units across the way.

It is unclear why William was so quick to drop his American companions and befriend Plante. But one thing was certain, the older man had William's trust.

In fact, Michael reported that William had taken such a strong liking to his American cellmate that several weeks into his incarceration, he told Alex he could no longer join him at the legal meetings he was having with his attorney in the reception area of the prison. From now on, he was inviting Plante to sit in on the strategic sessions, which were also attended by William's mother when she was on the island. Being barred from the meetings was upsetting to Alex, but being replaced by the man he had dubbed "the elderly con man" was even more infuriating.

For a time, Barbara Labrador also seemed to trust Plante. At least she agreed to help him out with some of his personal business affairs. Plante had even given her a power of attorney to handle matters stemming from his ongoing divorce proceedings.

But the street-savvy Evan George distrusted Plante, and was very wary of the increasingly close relationship between William and his cellmate, although he did not voice his concern in the same boisterous fashion as Alexander Benedetto did. Evan had a softer, gentler way, and he tended to keep his opinions to himself. For much of the time, he stayed close to Michael, his longtime companion, and the man who was footing his legal bills.

Evan was born on June 1, 1977, in San Francisco, California. Soon after, his family moved to Salem, the capital of Oregon, a small, picturesque city south of Portland. Friends reported that Evan's family life was difficult, so challenging in fact, that at the age of thirteen he left home for good. No details of his childhood have been made public, other than that he has a sister three years his senior.

At first Evan secured a job at a gas station, and even tried to stay in school. But he soon dropped out of classes at the Salem-Kaiser school, and ended up homeless and living on the streets of Portland, and then the nearby town of Tigard.

Next, came a drug problem.

Records show that Evan used the address of Outside In, a social service agency in Portland that helps homeless youths, to apply for his driver's license, and when police asked for his place of residence for an arrest record. There, he had received much needed assistance and even made a few friends.

Juvenile records are sealed and not available to the general public. But it has been reported in the press that police records in Oregon's Multnomah County revealed that beginning in 1996, Evan was picked up for theft, criminal trespass, and other petty crimes. He was just nineteen years old when his adult criminal activity began. At age twenty, he was arrested again, this time charged with his first felony. Records show that in January of 1998, Evan was picked up for possession of a controlled substance, a felony that carries jail time if convicted. Soon after, he left Portland for San Francisco, where he had family. When he arrived in the Golden Gate City, he telephoned his first cousin, a cop in the San Francisco area. "He called me up and met my family and me in San Francisco," Jacob Westlie told a reporter from *The Sunday Oregonian.* "He said he had decided to try his luck down here."

What Evan failed to reveal to his cousin was that he had skipped out on a warrant in Oregon. Westlie reported that his cousin's time in San Francisco was no easier than his years in Oregon. He also said that for a while, Evan dropped out of contact. "It was tough for him, coming down with no support, having to start from scratch," Westlie explained.

Westlie described a visit that Evan made to San Francisco when he was fourteen years old. "My sister was around his age," he told the reporter. "Evan volunteered at the high school barbecue and was there the whole day helping, barbecuing hot dogs and making friends." Westlie said that on the way home, "thugs" approached Evan and his sister. "They said rude, sexual things to my sister," he recalled. "Evan said, 'You shouldn't be talking that way.' They broke his nose and blew out his ear."

Westlie said that in spite of the vicious attack, Evan did not fight back. "He's really a gentle person. He's always just had a lot of bad luck," he stated.

But Evan's luck took a turn for the better when he was introduced to Michael Spicer. Evan was twenty, and not regularly employed when he met the dashing Virginia man, who was fourteen years his senior. Instead, he was doing odd jobs and living paycheck to paycheck.

It was Michael's friend in San Francisco, Justin Cohen, who had introduced the two men. At the time, Evan was regularly cleaning Justin's house as a way to supplement his meager income. Like most young people in San Francisco, where rents are sky-high, and home prices even higher, he could not afford his own apartment. To stay in the city that he now loved, he lived on people's couches and in cheap residential hotels. Both men reported that their friendship was a special one. Michael even introduced Evan to his sister, Chris, when she came to San Francisco to visit with family there. But Chris admitted that she did not realize at the time the depth of the men's friendship.

Suddenly, Evan did not have to worry where his next meal would come from, or how he was going to pay his bills. Instead, he could just be a person, and enjoy life for a change. But, in order to be with his new special friend, Evan had to move once again. This time, it was to Washington, DC, where he was given his own apartment and a chance at happiness.

He and Michael enjoyed their time together in the Capital City, and during a visit to Michael's mother's home in Charlottesville, Virginia. Yet Evan's decision to quit school and adopt a "live for the moment" attitude would have a lasting impact on him.

For one, he was ashamed of his limited vocabulary and lack of proper knowledge of grammar and punctuation. His insecurity about his meager education also made him uneasy in social situations, fearing that people who were more educated than he might look down on him. In fact, Evan was rather intelligent.

Joseph Archibald, the lawyer who was representing Evan and Michael in their criminal case, recalled how he had been taken aback by the young man's incredible memory. In fact, he recognized Evan's ability to vividly recall events right down to the minutest detail, because he himself had the same gift. To test the young man, he even had him read certain passages, and then smiled knowingly when Evan was able to recall what he had read word for word.

Like Archibald, Evan George had a photographic memory. It was a blessing that made it even easier for Archibald to get through law school in London with honors. He could pick up any book in his office, no matter how thick, and recall verbatim a selected paragraph on any given page that he had read ten years earlier.

In addition to Evan's aptitude for detail, the young man from Oregon had also picked up different, but equally important skills during his years on the streets. He was good at reading people. In fact, the soft-spoken man with the almond-shaped eyes and bushy eyebrows had developed an uncanny ability to decipher a person's character. His talent was probably born out of necessity and a need for self-preservation.

At Her Majesty's Prison, Evan's radar was telling him to steer clear of the man sharing William's cell—that he was trouble.

Several months after Alex was moved from William's cell, Michael and Evan were also separated. It had been alleged that a guard at the prison caught the two men kissing in the shower, and word of their intimate contact had upset prison officials. On this palm-fringed island, homosexuality is accepted only if it is completely hidden from view. Many Tortolans refer to gay men as "anti-men." The recent law decriminalizing homosexual acts in private was met by blaring protests from residents in the BVI.

The young man was terrified when he learned that they intended to place him with another inmate in the remand wing. For much of his incarceration, Evan had stayed close to Michael, feeling safe in the company of his older friend. Now, faced with the reality of a move to another unit, he feared the worst: that prison officials might put him in a cell with one of the more violent criminals, or with one of the "Island Boys."

Several members of the ruthless Colombian drug gang were being held at the prison. They belonged to the group that had broken out of jail the past year in the wild shootout that claimed Police Inspector Jacob George's right eye. Michael and the others suspected that Lois' death was somehow linked to the group—that maybe she had found out about a drug deal they were planning and she was threatening to go to the police.

When guards arrived in the remand area to make the switch, Evan began a loud protest. Running to the rear of his cell, he refused to allow the officials to take him from Michael.

"Evan, there are some things in life that we can control, and others that we can't," Michael said, trying to console him. "This is one of those times that we have no control."

In the end, Evan was placed in the unit diagonally across the hall from Michael, and could still see his friend through the bars. His new roommate was Umberto Chavez, a Venezuelan man who had been picked up by police during a huge drug bust on the small island of Anegada. It was alleged that police found the Spanish-speaking man in possession of a two-way radio, and threads found on his clothing indicated that he had had drugs taped to his person. It was not alleged that Umberto was part of the "Island Boys" clan, a group that was extremely well known to law enforcement officials in the United States.

Umberto turned out to be soft-spoken and kind, and not the scary monster that Evan had envisioned. The slight, dark-haired man spoke almost no English, and for the most part, kept to himself.

Evan's move would not be the men's last change. During their incarceration, their living arrangements would shift several more times. At one point, Alex and Michael would even share a unit. But William's situation would prove the most fateful.

CHAPTER TWENTY-ONE

Waiting for the Preliminary Inquiry

Each of the four men found his own way to pass the time at Her Majesty's Prison while waiting for the Preliminary Inquiry, which was now scheduled for the third of May. For William, who was accustomed to working in an office, it was faxing letters back and forth to his attorneys and friends in New York.

He was also keeping a written journal of everything that had had happened since his arrest on January 15. It was later reported that he was planning to write a book and possibly interest Hollywood in his story. Michael reported that William kept lists of every detail of the men's incarceration, right down to the foods they were served at each meal.

Alex vacillated between periods of depression, during which he sat on his cot and moaned, and "highs," in which he complained about his unjust confinement, then exercised non-stop for his entire hour-long period outside. Evan was more moderate. He played basketball on the prison's court and jogged when he was outside, and in his cell, he devoured the books, magazines, and newspapers that Michael had requested from his sister. At one point, he read a book a day. He also wrote letters and faxed his friends on the West Coast. He found the whole experience terrifying.

Michael Spicer seemed to be handling imprisonment the best. He had never held a real job, and did not have the same difficulty adjusting to a sedentary day as William and Alex.

He was also a voracious reader, and seemed to lose himself
in the books and copies of *The New York Times* that his sister
Chris delivered and mailed to him. He had been a dedicated
reader of the *Times* since his childhood, when he used to
spend hours reading the paper with his dad. Lewis Spicer
was once a professional basketball player for the Providence
Steamrollers, and had enjoyed playing hoops with Michael's
older brother, until a diagnosis of Parkinson's disease that
left him wheelchair-bound starting when Michael was just a
young boy. Unable to play basketball or baseball with his
youngest son, Lewis forged a different relationship in which
he and Michael would spend time reading and talking about
everything from the news of the day to literature. Chris
recalled that the two seemed more like two adults than a
father and son.

Spicer and his friends continued to be held in twenty-
three-hour-a-day lockdown at Her Majesty's Prison and
began lodging formal complaints with authorities, writing
letter after letter to officials at the US Consulate about their
plight. They wrote that they had been detained for four
months without so much as a Preliminary Inquiry to determine if there was enough evidence to continue holding
them. And they complained about the manner in which they
were being treated in jail, and the confinement to their cells.

The men's families were writing similar letters. There
was not much that officials at the Consulate could do to
expedite the case, but authorities there did write a letter to
the governor of Tortola on the men's behalf, asking that the
four be given more time outside of their cells. They asked if
the men could at least be given the ability to walk inside the
unit in which they were being detained.

Prison officials had been reluctant to allow the quartet
outside with the other prisoners because of concerns about
their safety. Convicts at Her Majesty's Prison were allowed
to move about its grounds during the day. Spicer and the others were among the only white Americans in the facility and
prison officials did not want to risk an incident in which the
men could be injured or worse.

Ultimately, the officials reached a compromise in which the four men were allowed to leave their cells for up to four hours each day, either to roam the hallway just outside their units or to go outside in the prison yard to stretch and get some fresh air. But there was little the Consulate could do to move the men's case along. Instead, the foursome continued to be brought before a magistrate every Monday for their weekly remand hearing, often to learn that the Preliminary Inquiry originally scheduled for mid-February had been postponed once again.

Early on in their incarceration, a representative from the US Consulate in the Caribbean had visited the island, and had gone to see the men's lawyers, as well as the McMillens. But this case was unusual and required special handling as both the victim and the accused were Americans.

When the McMillens returned to Tortola in March, they were dismayed to learn that little had been done to advance the police investigation into their daughter's death. They found that the four men from Zebra House were still in custody, awaiting the Preliminary Inquiry (PI), which is the British legal system's equivalent to what is termed in the United States a Probable Cause Hearing. They were disappointed to hear that the PI scheduled for mid-February had been postponed pending the results of forensic testing on the evidence that had been submitted to the lab in Barbados.

Rumblings of previous associations in the States between the men and Lois McMillen, and suggestions that they were somehow linked by a modeling agency, had investigators on Tortola scrambling for information. These suggestions were never substantiated.

Whispers about a car accident on the island that had involved Lois and several of the men now under arrest was another angle they were pursuing. Police were learning that William and Alex had been passengers in Lois' car, and that there may have been a discrepancy over money owed for injuries or damages. Investigators were trying to locate records of the supposed crash that occurred during a previous trip to Tortola. But an in-depth search of the old police files turned up nothing.

Instead, William was sharing the details of the car accident with the only other American man besides he and his friends who was being detained in the remand wing of the prison at Balsam Ghut—Jeffrey Plante.

Upon their return to the island in mid-March, the McMillens were troubled by the police department's handling of a strange incident the couple encountered and reported to police. Soon after their ferry landed on Tortola, they received a mysterious telephone call from a man who identified himself as Stephen Esses, a private investigator.

"He said that he had come down to 'help us with our problem' and he wanted to meet with us," Jo McMillen recalled of the cryptic phone call. "We agreed to meet with him at the Prospect Reef hotel at ten thirty or eleven o'clock the following morning."

According to the McMillens, when they arrived at the sprawling two-story waterfront complex, they were immediately turned off by what they saw. Waiting for them at one of the plastic tables of the hotel's outdoor restaurant was a thirtyish man who appeared to be suffering from a horrible hangover, and looked a wreck. During their meeting, Mr. Esses told the couple that he was on the island to investigate their daughter's murder. It was unclear to the McMillens who he was working for—if anyone. At one point, he indicated that he worked for the United Nations, and provided the couple with several telephone numbers where they could supposedly contact him in the States. He said he knew all of the men in custody, and that he had also known Lois, who had been a good friend of his. The slender man with the dark hair said he had met their daughter in the Hamptons during the summertime, and then went on to accurately describe her to her parents.

Mrs. McMillen observed quietly, wondering when this guy and her daughter may have come into contact. One thing she believed was clear, Lois would not have been a friend of this man. He claimed the police were withholding information from the McMillens, and that he could find the real killer and bring him to justice. He pointed to a deposition given by Inspector Jacob George that had been filed with the court. In it, he said, was evidence that the four men in custody were innocent of their daughter's murder. A subsequent review of the deposition by the police revealed no such evidence.

Later that day, Mr. Esses telephoned the McMillens at their villa and told them it was extremely important that they meet right away. Mr. McMillen agreed to see the American gentleman for a second time back at the Prospect Reef hotel that evening. This time, the investigator allegedly told Mr. McMillen that he and his wife were in danger and that he could help them to get back to the States—for a fee.

Russell McMillen was angry at the idea that this man was looking for money and told him he was not interested in his services. His fury grew when, according to McMillen, the man announced that it was "easy" to bribe people on Tortola, and then pulled a wad of hundreds from his pocket. He fanned out the bills to show how much he was carrying, and said, "This is all it takes." Mr. McMillen said Mr. Esses then indicated that he intended to fly to Barbados, where the evidence in Lois' murder case was being tested.

Mr. McMillen was fuming when he returned home to the villa that evening, Mrs. McMillen recalled. The meeting had upset him, as had the thirty-minute drive to Road Town in the dark on the precipitous roads on what he deemed a wild goose chase.

The next day, the older couple went straight to police. They filed a report with Inspector Jacob George about their bizarre meetings with Stephen Esses. But they were upset when days passed and it appeared that police were doing little to follow up on what the couple perceived to be a veiled threat.

Frustrated with the lack of progress in her daughter's case, and about the police investigators' failure to follow up on their report about Mr. Esses, Mrs. McMillen went to see the attorney general. Attorney General Cherno Jallow agreed to meet with her and listened as she told him that she

"knew something that he did not." She later recalled that Jallow, a serious-minded man from Gambia, in West Africa,
expressed dismay that police had failed to tell him about the
couple's contact with Mr. Esses and made his disappointment known to the department's top brass.

Next, the McMillens heeded the advice of several local
friends and hired a private investigator to help island police
with their daughter's case. It was not their usual modus
operandi to challenge people in authority, but the McMillens
wanted justice for Lois, and were anxious to do whatever
they could to help find the person or persons responsible for
killing their daughter. They wanted reassurances from an independent third party that police were doing everything possible to learn the identity of the person who had hurt their
only child. The couple took the unusual step of seeking and
obtaining permission from the island's governor, Frank
Savage, before retaining an investigator.

The couple went to Kroll Associates, a private international security firm based in Manhattan, and with sixty
branch offices around the world. The McMillens had chosen
Kroll not only for its stellar reputation, but also because an
executive at the firm was a close personal friend of the couple. It was decided that since their daughter's murder had
occurred in the Caribbean, an agent from the firm's Florida
bureau would be dispatched to look into the matter. They
even told the investigator about their visit from Mr. Esses,
and asked that he look into the man's credibility for them.

The prosecutor in the McMillen case, Senior Crown
Counsel Terrence Williams, troubled by pieces of the police
investigation that appeared to be incomplete, asked a detective from the Royal Virgin Island Police Force's drug squad
to look into the matter for him. For Williams, who was
accustomed to the aggressive police work he had seen in
Jamaica, the idea that investigators had not interrogated the
four men before arresting them was contrary to his experience. He understood that many of the officers had limited
experience in murder interrogations, but he wondered why
the investigators did not invite one of the British officers on

the force, either Deputy Commissioner Johnston or Inspector Mike Wickerson, to take a crack at the four suspects.

It was no secret that there existed a strained relationship between the local British officers and the black officers on the force. The British officers were better paid, and the monetary gap was a source of tension among members of the RVIPF. Additionally, murder cases in the BVI are put in the hands of the Superintendent and Chief Inspector of Police, and Johnston was careful not to jump the chain of command.

Yet, in situations where there is a lack of experience, Williams always believed it best to ask for help. He was aware that the British officers were well qualified, and might be better trained at extracting information from murder suspects, using methods they had gleaned from decades of service in the UK, where crimes such as murder were more commonplace.

Even Michael Spicer said that he wished he had been given an opportunity to speak with a British officer, feeling that the cultural differences between the West Indian investigators and he and his American friends might explain why police focused in on them so early in the investigation. He believed it possible that officers may have misread nuances and subtle differences in the English language, which in turn led to their suspicions and ultimately to the men's arrest.

The thirty-five-year-old Williams had been appointed to prosecute the high-profile murder, and several other big cases in the Territory. In a bizarre twist, Williams' arrival on Tortola on January 15 coincided with the grisly discovery of Lois' body.

Williams recalled that Stuart Best, his old neighbor in Barbados, where he had attended school, greeted him at the airport when he landed in the Territory. Williams had been hired to serve as a prosecutor with the island's attorney general's office, and was slated to start work later that day. He had not seen Best since their time in Barbados in the late 1980s. "You've arrived at an opportune time," Best told the compactly built man with the multiple suitcases. "There's been a murder."

The lawyer's eyes widened in acknowledgment of what his friend was telling him. Williams was short in stature, but tall on knowledge and good wit. Yet he was not quite sure how to best respond to his friend's pronouncement.

He was accustomed to prosecuting murder cases. It was what he did best.

Upon graduating from the Norman Manley Law School in Jamaica, Williams had been invited to remain in the balmy Caribbean country as a member of the prosecutorial team in the AG's office. He had enjoyed the job's fast pace, and the office's large chamber of council afforded opportunities for discussion and the ability to learn from the other attorneys on staff. It was not unusual to be given just three weeks to prepare them all for presentation to a magistrate during the island's twice-yearly circuit, at which cases were heard over a three-week period.

During his five years with the attorney general's office in Jamaica, there were times when he would be prosecuting fifty cases at a time—nearly seventy-five percent of them murders, rapes, and gun crimes.

But he would soon learn that on Tortola, anything more than one murder a year was an extraordinary occurrence. On this West Indian island, domestic abuse and theft were the dominant crimes, although it appeared to him that drug smuggling cases were on the rise.

In spite of his experience with the AG's office in Jamaica, and his years in private practice defending the kinds of criminals he once prosecuted, Williams was not given the high-profile McMillen case right away. It would be ten days before the file would land on his desk in a second-floor office of the sprawling glass-and-cement headquarters of the attorney general's complex.

When he initially reviewed the matter, Williams immediately noticed the stark difference in the way police work is carried out on Tortola in comparison to the methods on Jamaica. He was astonished that investigators had not aggressively interrogated the four men they had in custody, nor had they actively pursued and re-interviewed important witnesses such as Salo, the taxi driver. He noted that statements had been taken from the men from Zebra House, but there had been no follow-up question-and-answer period or police interrogation.

"They had enough to arrest them," Williams later explained. "It is enough to have circumstantial evidence under our law, to add up the circumstances and say what they mean. Not what they mean by themselves, but collectively what they mean.

"Lois McMillen was murdered in shallow water and these are men who were with her consistently in the days leading up to it. These men have marks on their bodies, and wet and sandy shoes, and explanations you don't believe. And they were reluctant to mention the fact that they had been in the area where McMillen was killed. That is circumstantial evidence."

The new police investigator that Williams brought on board to help with the McMillen case was a local man named Alwin James. The beefy veteran officer had just worked with Williams on a drug case and his investigative skills and honest character had impressed the young prosecutor.

Interestingly, a guard at Her Majesty's Prison also thought highly of Alwin James. In fact, the ex-police officer turned prison employee decided to contact James when an inmate at the facility—Jeffrey Plante—came to him in early May requesting to speak to police.

CHAPTER TWENTY-TWO

No Forensics

Unbeknownst to the four men from Zebra House, the fifty-three items that had been delivered to Barbados for examination were returned in mid-March to authorities in Tortola with "unsatisfactory" results. Cheryl A. Corbin of the Forensic Sciences Centre in the Office of the Attorney General in St. Michael, Barbados, informed investigators that her facility was not equipped to conduct DNA tests on the materials that had been delivered by Sergeant Harley in late January. Instead, she recommended that the items, and other articles that had not yet been analyzed for DNA, be forwarded to a more sophisticated laboratory on the island of Jamaica, where DNA tests could be performed.

Among the items not yet tested were blood samples found on the rocks at the Drake's Highway crime scene and fingernail clippings and scrapings that had been taken from the four accused men, as well as those of Alvin Martin. Martin was the man who had been seen driving with a blond woman on the night of Lois' murder. The vaginal and rectal swabs taken from the body of Lois McMillen, which police would use to determine whether she had been sexually assaulted, had also not been analyzed. Nor had the urine sample that the medical examiner had collected from her during a post-mortem exam.

The tests performed on Barbados did reveal that one of the sneakers belonging to William Labrador had a brown spot on the tongue that tested positive for blood. A piece of "folded sticking paper"—better known in the United States as adhesive tape—that had been collected from the wastebasket in the room of Michael and Evan also came back positive for blood.

In her official report, Corbin wrote that she had found "sand" on the Kastels belonging to Evan George. There was no mention of the shoes taken from Alexander Benedetto. It would turn out that Michael Spicer's K-Swiss sneakers with the holes in the soles had also been sent to the laboratory, but they did not appear wet and therefore no tests had been conducted on them.

In her written statement, dated March 14, 2001, the forensic scientist also noted that during her examination of the articles the previous year, she had observed black, red, and brown particles on some of the fingernail pieces found in the men's garbage pails at Zebra House. She had also found blood on some of the stained tissues taken from the wastebaskets. But she could draw no further conclusions.

Corbin's recommendation that she forward the items to the prestigious Forensic Science Laboratory in Kingston was met with mixed reaction by authorities on Tortola. On the one hand, police in the BVI wanted to get results in an expeditious fashion. Already, they had lost more than one month by sending the items to Barbados, where the facility was not equipped for DNA testing. Investigators knew that there was a fully equipped and ultra-modern lab in Great Britain at their disposal. They also knew that Jamaica had its own caseload. Now they were forced to weigh the political ramifications of harming relations with officials on Jamaica against opting for the most expeditious testing available. Police also did not want to leave the impression that the four white Americans sitting in Her Majesty's Prison were being treated any differently from residents of the Territory.

On March 2, 2000, authorities gave the green light for Corbin to deliver twelve items to the forensic lab in Kingston, Jamaica, for DNA testing. Among the articles were two pairs of men's sneakers, the Kastels that belonged

to Evan George, and the Adidas with the bloodstained
tongue that belonged to William Labrador. The scientist in
Barbados had cut the tongue from the shoe, and it was this
section that was forwarded for further analysis. The fingernail pieces and stained tissues found in the garbage pails
taken from Zebra House, and the folded "sticking plaster"
from the men's garbage that had tested positive for blood
was also sent, along with the vaginal and rectal swabs taken
from Lois McMillen's body. A blood sample retrieved from
Lois post-mortem had tested negative for cocaine, cannabi-
noids, and alcohol, and the forensic expert on Barbados had
decided that it was not necessary to test her urine.

Several more items would be forwarded from Barbados
to Jamaica on April 17: the fingernail scrapings and clippings from Lois McMillen, the tampon the medical examiner had found in her body, and a white Nike shirt that
belonged to Michael Spicer. Corbin had observed brown
spots and "earth" stains on the garment and reported that the
patches had tested negative for blood. Nevertheless, it was
sent on to Jamaica for further examination. It was not clear
who decided when to forward items and which items should
be forwarded.

Meanwhile, in mid-April, members of the Royal Virgin
Islands police were called to the scene of another fatal
shooting, not far from the location where Lois' body had
been found. A local man named Euan Watkins was brutally
murdered, shot numerous times as he stood tending bar at
the pub adjacent to his home in Sea Cow Bay. Watkins had
spoken to police and was expected to identify the shooter in
the Jason Bally murder last November when he was gunned
down in cold blood. News of the chilling execution-style
killing had island residents alarmed.

In mid-May, authorities learned that tests performed on
the forensic evidence in the McMillen case submitted to the
lab in Jamaica for DNA testing had also failed to link any of
the men in custody to the crime.

In a report dated May 18, 2000, Sherron R. Brydson, a
government analyst at the island's laboratory, wrote that the

DNA profiles she had obtained from samples taken from William Labrador and Alexander Benedetto "had not been found on any of the other items submitted for testing." The forensic expert reported that the fingernail scrapings that had been obtained from Lois McMillen did not reveal any DNA from a second party. That meant either that Lois did not make physical contact with her attacker during her attempts to flee, or that the material's exposure to seawater might have destroyed critical physical evidence in the case.

The scientist also stated that Lois' DNA had not been found in the fingernail clippings and scrapings obtained from Alex and William, or on the stained tissues taken from the men's waste bins at Zebra House. DNA screenings on fingernail clippings and scrapings taken from Michael Spicer and Evan George had not been conducted.

In her report, Brydson also wrote that she had detected "no blood" on Michael Spicer's "worn and soiled white knit shirt with blue and white trimmings, labeled Nike, received with earth and brown stains on front and back." There's no indication in the record as to whether tests where run to determine if the stain was indeed barbecue sauce, as the men had claimed.

But there was one stunning revelation in Brydson's summary: a screening of the tampon the medical examiner had removed from Lois' body revealed the presence of semen.

"Semen present. Spermatozoa found," Brydson wrote in her report. But she also explained that seawater contamination could explain why tests could not identify any foreign DNA material on the tampon.

Based on the finding, it was reported that Lois McMillen had engaged in sexual relations within forty-eight hours of her death. But with whom? That is what police now intended to find out. Michael and Evan had already publicly declared their homosexuality. Investigators were still unclear about the sexual status of William and Alex—although Alex had already told them about his intimate relationship with the deceased.

Authorities on Tortola had already postponed the men's Preliminary Inquiry twice because of delays in the testing of the forensic evidence that had been collected in the case. They were also receiving behind-the-scenes pressure from the US Consulate to move the matter along. The burden was taking a particular toll on the island's governor, Frank Savage. Soon after the men's arrest, Savage began suffering from bouts of stomach distress that would only worsen as the mishaps that had plagued the investigation from its onset continued in the weeks and months ahead. Yet the senior British official was determined to see the case through to its rightful end. He even told the McMillens that it had become a matter of principle, and that he felt the entire British legal system was being challenged. Savage vowed to the couple that he would seek justice for Lois.

In early June, the Preliminary Inquiry scheduled for the fifth of the month was postponed once again after a failed start. Soon after the hearing began, Terrence Williams asked for and was granted more time to prepare his case. Williams wanted to send several additional pieces of evidence to a lab outside of London for further forensics tests. The laboratory in Chepstow, England, affiliated with Scotland Yard, was considered to be the best in the world. Little had been accomplished during the June hearing; just two of the witnesses for the prosecution, Winsome Manning and Jocelyn Rhymer, had given their depositions. Manning testified to her ghastly early morning discovery and Rhymer to her role as the first police officer on the scene that January day.

On the twenty-first of June, and then on the fifth of July, a number of items were transported to the London Laboratory of the Forensic Science Service, also known as FSS Chepstow Laboratory. Police were hoping that the scientists there could employ cutting-edge techniques to extract results from the samples that had thus far failed to link the four men in custody to the crime.

Michael Paul Jonathan Appleby, a forensic scientist who specialized in cases involving the identification and characterization of biological matter, was asked to take charge of the articles. Appleby had been employed at the Forensic Science Service for nineteen years and was considered an expert in his field. In a signed statement, he explained that he had been asked to examine the items relating to Zebra House and the four men for "the presence of body fluids attributable to Lois McMillen."

Among the items that had been transported to the lab in England was the tampon that the M.E. in Tortola had retrieved from Lois' body, as well as the vaginal, rectal, and oral swabs taken from her body post-mortem. The laboratory in Jamaica had found semen on the tampon taken from the body of Lois McMillen, but could provide no further details. The tampon had been wet with seawater when it had arrived at the lab for analysis, and was still in a damp state when it reached London.

The multicolored topsheet confiscated from William's bed at Zebra House, along with the gray topsheets taken from the beds of Evan George and Michael Spicer and the green-and-yellow one taken from the bed of Alex Benedetto were also included in the delivery. The three tampons in Alex Benedetto's garbage pail, which were found without their wrappers but seemingly unused, and the "sticking plaster" and slivers of fingernail clippings that were attached to it also arrived, as well as fingernail scrapings and clippings taken from Alex, William, Michael, and Evan. William's right sneaker was also forwarded to the lab for further examination. The tongue of the shoe that had been cut for separate testing had seemingly disappeared. It remains unclear what exactly happened to the piece of evidence, but rumors alleging that one of the accused had paid someone to remove it from the lab began swirling around the island. These allegations were never substantiated.

The Preliminary Inquiry had first been scheduled for February 23, and was then postponed until May 3, and again until June 5. But the proceedings were never completed on the fifth. The prosecution had asked for another postponement just hours after the PI had begun, and the court granted their request. Five-and-a-half months after the four men were initially jailed by police, they still knew virtually nothing about the charges against them and had no idea what evidence, if any, the police held.

As the evidence made its way to England, the four men from Zebra House continued to wait at Her Majesty's Prison for their day in court. The delay was particularly difficult because the men's lawyers could not view any information about the police's case, and repeated requests for official documents went unanswered.

Even more frustrating was that the men believed that police had in their custody a small instant camera that could prove they were not involved in Lois' murder. Alex Benedetto, in particular, was raising a fuss over the Fuji pocket camera police had confiscated during their search of Zebra House. He was convinced that photographs he had taken with Michael's camera during their early morning hike around Belmont on the day of Lois' murder might clear them of suspicion. Alex was hopeful that the photos would show the scrapes sustained when he fell, and the "sun blister" on William Labrador's nose, and disprove the police theory that he was injured during a fight. But his request to have the camera returned to him yielded no immediate response.

Officials at the facility had come to like the men from America, or at least were amused by them. The men later reported that, for the most part, the guards treated them fairly. It has been alleged that William Labrador took advantage of their kindness when he asked for permission to call his mother in late June, and instead dialed into a Court TV studio to participate in a live broadcast with host Catherine Crier.

During the on-air interview with Crier in late June, William talked from the prison about his plight. The station had given him an 800 number that enabled him to dial into the already-in-progress cable news program. His mother, Barbara Labrador, and attorney, Michael Griffith, from William's hometown, were in the studio at the time and also being interviewed by Ms. Crier.

Griffith, an advocate for Americans imprisoned abroad, had taken Labrador's case pro bono. The stout, gray-haired lawyer was best known for his representation of the American man, Billy Hayes, whose gripping story was portrayed in the movie dramatization *Midnight Express*. Hayes was the Long Island man who was allegedly caught by Turkish authorities trying to smuggle hashish out of the country by strapping it to his body, and who had received a lengthy sentence in a Turkish prison.

During his career, Griffith had also represented Americans imprisoned abroad in over twenty-five countries, and was a partner in the International Legal Defense Council, based in New York and Philadelphia. Labrador's plight had appealed to him, and he agreed to work on William's case for free. He could not be William's sole legal representative, as it is customary in the BVI that a Caribbean attorney tries cases in the British Territory's court of law.

Already, William had retained and fired his attorney Gerald Ferara because of disputes over the way in which the Queen's Counsel was handling his legal representation. He had since secured the services of a second Caribbean lawyer, Ralph Gonsalves, a prominent Caribbean figure who would soon excuse himself from William's case to make a run for the position of Prime Minister of St. Vincent and the Grenadines. Ironically, Dr. Gonsalves would win the election in a landslide victory on the same day that William's murder trial would begin in Tortola.

During the live interview on Court TV, Griffith told the show's host that he was acting as William's "New York" lawyer. He said that he had advised the Labrador family to launch a media campaign in the United States that included a boycott of the British Virgin Islands. He then went on to announce the boycott, urging tourists and yachtsmen to avoid the British Virgin Islands until William Labrador was freed from jail.

"We are now announcing a campaign to boycott Tortola," the lawyer told the cable television audience. "We are going to make sure that Americans don't go there until William is released." Griffith went on to make several inflammatory remarks about the authorities in the BVI and ended by calling the prosecutor's office in Tortola "a bunch of incompetent bumblers."

In response to a question from Crier, Mrs. Labrador told the host that she believed that the prosecutor's repeated delays in bringing her son's case before a magistrate was a sign that authorities in the BVI were withholding information about her son and the other three men in custody. She spoke of the lag in receiving the autopsy report, telling Crier that the document had been presented to the attorney general's office in early May and then held for eleven days before being turned over to the defense counselors in the case. She then alleged that Lois McMillen was not murdered as police had said, but that she "simply drowned."

Mrs. Labrador appeared nervous during the interview, in which she told Crier that she had hired an independent pathologist to review the autopsy report on her son's behalf, and the independent consultant had determined that Lois McMillen did not die as a result of foul play. "She was not beaten, she was not strangled. . . . She drowned," the platinum-haired woman in the bright red suit told Crier in conclusion. "She drowned. This is not a homicide."

William Labrador's first comment to Crier when she asked him how he was doing elicited a half-chuckle from the pretty blond host.

"Fantastic," William replied in a laid-back style. "Another great day to be alive. Another perfect day in paradise."

In response to Crier's questions about recent press accounts that reported the quarter-size bloodstain on Michael Spicer's shirt, and some "twenty-one phone calls" allegedly made to Salo the cab driver from Zebra House on the morning after Lois' murder, William told the interviewer:

"I can only comment on myself, and commenting on myself, I would not know."

When Crier asked the Southampton man about his friends' night at Quito's, William distanced himself from the three men in prison with him for their alleged role in the crime. He told the host that he had no idea if the three had actually gone to the nightspot in Cane Garden Bay that Friday evening as they had told police.

William's attempt to separate himself from the group would not bode well for him in the months ahead. As he sat on the phone distancing himself from his buddies, he was unaware that his three friends had located witnesses to back up their allegation that they were at Quito's that Friday night.

In addition, the police had recently determined that Moon Williams, the marina worker who'd told them he had seen three men trailing behind Lois as she walked along the beach on the eve of her murder, was not a reliable witness. Follow-up interviews with the Rastafarian led police to conclude that he could not have seen Lois at Quito's that Friday night because she was most likely already dead at the time he claimed to have seen her. Additionally, police believed that Moon might have been drinking that night, and was most probably confusing his account of Friday evening's events with a previous night that same week.

The Court TV program infuriated authorities and locals alike on Tortola. Griffith knew that tourism was the country's number one source of income, and that his campaign to stop tourist dollars from flowing into the island's economy would strike a chord with authorities. But what he did not consider was the backlash his comments might have on the men's case, and on the people in the BVI, who depended on tourism dollars to feed their families—or that nine BVI residents would sit as jurors and rule on William's guilt or innocence.

As Mrs. Labrador sat in the New York studio criticizing the island's legal system, and insisting that no homicide had occurred there, she was unaware that police in Tortola had new evidence that they believed directly tied her son to Lois' murder. William, too, was in the dark about the latest twist in the case as he sat in Her Majesty's Prison as a call-in guest on Crier's show.

CHAPTER TWENTY-THREE
Prison Informant Breathes Life into Crown's Case

William Labrador was unaware that on the 116th day of his incarceration at Her Majesty's Prison, his cellmate was at police headquarters in Road Town, telling an investigator a bare bones story about the Southampton man's alleged confession to drowning Lois McMillen.

It was on May 11, 2000, that Alwin James of the Royal Virgin Islands Police Force conducted the first of several clandestine meetings with Jeffrey Plante of Plano, Texas. During the covert conference at police headquarters, Plante reportedly told James that William Labrador had confessed to the murder of Lois McMillen the previous month, during the week of Lent. It was a startling revelation, and one that added a substantial new dimension to the case. The six-foot-tall man with the thinning brown hair and thin upturned eyebrows told police that he feared reprisal if his cellmate were to learn of Plante's informant status, and asked that his conversations with police be kept confidential.

"Go back and take a written statement from this Mr. Plante," is what Deputy Commissioner Johnston told Alwin James when the police investigator told him of the Texas man's insistence that Labrador had confessed to him the previous month.

In a second meeting, held on June 3, Plante described to James how he had first befriended William, and how the two of them subsequently started to talk more often about personal matters. He said they had gotten to know each other well during their four months of incarceration, in part because they were sharing a tiny cell twenty-three hours a day, seven days a week.

"I am Roman Catholic. Mr. Labrador is also Roman Catholic," Plante told police. "I like to consider myself a good Roman Catholic. I pray often and had a lot of material in the cell. A few days prior to Good Friday during Lent, I was praying and Mr. Labrador asked me whether I felt if God would forgive him if he was involved with killing someone. My answer was that I know a priest here in Road Town, Father Peters, and I would introduce them because I was not comfortable answering that question.

"I asked Mr. Labrador specifically if he had anything to do with Ms. McMillen's death. His answer was yes. I asked him what happened. He said that they were driving and that they were arguing. That she attempted to pull into a police station, and he prevented that and that the argument got heated and out of control. I asked him what happened to the girl, and he said she was drowned: that 'I had my foot on her neck.' I asked him why, he said that it was over money and that she was no good."

In one of his three statements to police, Jeff Plante alleged that William Labrador had boasted that both he and his friend Alex had shared a sexual encounter with Lois on the night the three were first introduced. Plante told investigators that the alleged act of passion occurred after a night of drinking at a Full Moon Party at Bomba's Shack.

For the next six weeks, Plante remained in the cell he shared with William at Her Majesty's Prison—keeping his informant status a secret.

Michael later recalled that he and the others were aware that Plante was meeting with police, but had no idea why. He said that upon his return from Road Town, William's cellmate was telling them "not to worry," that he was "helping them" in their plight.

Both Michael and Alex later claimed that Plante was telling William that he was meeting with Alwin James and

Senior Crown Counsel Terrence Williams concerning "information on the other three in the death of Lois McMillen." According to Michael and Alex, Labrador never warned them about what his cellmate said he was doing.

Meanwhile, police were following up on leads Jeff Plante had provided to them. One was that he overheard the men talking about some twenty-one phone calls that had been placed from Zebra House to Salo, the cab driver, on the morning after the murder in what police thought might have been an attempt to come up with an alibi.

Police did in fact pull phone records on calls made from Zebra House, and found that twenty-one calls had been placed to Salo's telephone number—over a two-week period, and none on the morning that Lois McMillen's body was found on the beach. The records showed that the first of the calls from Zebra House to Salo was placed on January 4, the day after Alex and William joined Michael at his family's vacation residence. The last call to Salo was made on the evening of Lois' murder, January 14. The phone records show that the cab driver's number was dialed at 21:48, or 9:48 p.m., as the men had said in their statements to police.

Based on additional information Plante provided, investigators also tried to pull bank records on David Blyden to learn if wire transfers or large deposits had suddenly turned up in his account. They were trying to confirm reports that the taxi driver had been paid off by the foursome to keep quiet about their whereabouts on the night of Lois' murder.

Deputy Commissioner Johnston said attempts to view bank records dead-ended when police learned there were a number of men named David Blyden in the BVI and officers could not determine which accounts belonged to David "Salo" Blyden the taxi driver.

In the months to come, police would arrest Salo on a drug-dealing accusation. It has been suggested that investigators were hoping to strike a deal—no jail time if he agreed to testify against the four men jailed for Lois' murder. But

Salo never deviated from the original story he told police. Ultimately, he served a one-year sentence after being convicted on a minor drug charge.

When Barbara Labrador arrived at Her Majesty's Prison in early July she was called into a meeting with her son's lawyer in which she learned what new evidence police had against her son. It was at that Friday afternoon conference that the attorney presented both William and his mother with Plante's lengthy deposition.

Mrs. Labrador was flabbergasted to find out that the man who had sent her a Mother's Day greeting card back in May, wishing her a good day and telling her not to worry, had gone to police alleging to have heard her son confess to Lois' murder. It would turn out that Jeff Plante penned the Mother's Day wish to Barbara three days after he had already gone to police with his explosive information.

The note to William's mother read as follows:

> Barbara, Happy Mother's Day!
> I pray the next one will be under much better circumstances. You are aware that I am helping William as much as possible I am sure. Hopefully, it will all work out soon. . . .

The relationship that Plante had forged with William's mother was an odd one. Since March, the savvy Long Island businesswoman had been going to the island frequently to visit William and to try to get him out of jail. Over a period of time, Plante grew to know Mrs. Labrador, and according to William's own testimony at trial, had given her power of attorney to handle his affairs in Texas concerning his divorce, and also to assist in the process of wiring money from his account in the Cayman Islands to William's defense fund, and for Plante's own use. Plante also claimed that Barbara Labrador prepared a series of wire transfers for him to authorize, but there was conflicting testimony as to whether these were to be loans or contributions by Plante to William's defense fund.

In any event, Plante told police that he changed his mind about contributing to William's defense "after talking with the other guys at the prison.

"I told him that I could not understand, if he was innocent, why he wanted to hire such a high-profile attorney," Plante said. "Mr. Labrador is persistent and badgered me for this money."

Unlike the Spicers and the Benedettos, the Labradors did not have a family fortune. To raise money to fund her son's mounting legal expenses, Barbara Labrador had already held a series of fundraisers on Long Island's East End. Local merchants and members of the community with large private homes had donated the use of their restaurants and residences to host the affairs, and then those in attendance were asked to reach in their pockets and give what they could. It has been reported that donations totaled in the hundreds of thousands.

Alex learned of Jeffrey Plante's statement to police at a jailhouse meeting with his attorney, Paul Dennis, that same Friday afternoon that the Crown released it. He was fuming when he came back to the remand wing to report the news to Michael and Evan. It was an electrifying start to the July Fourth weekend.

Evan immediately blamed William for the mess. He was furious that he had been dragged into what he now believed to be an unending nightmare because of William's sheer stupidity. What was William thinking when he befriended this elder American gentleman? Did he not realize that the man was in prison for a reason, and that jail is not a place to cultivate new friends?

For the past five months, Evan had done his best to be patient, believing Michael and their lawyer, Mr. Archibald, when they told him that he needed to hold on, it would all be over soon. He was certain that police could have no evidence to tie him to the crime, and insisted that he knew nothing about what had happened to Lois.

Evan had liked Lois. And he was sorry that she was dead. During their brief outings, he had been amused by her zany personality, and had admired her wild style of dress. Actually, he found her a pleasant alternative to Michael's two other friends, Alex and William, who he thought were much too emotional.

In spite of his countless attempts to tell his captors of his innocence, Evan was frustrated that he was still sitting in the Caribbean jail awaiting a hearing to determine his culpability in Lois' death. Now, it looked as though they were all in for more trouble. Evan was sickened as he thought back on how William had acted over the past five months, writing his unending faxes, planning his legal strategy, and keeping lists of every meal he had been served for the "big" book he was going to write upon his release. What kind of person cuts off all contact with his travel companions and then befriends a fellow inmate in a Caribbean jail?

In late June, more than one month after Jeffrey Plante had gone to police with his stunning allegations, and weeks before his revelations were made public, Evan had faxed a letter to a friend in the Pacific Northwest, a portion of which was published in *The Oregonian* some months later. The quiet young man had just celebrated his twenty-third birthday as a ward of Her Majesty's Prison, and continued to pen letters and faxes to friends as a way to help pass the time.

"To put it BLUNTLY I had nothing to do with this," Evan wrote in his letter. "I didn't even know the girl's last name. I came to a vacation paradise . . . and then I got thrown into this chaotic horrific nightmare which does not seem to be ending. I am surrounded by drug dealers, armed robbers, murderers, also a child molester and rapist. There is a gang here called the Terror Squad. . . . Also we have a man with little mind left who screams constantly. We are continually harassed, threatened, pushed around. . . . We are sport for these people."

Michael reported that William was subdued and said

nothing when he returned to his cell after learning that Jeffrey Plante had betrayed him. For months, he had not spoken a word to Michael or Evan. Now, faced with his current predicament, what was there to say?

Deputy Commissioner John Johnston said that Jeffrey Plante's information appeared to be credible. "He came forward and gave us such unique knowledge," Johnston would recall of the Texas man's testimonial to police. "He could only have obtained it from the person who did it."

Johnston pointed to two statements in particular that Plante made to police. The first was pertaining to the manner in which William had allegedly confessed to killing Lois McMillen. Plante had told police that William reported that he had put his foot on Lois' neck to hold her under water.

Johnston believed "contusions" or bruises the medical examiner had discovered on Lois' neck and chest were consistent with that statement. In his report, Dr. Landron referred to a bruise on the base of the right side of Lois' neck, and to two other bruises in the same area. Dr. Landron's autopsy report also revealed bleeding under Lois' scalp, which indicated an impact or "blunt force trauma" to Lois' head.

A pathologist from London who had been asked to give an opinion in the case would later testify that the bruise on Lois' neck could have been caused by someone squeezing as he held her under the water, or simply in a chokehold.

The second of Plante's statements to resonate with the deputy commissioner at the time was information about an argument that allegedly took place between Lois and William. Plante told police that William had told him that the two were in Lois' car driving east from West End when they allegedly got into a heated argument. Plante said William told him that Lois had tried to steer the car into the police station, but that he had prevented her from turning there.

Beulah Romney, the woman who lived in the pink-and-white hilltop house on Drake's Highway, had told officers that she heard a car come to a screeching halt on the road below her home on the night of the murder. Beulah said the vehicle was coming from the west, and traveling in an easterly direction toward Road Town when it stopped short and the screaming began.

Her statement to police had never been released to the media. To Johnston, it seemed that only the person in the car with Lois that night could know in which direction her vehicle had been heading.

Johnston's conclusions would later be criticized.

CHAPTER TWENTY-FOUR

Ducks in a Row

With the Preliminary Inquiry now set for July 25, police were scrambling to collect witness statements from people they had interviewed more than five months earlier. One was Beulah Romney. But getting her to speak with officers was no easy task. Officers did not take a written statement from Beulah when they had first interviewed her three days after Lois' body was found.

In the months following the murder, Beulah said, she received a never-ending stream of visitors to her home. The callers were police investigators and other parties including journalists who she could not identify for sure. She said the police and other investigators questioned her so many times about her recollections that Friday night, that she finally told them to leave her alone and not to bother her again. She was a local woman, who had never traveled out of the Caribbean, and recalled being afraid for her own safety. She worried that whoever had killed Lois McMillen might try to harm her as a way of keeping her from testifying as to what she'd heard that Friday evening.

When police asked why she did not call them on the night of the incident, she demanded to know why no one at the police station, just seventy-five feet or so from her home, had heard the howling and—more important—why they had not responded. She assumed that everything that she was hearing, they were hearing, too. She was apparently unaware that the West End substation closes at ten p.m. It's quite possible that the officer there had retired for the night when the murder occurred just before midnight and never heard Lois' desperate screams.

Beulah recounted that, in addition to the seemingly endless visits by police personnel, one afternoon she came outside to find a woman striding up her walkway and straight into her backyard. The woman, an American, said nothing to Beulah as she pushed past her on her own land. It infuriated the Tortolan woman that this female stranger was brazenly inspecting the grounds, almost as if she were trying to determine what a person could see and hear from the hilltop residence.

After that episode, Beulah refused to speak to anyone—including the police.

Without much success, investigators tried to assure her that she was in no danger. At some point before the trial in May of 2001, Beulah said she heard a noise that sent her ducking for cover. It was a helicopter hovering over her house. For a third time, she decided that she would not say anything more. It is not clear who was in the aircraft, possibly police to take aerial photos of the crime scene, or a media outlet to shoot video from the air. But it did not much matter to Beulah. When Commissioner Vernon Malone telephoned to advise her to cooperate with the investigation, she curtly informed him that she had no intention of speaking any further with police. Even the prosecutor, Terrence Williams, was told that his position held no clout with her.

But in the end, the four-time grandmother finally agreed to give her statement to the court—after being advised that she would be obstructing justice and be subject to arrest if she did not cooperate.

On July 24, the day before the Preliminary Inquiry was set to begin, Beulah did give a written statement to police, although the story she had first told officers had changed slightly. No longer did she describe the screams she heard that January evening as female, as police had logged in their diary. Instead, she was now reporting them as high-pitched "screams for mercy" that could have come from either a man or a woman.

Investigators were relieved when Beulah finally agreed to give her statement. Yet they knew that getting her to testify at the trial, if there was one, was going to be a challenge.

Police were aware that there were problems with Jeff Plante's testimony. For one, he was under arrest and charged with a crime when William had made the alleged confession to him, and he also had a history as a con man in the United States. In the BVI, he was facing charges that he'd overstayed his visa by one day. He had been recently released from a Texas prison after serving five years of a forty-five-year sentence for his role in a savings and loan scandal. And his estranged wife, who asked to be known only as "Shannon" for this book, was poised to file charges that he stole her credit cards and had made unauthorized charges to the tune of $100,000 that she was now responsible to repay.

Officials in the BVI knew they could not rely solely on the jailhouse confession of a prison informant. They were hoping that the results of the DNA testing now being performed in London would provide them with more evidence to take to trial. But on July 24, 2000, the day before the Preliminary Inquiry was set to begin, the forensic scientist at the lab in Chepstow, England, returned his results—and again they did not tie any of the men to the crime.

Michael Paul Jonathan Appleby reported that a general screening test for the presence of semen on the tampon that had been forwarded to him from the lab in Jamaica was negative. His tests had failed to isolate the male and female DNA on the tampon.

"It was also apparent that certain areas from the tampon's outer surface had previously been cut and removed. . . . Two areas of the tampon were examined microscopically. No spermatozoa were identified," Appleby wrote in his report addressed to Deputy Commissioner John Johnston. "The lack of detectable levels of semen staining on this item may be due to it not being present, or that the previous examinations undertaken on this item have removed it."

In relation to the vaginal, rectal, and oral swabs, he reported that "each of these items had been previously examined, and very little cotton was remaining.

"In respect to the vaginal and rectal swabs, the remaining cotton present on the swabs was examined. No semen was detected." Appleby went on to state that the oral swab did not have enough cotton remaining to perform an examination. Strangely, an appellate court later confidently related that there was sperm on the tampon.

The four sheets taken from the men's beds did not contain any DNA from Lois McMillen either. Short tandem repeat DNA profiles of the "used plaster with fingernail clippings" indicated that the cellular material on the items had originated from a woman, but did not match the profile relating to Lois McMillen.

The three tampons found in Alex' wastebasket together with their applicators tested negative for blood. Two appeared to be in their original condition—with the tampons still inside their cardboard sleeves. The third appeared to have been pushed slightly out of its applicator, and bore an area of "very light colored diffuse staining on the tip." Microscopic examination of this area failed to identify any cellular material. Chemical tests for the presence of blood also proved negative.

Appleby reported that the plastic bags labeled as containing the fingernail scrapings of Alex Benedetto contained "no material visible to the naked eye" and therefore no further examination was conducted. Tests of the fingernail clippings of Alex Bendetto revealed no indication of DNA from a second individual.

Upon examination of the right Adidas sneaker belonging to William Labrador, Appleby noted that an area of the tongue had been previously removed. By all accounts, the tongue had disappeared, and it was unclear what had happened to the "key" piece of evidence.

When authorities first obtained the sneaker, they noticed what appeared to be blood on the tongue of the footwear. Using a red marker, they drew a circle around the stain to emphasize its location. Forensic experts subsequently cut the tongue out of the sneaker for separate analysis. Later the tongue went missing. But authorities still had the sneaker and the area adjacent to the tongue still bore a portion of the red circle that authorities had drawn. Appleby opted to test that marked area for the presence of blood and reported that "none was found." But further analysis of the area "gave a weak positive chemical reaction for the presence of blood," he wrote. The scientist subsequently submitted the sneaker for further DNA analysis but wasn't able to report any conclusive findings.

When Appleby went to examine the fingernail scrapings and clippings taken from William Labrador, he found that considerable mold had grown on the samples. Investigators had made a mistake in packaging the evidence; by the time Appleby examined the material, it was covered with fungus—caused by the heat and humidity in the tropics. His forensic examination of the specimens showed only Labrador's DNA—and none from any other individual. The same proved true for the samples obtained from Michael Spicer.

The forensics scientist reported that DNA testing of fingernail scrapings and clippings from Evan George were unsuccessful because they were so moldy.

In his conclusion, Appleby wrote, "Body fluid staining attributable to Lois McMillen had not been detected on the items relating to Zebra House, Belmont, or on the samples taken from Alexander Benedetto, William Labrador, Evan George and Michael Spicer."

It was now clear that the tests conducted in England, as well as the ones that had been performed at labs in Jamaica and Barbados, had failed to isolate the genetic markers that forensic scientists often employ to connect suspects or defendants to a crime scene.

CHAPTER TWENTY-FIVE

Preliminary Inquiry

With no forensic evidence directly linking the men to the crime, Prosecutor Terrence Williams nervously went to court the following day to present the Crown's case to British Magistrate Gail Charles. He would be relying solely on the depositions of the police officers who had investigated the case, and the testimony of witnesses such as Beulah Romney, Chris Crawford, and Lois' mother, Jo McMillen. He also had his "star" witness, con man Jeffrey Plante, waiting in the wings and ready to make a statement before the court. Gail Charles had been the arraignment judge in the case, and had sat on the bench at the men's weekly remand hearings during the past five months. The proceeding was to be closed to the public and the media, and the judge placed a gag order on all parties in attendance. The magistrate made it clear that what occurred in the courtroom was not to be discussed in public until trial and warned that any person who violated her order would be banned from the courtroom.

Lawyer Oscar Ramjeet was in court on behalf of Michael and Evan. Ramjeet had visited with the men at Her Majesty's Prison every Friday and knew their case well. Paul Dennis was there to represent Alex. William was represented by Ralph Gonsalves.

Barbara Labrador was among those in the ground-level

courtroom, along with Michael Spicer's sister, Chris, who sat nearby. Normally, the hearing is closed to the public, but the two women had been granted special permission by the court to attend several days of testimony.

The site of stone-faced security personnel clutching submachine guns frightened Michael Spicer when he stepped out of the shiny white police van with the tinted windows. In his two decades on the island, he had never seen armed officers. Now, suddenly they were out in force, lined up along the street in front of the weathered, one-story Magistrate's Court where the Preliminary Inquiry was to be held. The building, which was adjacent to police headquarters in the center of Road Town, was in a state of disrepair and looked more like a trailer than a courthouse.

Because of the high-profile nature of their case, the Crown had posted extra security around the courthouse. Armed officers wearing dignified tan-and-white police garb led Michael and the others into the low-slung building with the peeling paint. The silver shackles that encircled the four men's wrists were a stark contrast to the breezy suits and leather shoes they wore to go before the magistrate. All four of the men were exceptionally well groomed, but William Labrador stood out in his loud, red pants. Alex later said he had tried to persuade him to leave the bold-colored slacks—which he insisted on wearing to his court appearances—in his cell and be clothed in something more conservative for court. But he refused.

Even faced with Plante's damning statements to police, Labrador was certain he could negotiate his release. He believed that once he showed the judge all of the paperwork he had collected on Plante during the time that the two men were sharing a cell, there would be no question as to who was lying.

Unlike in the United States, proceedings held in the Magistrate's Court are closed to the public, and spectators can only gain admittance with special permission from the court. Another difference is that defendants in the BVI do not sit with their attorneys. Instead they are directed to a wood bench in the rear of the courtroom that is referred to as the "dock." The courtroom had an odd shape: the distance from side to side was much wider than the room's depth.

Beulah Romney would be the first to testify at the pre-trial hearing. Dressed in a tasteful dress and matching footwear, the fiftyish grandmother took the stand to establish the time of McMillen's death. Chris Crawford, the marine surveyor from Massachusetts, took the stand next to establish that Lois had been at the Jolly Roger in the hours before her murder.

William's new attorney, Dr. Ralph Gonsalves, chose not to cross-examine Romney, focusing instead on the "black man" whom Chris Crawford said he had seen talking to Lois at the Jolly Roger in the hours before her death. The lawyer wanted to know if Crawford had told police about the man, and if Superintendent Roy Stoutt had been there when he did. Crawford testified that he did tell police about the heavy-set man in the dark-colored T-shirt and said that Stoutt was in earshot when he made the man's existence known.

Michael and Evan's Guyanese lawyer, Oscar Ramjeet, also wanted to know about the mysterious man Crawford had seen talking to Lois. Under cross-examination, Crawford said that the six-foot-tall black man was not at the bar when Crawford had returned to the Jolly Roger later that evening to retrieve the purse that his friend had left behind.

Attorney Dancia Penn was also present, representing the McMillens. The couple had hired Penn to observe the proceedings after Court TV reporter John Springer suggested that they find local counsel to look out for Lois' interest and help them deal with the media inquiries they were receiving in regard to their daughter's case. They took his advice and retained Ms. Penn, a former attorney general in the BVI. She had an esteemed reputation on Tortola, and having her as a representative gave the family added clout in the courtroom.

Josephine McMillen was the third person to testify. She and her husband had come to the Magistrate's Court that morning with a mix of trepidation and curiosity. She and her husband had never before laid eyes on three of the men accused of killing their daughter and were anxious to glimpse the "monsters."

Russell was having difficulty walking, and had entered the building with the assistance of a wooden cane. Once inside, the couple's attention was immediately drawn to the rear of the room, where a dark-haired man sat, his head bowed. They noted that the gentleman was sweating profusely, jotting down notes on a pad with a pen he held in his left hand. "He looked absolutely sinister," Mrs. McMillen recalled later.

Lois' mother said she was surprised to learn that the man was William Labrador. She hadn't been aware that the custom in the BVI was for suspects to sit in the rear of the courtroom. She noted that Labrador never made eye contact; nor did he offer condolences for Lois' death. Even when she rose to take the stand to testify, Mrs. McMillen observed that William Labrador did not look up.

Lois' mother was poised and dignified as she stood before the magistrate in a tailored black suit and prepared to respond to questions from the prosecutor. It was difficult for the grieving mother to face her daughter's accused killers, but she was determined to do what she could in the name of justice for Lois.

Dressed in a dark suit, Russell McMillen appeared worn and frail as he looked on from his hard wood seat, listening to his wife tell the court about her "unusually close relationship" with their daughter.

"She is my only child and daughter," Mrs. McMillen told the magistrate.

Prosecutor Terrence Williams asked her if she could tell the court when she and her husband realized that Lois had not returned home.

"We had been waiting for her all night long . . . On Saturday morning, we probably woke up about twelve a.m. She was not home. We went back to bed, but kept waking up every hour on the hour and realized she was not there. As the morning progressed, we got dressed and I would say that about quarter to six we were ready for the day," Mrs. McMillen said.

"We decided that the people who could help us the most were Mr. Spicer and his houseguests," she continued over the dull hum of the air conditioner. "We decided to call them up to find out whether they had seen her the previous evening. We called Mr. Spicer's home at about half-hour intervals. We made the calls starting from eight thirty. We did not want to wake them too early. There was no answer to any of the calls. They have a machine, but we left no message."

When the prosecutor asked Mrs. McMillen if Lois was the kind of person who would offer a ride to a stranger, she was indignant. "Absolutely not," she responded. "My daughter is not someone who would invite persons she did not know well into her car."

One of the questions raised by attorneys for the four men was whether Lois could have come into contact with someone else who did her harm. But Mrs. McMillen insisted that her daughter had not gone out much on this trip because she was not feeling well, and that the only people she had socialized with were the foursome from Zebra House.

She next recounted the trip she and Lois took to St. John that fateful Friday.

"After supper, my husband and I went upstairs and left my daughter doing the dishes," she recalled in a matter-of-fact tone. "Then my daughter left home at about nine thirty . . . she took the rented car, I saw her before she left.

"When I saw her the next day at the Davis Funeral Home, I just remember seeing my daughter's body there, broken." Mrs. McMillen looked down at the ground as she recalled the grim moment, possibly in an effort to fight back a flood of emotions she had been successfully holding at bay.

Ramjeet, who was in court on behalf of Evan and Michael, rose from his position at the defense table. He began his cross-examination by asking Lois' auburn-haired mother about her daughter's outings during the family's Millennium visit to the island. He, too, wanted to explore who else Lois had socialized with in the days just prior to her murder.

"My daughter only went out by herself a couple of times on this trip," she said. "When we came down she had the flu.

On a couple of occasions, she went out by herself, but she came back early."

Ramjeet also raised questions about Lois' former boyfriend, Luigi Lungarini, and inquired about her daughter's state of mind when she arrived in Tortola. Some had theorized that Lois may have committed suicide—a theory police dismissed as ludicrous given the evidence they had in the case.

"My daughter came down to the BVI because my husband was very ill, and she was very concerned about him," Lois' mother said in response.

"Do you remember telling the police in a statement that your daughter was depressed?" the lawyer asked her.

"I gave a statement to the police on the day after the body of my daughter was found," Mrs. McMillen said, speaking in measured tones. "My daughter was concerned about her father when she came down. I would not say that she was depressed. That is a mistake. She was concerned about her father. If I said 'depressed' when I spoke to the police, I meant 'concerned' about her father."

Alex's lawyer, Paul Dennis, asked if Lois' mother could say for certain that she knew everyone her daughter had come into contact with during their trip.

"I cannot completely say from my own personal knowledge who she associated with when she went out alone," Jo McMillen told the tall, slender attorney.

After a short pause, William's attorney advised the court that he had no questions for the victim's mother.

"Thank you, Mrs. McMillen. You may step down," the magistrate instructed.

Lois' mother would later recount that her experience on the stand had been excruciating, and that inside, her heart was breaking as she spoke about her daughter's final hours at the villa. She said she was disappointed but not surprised that during the five-day proceeding, William Labrador never once glanced in her direction.

Next it was Jeffrey Plante's turn to take the stand. As the gray-haired man with the deep-set eyes made his way to the front of the courtroom, many of the chamber's occupants turned their gazes to William Labrador.

It was easy to spot Labrador in his red pants, which looked very much out of place in the formal courtroom setting. It was almost as if he thought he were back at home in Southampton and had dressed to go out for cocktails at one of the South Fork's tony golf clubs. Bright red pants were in fashion for the summer crowd there. He appeared to be taking notes for much of the hearing. In his left hand, he held a pen and continued to jot words on a pad that he had brought with him to court.

"My name is Jeffrey Plante," the man in the suit and tie told the court in response to Terrence Williams' opening question. "I am fifty-eight years old. I am an American citizen. I am now living in the British Virgin Islands."

Looking on from the back of the courtroom were Michael, Alex, William, and Evan. Their expressions revealed nothing as they sat listening to the man who had shared the remand wing with them for nearly six months.

Plante was no stranger to Magistrate Charles. On June 30, she had dismissed the forgery charge that had landed Plante in the Road Town jail. He had been accused of illegally using his wife's credit cards, racking up nearly $100,000 in unauthorized charges before he was taken into custody. But before the case was to go to trial, his wife decided she no longer wished to press charges against him. Shannon's con-man husband had convinced her to give their relationship one more chance. With the fraud charges cleared, all that remained was the visa violation charge, which the magistrate commuted as "time served."

Plante was now free of all criminal charges—and technically free to leave the Territory and return to the United States. Yet he was now a key witness in a murder case. Authorities in the BVI wanted him to stay there, and Plante was not too keen about leaving anyway, since he was expecting to be arrested upon his return to the States for violating the conditions of his parole in Texas. In addition, he had no source of income, and to top it off, Plante was claiming that

William Labrador had threatened his life. He told police that Labrador had wrapped a section of wire coat hanger around Plante's big toe and threatened to hurt him—all because Plante had offered to loan him money and had then changed his mind. He also alleged that William had a knife in his cell that he had obtained from a fellow inmate, and feared that the younger man would use it on him if he learned that Plante had gone to police with the alleged confession.

Since coming forward, police had made arrangements to put Plante in "protective custody." There was no departmental protocol for protective custody in the BVI's police force, since they'd never had to worry about creating a safe haven for a witness on Tortola in the past. But police were concerned enough about Plante's safety to cobble together a program for their "star" witness.

After discussions with the governor and the attorney general, it was decided that Plante would be provided with housing and a small weekly sum of money for living expenses. It was also decided that Plante would stay at a complex of villas on the island's East End that was owned by the wife of the commissioner of police, Icis Malone.

By all accounts, Plante's quarters at the Icis Vacation Villas were rather luxurious. He was given a deluxe villa at the quaint hotel on Brewer's Bay, which featured a pool and waterfall.

"On the eleventh of October last year, I was in the British Virgin Islands," William's former cellmate told the court. "I was arrested on that day. I was eventually remanded in custody. I stayed at Her Majesty's Prison in Balsam Ghut during my remand. I was at Her Majesty's Prison until June thirtieth, 2000. I was convicted for an offense here in the BVI. That case was dismissed."

Holding one of Plante's statements to police in his hand, Terrence Williams skimmed the document before rattling off a series of questions. Williams was no stranger to a courtroom, having handled dozens of cases in his long and distinguished career on the island of Jamaica, where he was born and raised. The prosecutor's style was animated and direct.

In response to one of Williams' questions, Plante told the court that he had a felony conviction in the United States. He said it was part of the Savings and Loan Scandal, and that he had been charged with theft.

"I was sentenced for that offense to a period of imprisonment of forty-five years," he said matter-of-factly. "I served five years. I am currently on parole for that charge. I am currently in violation of the terms of the parole—for not reporting. I have not been able to report because I was incarcerated here."

"Mr. Plante," Terrence Williams continued, "do you see the accused in the courtroom today?"

"I see the accused in the dock," Plante responded, his husky voice the product of years as a chain smoker. "I know them all. I met them at Her Majesty's Prison. I was in a cell at HMP for my arrest. I was there alone and then towards the end of January, I shared a cell with Mr. Labrador."

"Do you see Mr. Labrador in court?"

"I see Mr. Labrador in court; he is wearing the red pants."

"Do you know why you were sharing a cell with Mr. Labrador?"

"Yes, I was present in the area and I was told something by the prison officials," he said, referring to a conversation he had had with authorities at HMP. "There were constant arguments and disagreements between Mr. Labrador and Mr. Benedetto. Primarily the arguments were about who had more guilt in the crime they were charged with."

"Physical altercations?"

"I only witnessed verbal arguments."

"Can you tell us, is Mr. Benedetto in court today, sir?"

"The man I call Benedetto is sitting beside the gentleman in the red pants," Plante responded, pointing his finger at Alex.

"Thank you, sir, please continue."

"When the four gentlemen came to HMP, Mr. Spicer and Mr. George shared a cell and Mr. Benedetto and Mr. Labrador shared a cell."

"Mr. Plante, do you see these gentlemen in court today?"

"I see the man I call Spicer in court next to Evan George. He is in the tan blazer."

"When you overheard these arguments between Mr. Benedetto and Mr. Labrador were you sharing a cell with anyone, sir?"

"I was in a cell alone at this time," Plante replied. His demeanor was cool and relaxed. "When I heard these arguments between Labrador and Benedetto, they were in their cell and they were outside when there was recreation. I was able to hear them when they were in the cell because it is a very closed area. The remand area is extremely small, about twenty-five feet.

"There was a lot of hollering and yelling in the remand area. Mr. Benedetto and Mr. Labrador were hollering and yelling. Mr. Benedetto would accuse Mr. Labrador of having complicity in the crime they were charged with and constantly reminding Mr. Labrador that he did not have any kind of an alibi. In response, Mr. Labrador would scream at the top of his lungs back at Mr. Benedetto. He has a volatile temper."

"What would he say, sir?" the prosecutor inquired of the witness.

"I don't remember the exact words, but it was generally who had more guilt, more complicity, and more involvement. A time came when my cell arrangements changed. The new arrangement was that Mr. Benedetto was moved out of the cell with Mr. Labrador to where I was, and moved in with Mr. Labrador. Prior to the change in the living arrangements there was a major argument between Mr. Benedetto and Mr. Labrador."

Next, the prosecutor asked his key witness to tell the court about what a normal day at the prison would be like.

"On a normal day at HMP, for the first time—four or five months—that we were together in the cell, we spent twenty-three hours a day together, seven days a week," Plante recalled. "That other hour in the day would be used for showering and what little recreation we could get. After the first four to five months, they allowed us out for approximately three hours a day, including shower time. About one hour was designated outside time, and two hours inside time, which included the shower. During those months, in my opinion, there was empirical trust between us, which developed over months. We spoke all the time during the period."

"Mr. Plante, what did you speak about?"

"We talked about Mr. Labrador's strategy. Strategy included attorneys, it included separation—too, [sic] he felt that he was the only one who had no circumstantial evidence, and the others did. He felt that separation from the other three men charged would exonerate him.

"The discussions around attorneys centered around problems he had with Mr. Ferara," Plante continued. "He felt that Mr. Ferara believed he was involved and/or Mr. Ferara would not seek information to substantiate his alibi.

"We also spoke of the press—Mr. Labrador set forth on a mission to get the press—US and others to bring pressure on the BVI in hopes that that would help in obtaining his release. He probably spent three to four hours a day writing faxes and letters to different members of the press. He had a Web site set up by a friend of his for the specific purpose of telling people his situation here, as well as he had numerous disposable cameras he had brought to him. He had taken pictures of the facilities, inmates, and prison guards, which he sent out through various sources. Some of the pictures I understand were to be put on the Web site." Plante paused.

"I also had further discussions relevant to this matter. At the point where he felt he had sufficient press coverage and he felt that Mr. Ferara was not complying with his requests . . ."

"Excuse me, sir, can you tell the court how you know how Mr. Labrador felt?" Terrence Williams interrupted.

"I knew how he felt because he told me—he fired Mr. Ferara and hired Dr. Gonsalves. We talked endlessly about those specific things. He would ask for my suggestion, we would banter back and forth.

"His mother was intimately involved with Mr. Labrador's case and was down here quite often. I had a number of discussions with Mrs. Labrador about money. Mrs. Labrador took a wire for me for fifty thousand dollars to be put in an account that I would have access to. Subsequent to that, Mr. Labrador asked me if I would loan him twenty-five thousand dollars to help pay his attorney. At that point, Mrs. Labrador had a number of wire transfers made up and brought them to me for me to sign," he said.

"I explained to Mr. Labrador that I would consider his request, but I told him that I could not understand, if he was innocent, why he wanted to hire such a high-profile attorney. Mr. Labrador is persistent and badgered me for this money," Plante said, detailing the alleged involvement of William's mother, who he had given a power of attorney to act on his behalf. Plante said that because of conversations with the other defendants, he did not feel comfortable with the loan to Labrador.

The trio of defense attorneys began scribbling notes as Plante testified about a conversation with Labrador in which the Southampton man purportedly admitted to an argument with Lois McMillen that "got heated and out of control." Plante indicated that the conversation had taken place a few days before Good Friday.

"He [William] said that after the young lady was drowned, he said that the Jeep was taken to the ferry landing and that a trail or path was taken to Belmont, which took about forty-five minutes," Plante continued.

The prosecutor stopped Plante for a moment to ask if he had had conversations with Evan, Michael, and Alex during his period at the prison at Balsam Ghut.

"I have had discussions with the other men," Plante responded, his words striking a chord with Evan and Michael, who sat silently staring at him from the wooden bench in the rear of the courtroom. "In the first part of May, Mr. George had been moved out of Mr. Spicer's cell. I was talking to Mr. George during the recreation period. I was outside and talking to him through the bars of his cell. Mr. George told me that he and Mr. Spicer and Mr. Benedetto, on the night of the murder, had consumed a lot of drugs.

"They came home. Mr. George said that he had found Mr. Labrador fully clothed on his bed [Mr. Labrador's bed] with wet shoes," he said. "He said he—Mr. George—went outside and was sitting, trying to clear his head and that he heard a car drive up. Shortly thereafter he said Mr. Benedetto and Mr. Labrador left the house. He heard the car drive away, but did not know who it was because he did not see the car. Mr. Spicer and Mr. George are lovers. They were living together for almost three months.

"At the time Mr. George spoke to me, he was not sharing a cell with Mr. Spicer," Plante told the court, referring to the time when guards moved Evan out of Michael's cell and in with Umberto Chavez, the Venezuelan man who did not speak much English. "Before the time when he left Mr. Spicer's cell, I was included in a number of conversations with Mr. George and Mr. Benedetto and Mr. Spicer and Mr. Labrador. Sometimes the conversation took place with all of them, sometimes with two or three of them."

Michael Spicer looked on from the dock. He was doing his best to hide his frustration as Plante proceeded to tell the court about alleged conversations he had had with the others during the five months that he occupied William's cell. Spicer thought back to that first afternoon when Plante had called him over to the window to introduce himself and grub a cigarette.

"Apart from when we were all together," the sound of Plante's voice, and his unmistakable Southern twang, interrupted Michael's recollection of that first meeting with the con man who now stood before him in a court of law. "Mr. George would start to speak to me about this matter. He would start a conversation about different facts and issues about himself and Mr. Spicer, or about the case, and Mr. Spicer would threaten and cajole him to keep his mouth shut and he would stop."

Mrs. McMillen sat up and listened intently to the Texas man's testimony, particularly distraught over the allegation that Spicer, her longtime neighbor at Belmont Estates, could have been involved in her daughter's death.

"There were a number of occasions where Mr. Labrador initiated what could be referred to as mock trials in the remand area," Plante continued. "I also spoke to Mr. Spicer about this matter. On one occasion, Mr. Spicer, Mr. George, and Mr. Benedetto were outside during recreation and they were discussing a local cab driver named 'Salo.'

"Mr. Spicer had said that Salo had sold them all the drugs that they were taking while they were here," Plante continued. "He said that he hoped that Mr. Salo had been given enough money to either disappear or leave the island. Mr. Benedetto added that he felt that Salo had gone—left.

"On another occasion, Mr. Spicer had asked me how he should get more money to Mr. Salo while in prison. Mr. Spicer said that he had received a message from Salo that he wanted more money. Mr. Benedetto, Mr. Spicer, and Mr. George said—by this time Mr. Labrador had separated himself— that Salo had made an agreement with them to leave. They mentioned to me that there was evidence that there were twenty-one phone calls made to Salo on the morning of the murder. I believe it was Mr. Benedetto who said this.

"On one occasion, I was asked by Mr. Benedetto—when Mr. Benedetto was living with Mr. Spicer, and Mr. George at the time was with a Venezuelan gentleman—Mr. Spicer was present at this time, Mr. Benedetto had asked me what the ramifications were of gay rage. I believe Mr. Labrador had showed me some press articles that referred to the possibility of something called 'gay rage.'

"While the conversation was taking place with Benedetto and Spicer, Mr. Labrador came up to Mr. Spicer's and Mr. Benedetto's window. Mr. Labrador started yelling at Mr. Benedetto and Mr. Benedetto started yelling at Mr. Labrador. Mr. Labrador was telling Mr. Benedetto to keep his mouth shut. Mr. Benedetto said in response that Mr. Labrador had had the girl up to the house that night. Mr. Benedetto said that to Mr. Labrador."

At the conclusion of Jeffrey Plante's testimony, the defense counselor who was representing William Labrador asked for a recess. Dr. Gonsalves wanted time to research this American man's past. He was confident that he would find plenty of ammunition to challenge his credibility as a witness.

Under cross-examination, Plante faced questions from Gonsalves about an account he held in the Cayman Islands. But the questioning produced little of note and Dr. Gonsalves again asked the magistrate for more time and an opportunity to bring Plante back for further questions about his financial dealings and prior convictions in the United States. Before leaving the stand, defense lawyers also questioned Plante about an admission that a hearing problem had precluded him from hearing portions of his Preliminary Inquiry on June 30 on the charge of credit card fraud.

"When the charge before the Magistrate Court was terminated, I did not hear much of what was going on because I have a hearing problem," Plante testified. In response to further questions, he said that he had had the problem for about ten years, but insisted that at Her Majesty's Prison, he had heard William Labrador and the others just fine.

"In the case of Mr. Labrador, most of our conversations were three feet apart; I clearly understood him," he added. "I also spoke of things I overheard at Balsam Ghut; of things being shouted in the yard."

CHAPTER TWENTY-SIX

Police Take the Stand

On July 26, 2000, Terrence Williams called a series of police investigators to the stand to bolster the case. Among them were Chief Inspector Jacob George and Police Sergeant Duncan Williams.

The inspector took the stand first. In a low voice, Jacob George began by providing details of the "fingertip" search that officers carried out on the boulder-strewn beach where Lois' body had been found. He described the items that police had collected during the hunt, and created a mental picture of the scene by explaining their locations in relation to the body on the beach. He also testified to his initial visit to Zebra House that Saturday afternoon, and told of his initial conversation with the men about the "wet and sandy" sneakers he observed by the pool.

William's attorney rose to cross-examine the police witness, first asking the long-legged investigator if *he* was the "officer in charge" of the case. When the inspector responded that he was, Dr. Gonsalves wanted to know if he had read *every* statement that had been taken by his officers in regard to the McMillen investigation.

"I would not necessarily have seen every statement taken by an officer on my instructions in this case," the inspector responded in a low voice. The attorney met his response with an incredulous stare.

Dr. Gonsalves next asked Inspector George if he believed

that it "would be of significance" to follow up on any person who had spoken to or was in the company of the deceased on the night of her murder. Gonsalves' lively courtroom style was in stark contrast to the laid-back demeanor of the police inspector, who stood before the court in plainclothes and polished shoes and spoke in hushed tones.

"Yes, it would be in my best interest to speak with individuals who had come into contact with Lois McMillen on the night of her murder," the inspector responded.

The lawyer followed up his response by asking, "What has been done to locate the black man that Chris Crawford had seen in Lois' company at the Jolly Roger on the Friday evening before her death?"

"I personally did not follow through to make enquiries about this black guy," said George, who is also black. "I asked Station Sergeant Blackman and Acting Inspector James to make enquiries into this. To date, through these enquiries, I have not been able to identify this black man."

William's lawyer next grilled the inspector about his reason for filing formal charges against the men from Zebra House when he did. Gonsalves suggested that George had rushed to judgment, and filed the charges before he had completed his investigation, after learning that the men were going to court in an effort to win their release from custody. He asked what knowledge the inspector had of the men's plan to obtain a writ of habeas corpus, and whether or not that influenced the inspector's actions.

But Inspector George contended that the men's legal maneuver had nothing to do with his decision. He explained that he did not have confirmed information about the petition at the point when he brought the men before the magistrate, and insisted that he did not learn about the application until January 21, two days after he'd formally charged the men with the crime.

"The habeas corpus application was in the air," the inspector stated in a bland tone. "You heard rumors about the place."

Michael and Evan's lawyer, Oscar Ramjeet, pursued

another line of questioning. He focused on several items police had taken during their search of Zebra House that Saturday afternoon. He first wanted to know precisely what the inspector had observed in regard to the shirt that Michael Spicer had been wearing that morning. For months, the defense had been contending that the stain the officer had sighted was not blood but barbecue sauce.

"What I observed on Spicer's shirt appeared to be blood," the officer responded. "I cannot say whether it was barbecue sauce."

Ramjeet next asked about specific items that had been taken into custody. He wanted to know about a portable camera that he suspected might have been removed by police during their search of Zebra House.

"No, they did not give me any portable camera," the inspector replied. The camera that Mr. Ramjeet was referring to belonged to Michael Spicer. The Virginia man was certain that police had taken the Fuji during their search of his home.

"Would you say that Michael Spicer cooperated with you?" Mr. Ramjeet continued with his questioning of the police inspector.

"Yes, I would say that Mr. Spicer cooperated with me."

Police Sergeant Duncan Williams was the last witness of the day. He had been called to testify to his role in the collection of evidence at the Drake's Highway crime scene, and to his interview with Spicer on Sunday, the sixteenth of January at the Road Town police headquarters. Defense counselors had few questions for the sergeant, and court was adjourned until the following day.

Rays of early morning sun warmed the courtroom as forensics expert Julian Harley strode to the witness box on July 27.

Defense counselors again raised the issue of the as-yet missing disposable camera with the tall, graying sergeant.

"I believe we all knew about the camera—Mr. Jacob George, myself, and other members of the team," recalled the well-spoken investigator with the curly hair and thick sideburns. "I can't remember the existence of film in a camera being discussed. Everything that was collected is still in my possession."

The lawyers intended to request that the camera be released into their custody, or at the very least, ask that the film it contained be developed for review. The defense also posed questions to Harley about Alvin Martin, the black man whom police had brought in for questioning early in the investigation. They were still in the dark as to why he had been picked up by police; they were unaware that he had been spotted with a blond woman in a car similar to the one that Lois had been driving on the night of her murder. The responses the lawyers received from police in court still did not illuminate why the rangy man with the thick dreadlocks had been brought in to speak with investigators, or why officers had decided to collect samples of his hair and fingernail scrapings for testing purposes. Instead, the responses given just affirmed that he had been questioned and that samples had been obtained.

The next police witness to take the stand was Constable Adrian Kartic. He, too, was questioned by the defense about Alvin Martin. Kartic could not recall why Martin had been brought in for questioning, again leaving the defense with unanswered questions about Martin's involvement in the case. Even after the trial, the defense remained in the dark as to why Martin had been picked up and questioned early in the investigation.

William's lawyer also questioned Kartic about a visit he and another officer, Constable Johnny, had made to the prison to see Labrador the previous week.

"Almost a week ago, I went to the prison with Inspector Blackman and Detective Constable Johnny," the youngish officer told the court. "Inspector Blackman had a warrant in his possession; with the warrant, I paid him [Labrador] a visit. We went to execute a warrant to see if there was anything of evidential value in relation to this case. Specifically, we were looking for clothing and shoes."

Kartic told the court that he remained outside while his superior, Anderson Blackman, went inside the nine-by-twelve-foot cell to search it.

"I know some shoes were taken to the outside of the cell; by the door by Inspector Blackman," Kartic related. "There were about five pairs of shoes. There were hard shoes and sneakers. I can't say how many of each."

The constable recalled that the three officers left the prison without a single item of clothing or shoes. They had been looking for a specific kind of shoe, one with a sole that would match the shoe impression that had been found on the rear door of the rental car.

Kartic's colleague, Kendolph Bobb, was also called to testify that afternoon, as was Sheena Andrews, the young girl who had directed police to Lois' body.

On the twenty-eighth of July, the medical examiner from St. Thomas, Dr. Francisco Landron, was called to the stand. After reciting his credentials, the magistrate deemed the doctor an expert witness, and granted his request to refer to notes that he had taken during the autopsy of Lois McMillen on Tuesday, January 18.

"The finger- and toenails are painted red," he began. "The body cavities . . ."

The doctor's testimony would span the entire day's proceeding and include a lengthy discussion of the autopsy, and the cause of death.

"I would say that the cause of death was compatible with drowning," the well-dressed man with the jet-black hair told the court.

Landron next responded to a question from one of the defense counselors in regard to bruises he found on Lois' body. The medical examiner had testified to three contusions he had seen: one in the right anterior of the neck, one beneath her left clavicle, and another in the middle of her chest. The lawyer wanted to know if the doctor had found any bruises directly on the back of Lois' neck.

"I found no abrasions or contusions to the posterior of the neck," Dr. Landron replied.

The medical examiner was next asked whether there would be bruising to the back of the neck if someone were held under water.

"If one was to hold someone face downward from the back of the neck, there could be abrasions or contusions there, as well as there might not be," the pathologist replied. "If you held the person the other way, from the front, holding the head down, you would expect the abrasions to be at the back of the neck."

Dr. Landron was also questioned about his findings in relation to the "incised wounds" that he had seen on both of Lois' hands. Attorneys for the men questioned the doctor about the probability that the razor-thin scratches he found on both palms could have been caused by a sharp object on the beach where her body had been found. The lawyers wanted to know if the protracted exposure to the effects of seawater could cause the skin on Lois' hands to soften, and therefore become more susceptible to "incised wounds." They suggested that the wave action at the scene where Lois' body was discovered could have caused Lois' hands to come in contact with a sharp object.

"In these circumstances, theoretically, the injuries could have been caused by a sharp object on the beach or in the sea, but in my opinion it is not probable," Landron told the court. "The probability of an event has to do with factual circumstances. I went to visit the scene a week or two after the post-mortem [autopsy]. The probability I am asserting is not based on the physical evidence circumstances as I saw them two weeks later."

At the end of the lawyers' cross-examination of the medical examiner, Prosecutor Terrence Williams stood to reexamine the doctor on several points. He first asked Landron if he could offer a possible cause for the incised wounds on Lois' hands.

"Theoretically, these injuries may also be defense-type injuries, meaning that the deceased could have been defending herself," Landron told the court. "I only noticed the incised wounds on the inside of the deceased's hands, her palms. There were no other incised wounds on any other part of her body. It is not likely that, if there was a sharp object at the scene and the body was being washed against it, it would not be probable to see incised wounds only on the palms. I would expect to see them on other parts of the body in those circumstances."

Williams next asked what role "rigidity," the stiffening of the body after death, could have played in regard to the slice-like wounds found on Lois' palms.

"Regarding the rigor mortis having set in—as I mentioned in those circumstances, a body that is being moved by the action of the waves, if the wave action caused the hands to be in contact with a very sharp object producing these wounds, I would expect to see the wounds on other parts of the body," the pathologist explained. "If rigidity had already set in, it would be even more unlikely because those portions [palms] would have been protected" as the muscles in her fingers contracted, forming two fists.

Five days after Dr. Landron testified before the court, two more police witnesses, Dennis Jones and Anderson Blackman, were called to the stand. Detective Sergeant Jones was at the Magistrate's Court to swear to his role in obtaining a statement from William Labrador. His superior officer, Sergeant Blackman, had been called to establish his role in the case. It had been Blackman's initial hunch that "something was not right" that had prompted police to focus their attention on the four men vacationing at Zebra House.

Labrador's attorney was anxious to ask the lanky officer with the moustache and goatee about the search warrant he executed at Her Majesty's Prison several weeks earlier, on July 17.

"I went to look for a pair of shoes." The investigator's

voice was so low that many in the courtroom strained to hear his response. "I'm not certain whether it was to match with an imprint at the scene of the crime."

"Why did you go to the prison, Sergeant? What were you looking for specifically?"

"I went for a particular pair of shoes, acting upon instructions," Blackman said in a mumble. "Specifically, I was looking for a pair of shoes with some tracks at the bottom. I had seen a visual of tracks. When I say visual, I mean I saw a photograph of a shoe print."

What went unsaid in court was that crime-scene investigators had photographed a shoe print inside McMillen's vehicle. The team was anxious to learn if any of Labrador's footwear would match that print. In addition, Jeff Plante had told police that Labrador had indicated that police had taken the wrong pair of shoes into evidence—and that the sneakers in police custody where not in fact the ones he had been wearing on the night of Friday, January 14, 2000. Plante had also claimed that William Labrador had given his mother some articles of clothing to take home on one of her trips to the jail.

Responding to questions from Labrador's defense attorney, Blackman said he had no idea when or where the photograph of the shoe print had been taken. He also acknowledged that Labrador might have told him at some point that he had another pair of shoes at the Spicer residence, but that he couldn't remember. Later, at trial, Inspector Jacob George testified that the shoeprint belonged to Lois McMillen and not to any of the defendants; the defense did not object to or dispute the inspector's claim.

Later that same day, Jeff Plante was called back to testify for a third time. Once again, Labrador's lawyer, Dr. Gonsalves, wanted to ask him about a felony conviction in the United States that Plante had mentioned in his earlier testimony—and about another one that he had not. In response to the lawyer's question, Plante admitted that his conviction on theft charges stemming from a savings and loan scandal was not his first felony.

"The first felony conviction was appealed and over-turned," the American man responded in a matter-of-fact tone. He told the court that he had been charged with "theft of over ten thousand dollars." "It was on that matter that I was retried and sentenced to forty-five years. The charge arose out of a savings and loan issue. I was one of the owners of a savings and loan. I was also a real estate developer and a general contractor.

"Four hundred and twenty-three persons were charged. I was one of those people. The issue was whether or not there were valid appraisals to support the loan portfolio of numerous banks," Plante told the court.

During his brief time on the stand, Plante gave incomplete and confusing responses to further questions by defense attorneys. He could not recall specific details of prior arrests and convictions—one involving the sale of Mexican adobe tiles that he had taken possession of and resold, but never paid for—although he did not deny that he had been found guilty of other offenses in the past.

"I don't recall exactly how many other offenses there were," he said. "I accept the responsibility for things that happened in the past. I did not leave Texas without knowledge of a parole officer. If I go back, I will not be serving out the balance of my term."

On the eleventh of August, Magistrate Gail Charles moved to charge William Labrador with Lois' murder and charged his three friends as "accessories to murder after the fact." The three men were also cited for "perverting the course of justice," similar to an "obstruction of justice" in the United States. She also denied Michael, Alex, and Evan's applications for bail.

The murder charge against William largely appeared to stem from statements made to the court by his former cellmate, Jeffrey Plante. There was no evidence admitted at the hearing that directly implicated the three other men in the murder, resulting in the lesser charges.

As the four men sat in the "dock" listening to the judge's decision, Michael thought back to something that William had said to him in prison. The dark-haired man from Southampton had told Michael that he had two goals—"one is to gain my release, and the other is to win Plante's release." Michael chuckled to himself as he sat contemplating the bizarre irony of William's statement, realizing that he had succeeded in achieving one of his aims—Jeffrey Plante was free.

Upon learning the charges against them, the four men from Zebra House were next read their rights. "Having heard the evidence, do you wish to say anything in answer to the charge?" an officer of the court asked the four men who stood shackled before the court. "You are not obligated to say anything unless you desire to do so, but whatever you say will be taken down in writing, and may be given in evidence at your trial. . . ."

"Counsel will speak on my behalf," Michael Spicer replied. He then signed his name to the legal document as proof that he had been informed of his rights. Inside, he was trembling at the idea that he was being committed to stand trial for a murder that he firmly denied any part in.

"I reserve my defense," Alexander Benedetto announced, and then, in perfect penmanship, marked his name for the legal record. Alex, too, was horrified that he was being remanded back into custody to be tried for a crime that he said he'd played no role in.

"No, I have nothing to say," William Labrador told the court. His signature beneath his printed name was illegible. It is unclear how William Labrador was feeling at that moment. It has been reported by those closest to him that William still had not comprehended the magnitude of his situation and continued to be outraged at officials on the island for what he deemed to be an unfounded accusation against him.

Evan George responded in the same fashion as Michael, "Counsel will speak on my behalf." He then penned his John Hancock under the line that bore his full name. His signature consisted of a series of elaborate scrawls; only the first letters of his first and last name were decipherable.

Fearing that they would flee the BVI if released, the magistrate refused to set bail and instead ordered them remanded to Her Majesty's Prison to await trial. The case was set for trial in October.

In a telephone interview, the McMillens told the reporter from *The Hartford Courant*, John Springer, that they were "relieved" to learn that the men accused of killing their daughter were going to stand trial.

"We have been there all the time," Lois' father explained to the journalist. "It's been difficult to listen to witnesses describe how our daughter was killed and found in the water. But I think it was very important for us to be there to show that we are interested in the case and want to see justice done."

Since no members of the press were permitted inside the courtroom, a motive for the murder was not made public. Russell McMillen told Springer that the prosecutor did present a motive at the pre-trial hearing. But Lois' father would not discuss it with the reporter, citing the magistrate's instructions. Even the attorneys in the case were bound by a court order not to discuss the evidence with anyone outside the courtroom.

Springer subsequently learned that the prosecution's witness—Jeffrey Plante—had testified that William Labrador killed Lois McMillen after a heated argument over money. To this day, it is Mrs. McMillen's belief that something happened between William and Lois that night that prompted William to kill her daughter in a fit of rage.

"I don't believe that he set out to kill Lois that night," Mrs. McMillen said later. "Something set him off. Maybe William or one of his friends asked Lois to do something that she didn't want to do, or maybe she threatened to go to the police about something that one of them was doing."

Reached at her home in Watertown, NY, Michael's sister told the Connecticut reporter that, since departing the island the previous week, she had been waiting by the phone for news about her brother.

"I completely believe in Michael's innocence," Chris Matthews said to John Springer. "I know that the three of them know nothing about William's guilt, because any of them would have broken [down] about his guilt to get out of there a long time ago."

Chris had no idea that the worst was yet to come. Less than one month after the Preliminary Inquiry, the attorney general for the BVI, Cherno Jallow, stepped in and upgraded the charges. Without saying why, Jallow announced that he was indicting all four men for the murder of Lois McMillen. Suddenly, all of them were facing the prospect of spending the rest of their lives in Her Majesty's Prison at Balsam Ghut.

It was not known if the Attorney General had received some new evidence in the case that had led him to upgrade the charges against Michael, Alex, and Evan. What was clear was that in his role as attorney general he had the power to make such a decree.

CHAPTER TWENTY-SEVEN

Ready . . . Or Not

The day had finally arrived. After nine months of detainment behind lock and key at Her Majesty's Prison, the murder trial of the four men from Zebra House was set to begin. Reporters from the United States and the United Kingdom had flown down to Tortola in preparation for the opening arguments. Correspondents from *People* magazine, *Newsweek*, *Newsday*, NBC's *Today* show, and CBS' *48 Hours* were among the journalists to touch down in the palm-lined Territory.

Mr. And Mrs. McMillen were prepared to be in court on December 1, 2000, to show their commitment to justice for their little girl. The couple knew that it would not be easy to sit in the courtroom and listen as prosecutors recounted the terrible events that led to Lois' death. Yet they believed strongly that their presence at the trial would send a clear message to the jury—that they had faith in the legal system in the BVI.

Just one week earlier, the McMillens' Tortola home had been burglarized. A thief had somehow managed to slip into their bedroom and go through Mrs. McMillen's purse as the couple sat relaxing on sofas in the living room two levels below. Remarkably, the murder of their daughter and the burglary of their home still had not spoiled the couple's love of the palm-fringed island and its people.

Mrs. Labrador and her New York lawyer, Michael Griffith,

waited on the steps outside of the pristine white courthouse, with its impressive courtyard and wrought-iron gates. Michael's sister, Chris, and Alex's father, Victor, were there, too, anxious to get inside for the proceeding. The High Court building where the trial was to take place stood prominently at the end of one of Road Town's main streets. The two-story courthouse was well maintained, with a fresh coat of paint and impressive busts of important people in the UK and the BVI gracing its exterior. The structure was strikingly different from the faded, almost trailer-like Magistrate's Court just a few blocks away.

Stepping out of the white police van with the dark-tinted windows, Michael Spicer and his three companions were rushed past the crowd of onlookers and then up the narrow staircase to the second-floor courtroom—never imagining what the prosecutor was about to ask of the judge presiding over their case.

Students in neatly-pressed school uniforms had assembled on the sidewalk and across the street from the courthouse to watch the officers usher the four American men into the building. Their case was the most spectacular event ever to take place at the white concrete building adjacent to their school.

The police personnel assigned to work security detail at the courthouse for this proceeding were not armed, as they had been at the previous hearing. Nevertheless, the officers were stern and made it clear to the reporters vying to gain admittance to the building that they would not tolerate any disrespectful behavior in the island's courthouse.

Other than those who had attended the Preliminary Inquiry in July, no one knew the name of the American man—the prison informant—who had struck a deal with authorities on the island, or what other evidence there was in the case.

Unbeknownst to the media and the families of the four defendants, Senior Crown Counsel Terrence Williams intended to ask the court for still another adjournment in the case. When the forensic material that had been collected by investigators failed to link the four Americans to the crime, island officials began to worry that they did not have sufficient evidence to make a case in court. Even though police remained convinced that they had the right men in custody, much of the evidence they had collected—and had believed would seal their case—turned up no result. Whatever forensic material there might have been on Lois' body had been contaminated by its prolonged exposure to seawater and the items taken from Zebra House were not tying the men to the crime.

Police were also aware that the testimony of one prison informant was not enough to secure a conviction. There had to be corroborating evidence from another source. Williams believed that a new method for analyzing DNA evidence might allow him to bolster his case. The seeds for the idea had emerged from an earlier meeting with investigative specialists with Scotland Yard.

Earlier in the year, the governor of the Territory had called a meeting with key members of the Royal Virgin Islands Police Force. During the briefing, Deputy Commissioner Johnston suggested that police call in the Murder Review Board from Scotland Yard to reexamine the files in the McMillen case. Normally, the board was invited to review cases that were at least five months old and in which the trail had gone cold. Their task was to take a fresh look at those cases and determine if the original investigatory team had missed something in its initial investigation of the crime.

In the McMillen case, police had already identified who they believed to be the parties responsible for the crime. But Johnston felt that it would help to have a third party review what police had done thus far. He argued to his team that maybe the Review Board's distinguished members could suggest other avenues that police could explore. The MRB was made up of highly-trained detectives who were up on all the latest investigative techniques and cutting-edge forensic tests.

The governor agreed to the idea, and the case files and all of the forensic results that had been obtained thus far were opened to the two-man investigative team, a superintendent and a sergeant, from the United Kingdom.

During their visit to the BVI, the two officers reviewed all of the police files and then toured the island, visiting "key" sites on the north and south coasts, as well as Zebra House and the beach where Lois' body had been found.

The two officers recommended sending items that had already been tested in the case to be reexamined using new methods. One was to test samples of sand from the crime scene and various other locations on the island. Samples had already been taken from the shower trap and the stone walkway at Zebra House, and from the men's "wet and sandy" shoes currently in police custody, but no testing had been performed on the sand particles that had been gathered. They arranged for the British Forensic Science Service to carry out these tests on exhibits that had been collected by police in January.

The board members pointed to a renowned geologist in Great Britain named Professor Kenneth Pye, who, through scientific means, might be able to link some of the material already in evidence.

They also suggested that a number of the items that had already been unsuccessfully tested for DNA be retested using a new technique called "Low Copy Number DNA." This very sensitive technique enables scientists to isolate DNA from samples that are deemed too small for standard DNA tests, and then to copy them for testing purposes. LCN DNA profiling, as it is commonly known, increases the sensitivity of the technique so that, in theory, only a few cells are required for successful analysis.

Johnston reported that at no time in the review did the two-man team suggest that police had detained the wrong men, or that they should be looking at other suspects. "They agreed that we had the right people in custody," the commander recalled in the months following the men's murder trial. "The team was satisfied that all other potential suspects had been eliminated—like the former boyfriend Luigi—and that no evidence pointed to anyone else."

At that time, a private investigator from Kroll Associates, who had been brought in by the McMillens to supplement the police effort on Tortola, also arrived at the conclusion that investigators had not erred in arresting the four men from Zebra House.

Inside the airy courtroom, Crown Counsel Williams stood before Judge Neville Smith, and a crowd of about five dozen potential jurors. The impeccably-dressed prosecutor began by telling the elder justice, attired in the court's traditional blond wig and black flowing robe, that the Crown needed more time to send the material that had been collected by police to England for Low Copy Number DNA. The attorney general's officer had decided to follow the recommendations that had been made to police by members of Scotland Yard's Murder Review Board. In a deep voice, peppered by a Jamaican accent, he explained that the procedure was both time-consuming and expensive—at $50,000—and that it would require a postponement of at least two months. If Williams' request was granted, it would delay the trial, this time pushing it back to the next court session, in March of 2001. In the British Virgin Islands, cases are heard just twice yearly during sessions called assizes.

The judge was incredulous, and made it clear that he was going to think long and hard before granting yet another postponement. After a long legal career, Justice Smith was set to turn in his robe in less than one month, at the end of the year, having reached the mandatory age for judges to retire from the bench. A postponement would mean that another judge would be assigned to preside over the case.

Alex's lawyer, Paul Dennis, jumped up to vehemently object to any further delays in the case. The tall, slender attorney implored the judge to stick to the time schedule that had been decided by the magistrate in July.

"We have been hearing since January that there are outstanding forensic reports that the Crown is waiting for," Dennis told the judge. "Deadlines were fixed, dates were given by the Crown. Those dates came and went. We are here this morning, hearing the same song the Crown has been singing since January about this elusive forensic evidence."

The lawyer went on to characterize the request for further DNA testing as nothing more than a "fishing expedition" on the part of the Crown.

A lawyer named Hayden St. Claire–Douglas was in court to act as counsel for William Labrador. William's primary attorney, Ralph Gonsalves, was running for the position of Prime Minister of St. Vincent and the Grenadines, and the demands of his candidacy had made it impossible for him to be in court for the proceeding; he had turned over the case to Douglas, his law partner.

"My Lord," the lawyer began, as is proper to address the judge, "it is a matter of record that the accused were taken into custody January fifteenth and charged January the nineteenth. On August 4 [sic], a magistrate ruled that there was sufficient evidence to go forward. . . . The Crown should go forward having presented evidence of a certain nature."

"My Lord, this is a complicated case in a Territory where there is no DNA lab," Terrence Williams argued. "It is not a fishing expedition, but to complete a test that has already been done."

The defense counselors also made their own request to the justice on the bench. Lawyers for the four men from Zebra House asked that the charges against their clients be dropped, citing a lack of forensic evidence and tainted testimony from a jailhouse informant.

Justice Smith adjourned the case until the following day, at which time he said he would render decisions on both matters.

Lois' parents were in the courtroom for the entire four-hour proceeding. Their normally stoic faces revealed no emotion as they sat in the front row behind the jury box. Outside, they seemed optimistic, telling reporters they were hopeful that the more sophisticated DNA test would prove, once and for all, that Michael and his friends had killed their daughter. They also expressed disappointment at the way in which their daughter had somehow gotten lost amid all of the legal wrangling that went on inside the courtroom that morning.

Clutching a cane for balance, Lois' aged father stopped in front of the pristine white courthouse, pausing long enough to say a quick word to John Springer, the reporter from his hometown newspaper.

"They never mentioned Lois McMillen," he told Springer. "She wasn't there."

The following morning, the court was called to order just as thunderclaps echoed through the gray sky over Tortola. It was nine forty-five a.m. on December 2, 2000, when the session began. To the sound of raindrops pelting against the windows and gusts of wind rattling the leafy palms that encircled the building, Judge Neville Smith issued his rulings.

Judge Smith ordered that the four men be sent back to Her Majesty's Prison to await the results of the LCN DNA testing set to get under way in England. He denied the defense's motions to dismiss the murder indictments against Michael, Evan, and Alex, citing a litany of statutes and case law that pointed to the attorney general's sweeping authority in the British Territory.

As the judge delivered his decisions to the packed courtroom, Michael Spicer could be seen wiping tears from his eyes. The reality that he and his friends would have to spend another five months in their tiny cells at Her Majesty's Prison was almost too much to bear.

The Virginia man did his best to smile as he was escorted out of the courtroom in shackles. But it was apparent from his expression that he was hiding a great deal of pain behind that smile.

Alex, too, put his best face forward, flashing a toothy smile for the photographers and cameramen who had lined up outside the building to capture the men's images for their newspapers and TV shows. Alex's once dark blond hair was now streaked with deep yellow highlights from his daily exercise sessions in the prison yard under the hot Caribbean sun. It was clear that he had lost a considerable amount of weight since his incarceration at the hilltop prison—so much so that the warden had sent a doctor to make sure he was receiving the proper nourishment. Wearing a tailored blue sport coat, Alex stopped in the courtyard to make a statement to the journalists yelling out to him for a comment.

"We're hostages," he told the crowd as guards rushed him toward the prison van. "We're political prisoners. That's what I think."

Michael's sister, Chris, stood a few feet away, watching as uniformed officers whisked her brother and the others away to Her Majesty's Prison in an American-made van. The sky had darkened since she had gone inside the building hours earlier, and light rain showers continued on and off throughout the afternoon. She was angered by the thought of what Michael would again have to endure.

"It is atrocious, the unfairness of this, considering there is no physical evidence," the fortyish woman in the dark-colored dress told Springer as the two stood talking under towering palms, their leaves blowing about in the wind. "These are men with families and jobs and loved ones. I feel as badly for the McMillen family as anyone. Even if the DNA evidence came back saying there is a connection, they were in her car."

William Labrador's mother was equally upset. The following day, she agreed to an al fresco lunch with Springer at the resort where they were both staying in Road Town. Rays of noontime sun glistened on the water as the reporter arrived at the hotel's waterfront restaurant and sat down across the table from the blond woman with the bright lipstick and colorful sundress. Springer immediately noted that the wait staff at the Prospect Reef hotel knew the American woman by name. He watched as Mrs. Labrador lit the first of many cigarettes. Holding it between her thick lips, she spoke about her son's ongoing ordeal.

"They framed them," she announced in a thick New York

accent. Taking a long drag on her cigarette, she blew the smoke in the direction of the crafts that filled the boat basin just in front of the restaurant. "They figured it is safer, as far as the tourist economy goes, to have Americans accused of an American's death than to really investigate and find out why this young woman is dead.

"They wanted to be able to say to American tourists, 'Come here, it is safe. There are no problems,'" she added through the haze of smoke rising from the ashtray in front of him on the table.

Springer watched as Mrs. Labrador poured some cream into her coffee and took a long sip before lighting up a second cigarette. She was direct, holding little back as she discussed the Crown's case against her son.

"I know for a fact—and not from just my heart as a mother—that my son had nothing to do with this," Mrs. Labrador insisted. "He would not hurt a fly, never mind a woman. If a woman was being attacked on a street, he would be the first one to come to her defense."

It was during that conversation that John Springer finally learned the identity of the prison informant who had come forward with information that her son had confessed to Lois' murder.

"Barbara Labrador was talking about him like I knew him," Springer recalled. During the meeting, she kept saying, "All they have on him is that prison plant."

"Who's this prison snitch you keep referring to?" the reporter asked the woman seated in the white plastic chair across the table from him.

"Plante," Mrs. Labrador responded in a gravelly voice.

When John first heard the name, he thought that Barbara Labrador was referring to a person who had been planted in the prison by police. "Okay, who's this 'plant' you keep referring to?" John asked again.

"It's Plante," the Southampton woman repeated.

"Okay, plant, who is this plant?"

"It's Plante!" Mrs. Labrador was growing agitated. "Jeffrey Plante. That's his name. Jeffrey Plante."

John would later chuckle about the conversation he had had with William's mother, saying it was reminiscent of the comical Abbott and Costello skit "Who's on First?"

Springer resolved to learn more from Barbara Labrador about the prison informant and his allegations against her son.

CHAPTER TWENTY-EIGHT

Who Is Jeff Plante?

On December 3, 2001, Michael and the others were again remanded to Her Majesty's Prison, where they would wait another five months for their day in court.

Meanwhile, Jeffrey Plante was free to move about the Territory. Yet it would not be long before he, too, was back in the custody of the Royal Virgin Islands Police Force. It seemed that more than a dozen BV Islanders had a bone to pick with the man set to take the stand at the murder trial of the four Americans. In mid-November, police learned that he was passing "hot" checks all over the Territory, and the Chamber of Commerce was pressing for his arrest. Plante was back to his old tricks as a con man.

In early August, government officials in the BVI had decided that it was too expensive to continue keeping Plante at the Icis Vacation Villas on the island's lush north coast. While there, he had enjoyed a private room with round-the-clock police protection. Plante had seemed to be behaving himself since his release from Her Majesty's Prison, so, to save money, they decided that it would be okay for him to rent a furnished accommodation in town. The government would continue to foot the bill for his living expenses, providing him with a small monthly stipend that he was supposed to use to pay his costs.

About the same time, Plante's estranged wife "Shannon" joined him on Tortola.

Always the charmer, Plante had telephoned the pretty Southern belle and convinced her to give their marriage one more chance. She recounted that when she asked him where he was calling from, he responded with surprise: "You don't know?"

Shannon said that Plante told her that he was "working for the government" of the BVI and begged her to join him.

"I still loved him so much," Shannon recalled in a telephone interview. "He begs me to come down. He tells me, 'Look, I do have the money I owe you.' I wanted to believe him." In what she described as a "weak moment," Shannon said she overlooked the tens of thousands of dollars that her husband had previously charged to her credit cards and hopped on a plane for the BVI.

Shannon was no pushover. Yet, she could only explain her actions by saying that love is an irrational emotion, and it sometimes leads people to do stupid things. In her case, it was returning to the Caribbean to be with the man she had married not once, but twice, in romantic and religious ceremonies in Mexico and the United States. Theirs had been a whirlwind romance that culminated with a spur-of-the-moment jaunt to Mexico where they exchanged vows in a local bar.

In her mid-forties, and never married, Shannon believed she had found true love. Upon returning to the States, the couple repeated their vows, this time before a Catholic priest in a church near Shannon's home.

Next, they were on a plane for the Texas coast for a one-week honeymoon. At week's end, Jeff announced they were going sailing in the BVI and they were off again. Shannon said they lived it up at the finest hotels and aboard elegant sailing yachts manned by a captain and crew. Her new husband had even presented her with a token of his love, a jewel-bedecked watch that he'd purchased on one of the islands for $2,000. She knew exactly how much the timepiece cost. It later became clear that he had charged it to her credit card, along with the hotel rooms and the charter boats and the mooring fees.

Shannon cut her honeymoon short when Jeff revealed that he had violated the terms of his parole in Texas, where he had been imprisoned for fraud, and was afraid to return to the United States. When she got home to her apartment and began opening the bills, she said she nearly passed out from shock. Her credit cards were charged to the max—one had a balance of $13,000, another $14,000, and there were more.

The attractive blond said she nearly had a nervous break-down when she realized what had happened. Her attempts to reach Jeff by telephone proved unsuccessful. When he finally contacted her, she let him have it.

"Baby, I'm gonna make plans to come back," Plante told her during their brief conversation.

After hanging up with Jeff, the phone rang again. This time it was MBNA, the bank that had issued her credit card. They were calling to ask if she was going to approve charges for $8,000 for The Moorings yacht club in the British Virgin Islands. Realizing she'd been had, Shannon broke down in tears. The bank had police in the BVI holding on another line, she later recalled.

Shannon drew a deep breath as she described how officers sent a police boat to The Moorings where her husband—whom she now called "the scoundrel"—was taken into custody and then brought back to Road Town to go before a judge. But with no real proof of his fraudulent use of her credit cards—they were husband and wife—police were poised to set him free. It was only at Shannon's insistence that they held him on a technicality—overstaying his visa by one day—until they could further investigate her claims.

"I'm sitting in Dallas, Texas, writing letters and faxes to Governor Frank Savage and Police Commissioner Vernon Malone, begging them to keep him there," Shannon recalled.

Once released from custody at Her Majesty's Prison, Plante gained access to a telephone and a computer and began contacting Shannon from the vacation villa complex in Brewer's Bay. She recalled that the sound of his voice infuriated her. For months, she had been receiving letters and pictures he had taken on their honeymoon with post-marks from Long Island and Miami. She had worried that somehow, Jeff had gotten out of jail and was back in the States to taunt her. Barbara Labrador had been the unwitting courier of the mail, sending off the correspondence on her way home from visiting her son in Tortola.

In e-mails, Jeff begged her to give him another chance, and somehow even talked her into believing that he had money in a Caribbean bank account and that he was going to pay her back. Again, he promised that everything was going to work out. "I am putting together a life for me here, and yes, I would love to have you by my side and enjoy the rest of our lives together," Plante wrote in an e-mail to Shannon on July 16, 2000. "Actually there's nothing that I would ever hope or pray for more than that."

Desperate to save her marriage, Shannon boarded a plane in mid-August to be with the man she loved. She was sur-prised by what she found upon arriving in the Territory and joining her husband at Maria's Hotel by the Sea, a resort on the harbor in Road Town. Shannon described their accommo-dation as "absolutely fabulous," an efficiency with a kitch-enette, full bath and terrace with views of the aqua-blue sea.

"Every couple of hours, police came to check on Jeff," she recalled. "They gave him envelopes full of money to live."

Within weeks of his move out of the Icis Vacation Villas—and away from the twenty-four-hour police surveillance—Plante had managed to open a joint checking account at Banco Popular by using his wife's name on the credit appli-cation. He then immediately began bouncing checks all over the islands. The debts were mostly for groceries, and for meals at good restaurants on Tortola and the neighboring islands of the BVI.

Shannon's stay on Tortola took a bizarre twist when police asked her to act as a decoy in an undercover sting operation to catch a "dirty" cop who was trying to extort money from her husband for protection. One of the officers on the force had come to Jeffrey Plante and Shannon shortly after he was released from Her Majesty's Prison with claims about William Labrador. "I've got it on good authority that Labrador is making inquiries . . . that he's looking for someone to put a hit on you," is what the constable reportedly told Jeff and his wife.

Frightened, Plante had immediately reported the officer's ominous warning to Deputy Commissioner Johnston. A plan was then set in motion to catch the department's wolf in sheep's clothing. Shannon was asked to use a small cassette recorder hidden in a Kleenex box and told that she must sit in on a meeting between the officer and her husband in their flat overlooking the Caribbean. An investigator was hiding in a back bedroom. He listened through a closed door as the officer told the couple that he could protect them for a fee and recommended they get a gun. Police verified Shannon's account and said the "bad" officer was apprehended and charged for the ruse.

Shannon said it wasn't long after that that she realized Jeffrey Plante was trouble, and would always be trouble. He would not let her out of his sight, and had lied to her about depositing the government money into their joint checking account. Based on Plante's assurances, she had been writing checks to the phone company and to the local supermarket for the couple's weekly grocery shopping—all the while unaware that not a penny was going into their account.

When police got wind of Plante's activities, Deputy Commissioner Johnston recalled that officers began collecting his fraudulent checks and eventually arrested him and charged him with the crimes.

Shannon spent a total of two-and-a-half months on the island with Plante. During that time, he told her about what he had allegedly overheard at the prison in regard to Lois McMillen's murder.

"Shannon, William Labrador confessed to me that they had a fight over money," she recalled her husband telling her. "She knew that he had a huge deal somewhere and had obtained some money through embezzlement and Lois knew about it."

Shannon said that Plante told her that William said, "He stepped on the back of her neck and drowned her. And he thinks he's going to get away with it."

Uncertain whether to believe her husband's revelations amid so many blatant lies, she asked him why he was coming forward to testify. "He said that it was the right thing to do, and because he couldn't live with himself if he didn't, and to help the government because 'they need my help' because it's going to hurt tourism." Plante described Labrador as "cocky, arrogant, and violent."

When asked about Alex, Evan, and Michael, Shannon recalled that Plante said: "I don't know anything about the other three guys, but I know Labrador did it."

Shannon explained that the idea that William had actually taken a life had upset her husband—even though he was a criminal himself. When she confronted him about his own past, he told her that he believed that murder was very different from fraud. He went on to explain that his crimes had not hurt anyone in a physical sense, but William's alleged act had ended a young woman's life.

"He never ever recanted," Shannon said of her husband's admission to hearing William confess to the murder. She also recalled that his story about what William told him never changed, no matter how many times he told it.

Shannon could not decide if she believed what her husband was telling her. After all, he had stolen more than $100,000 from her in the short time that she had known him. And, while he had begged her to give their relationship one more try, it was clear that he would probably steal from her again if he had the chance. She recalled that he was convinced that once he testified at the men's murder trial, the residents of the BVI would welcome him with open arms. He would be their hero for saving the island's precious economy. He even talked of getting a job in Tortola, and buying a house with an ocean view that the two of them could share.

Shannon described her husband as "grandiose" and said that he loved being at the center of the high-profile story—and in the spotlight in general. She said she continued to tell him that he was being unrealistic, and made it clear that police intended to deport him back to the States to face his parole violation in Texas as soon as he testified to what he had allegedly heard William Labrador confess to in prison.

Deputy Commissioner Johnston said that he, too, made it clear to Plante that he should expect no favors in return for his testimony in the McMillen case.

Yet Jeffrey Plante continued to dream of staying on in the Caribbean, or moving to England and setting up a home with his wife there. Not surprisingly, he also continued to get into trouble. He and Shannon were asked to leave Maria's by the Sea, and then escorted around the island by a CID officer to view potential apartments. But Jeff refused to live in the one that authorities ultimately selected for him, telling Shannon that it was not up to his standards.

When he finally agreed on a flat, he then infuriated the officer in charge of his safety by telling the couple who owned the apartment that he was in the "witness protection program."

Shannon said that much of the time, she and Jeff were entertaining guards and their wives at their island residences. The officers liked to stop in for social visits, and at the same time, were trying to keep an eye on Plante, and make sure he was not getting into more trouble.

Shannon recalled that in early October, she and Jeff got into a fight that ended in violence. She said her con-man husband restrained her, pinned her to the sofa, and told her that he would not let her leave the island. She said he even stole her passport in an attempt to prevent her from going home. But she managed to get a new one and then returned to the States to find an eviction notice from her landlord, and countless overdue bills.

Within weeks of Shannon's departure, Jeff Plante found a new woman willing to be his bride. Somehow he had rented a computer that he used to troll "singles" chat rooms. On the Internet, he met a woman who lived in Houston, then another from France.

In a series of e-mail correspondences, he convinced the

French woman that he was a wealthy businessman and then invited her to join him at *his* Caribbean flat. He told her that his private jet was in London to pick up some clothes he'd ordered, and that he "would be glad to have her picked up to meet him in Tortola." When she told him that she was not able to get away right then, he said he would send her a pre-paid ticket. Naturally, he failed to mention that he was on the island as a witness for the prosecution in an upcoming murder trial and that he had a long history as a fraudster in the United States, where he was wanted as a parole absconder.

It did not take long for the French woman to get the true picture, but not before she had agreed to charge expensive meals at the Sugar Mill and a rental car to her credit card—Plante told her that his "crazy" ex-wife had cancelled *his* cards in spite. She even agreed to a February 14 wedding after learning of Plante's "big real estate business with a hundred and thirty-five agents, his houses in Dallas, Rhode Island and Hawaii, and his family's castle in England."

In a letter to Inspector Charles of the Royal Virgin Islands Police Force, dated December 21, 2000, she told her story of woe. "Maybe you understand that under these circumstances, falling in love that fast and losing any common sense is very easy on your sunny, island paradise," she wrote.

In late December of 2000, Plante would be rearrested and remanded back into police custody. Before he was stopped, he had written over thirty bad checks to local merchants, had wrecked a rented SUV, and was behind on his rent. Police had no choice but to incarcerate him for his crime spree, placing him in a cell at the Road Town police station where he waited to go before a magistrate for the frauds. Just days after Christmas, he was ordered held without bail on an allegation that he passed a bad check for $600.

When he was told that he could stay in Road Town or return to the more modern Her Majesty's Prison to await trial, he chose the dilapidated holding facility in Road Town.

He was aware that at Her Majesty's Prison he would not be locked away for twenty-three hours a day, and would be served better food. He repeatedly declined offers to be transferred there, citing fears for his safety. William Labrador was still among those behind bars there. Police found it noteworthy that he opted to remain in the filthy jail cell in Road Town until it was time for him to testify in court.

From time to time, Deputy Commissioner Johnston said that Plante would make demands for better treatment. And when Plante's demands were rejected, he would threaten to leave the island without testifying in the case. Johnston recalled that it soon became routine for Plante to carry on in this fashion.

"We would tell him, 'Okay, that's fine, you are free to go,'" Johnston recalled with a chuckle. "The conditions were not the best at the Road Town jail where he was staying. He would whine a bit and then tell us that he had thought about it and that he wanted to give testimony and intended to stay and take the stand."

In December, media reports revealed that Plante had been a star witness for the prosecution before. One of John Springer's articles on CourtTV.com pointed to his role as a prison informant in a murder case in Hawaii in 1995. He had already been paroled and returned to prison several times before he provided testimony at the 1995 trial of a man who had been incarcerated in a cell adjacent to his on the island of Maui.

In that case, Plante told authorities that the inmate had confessed to the murder, citing "drugs and money" as the motive. The case ended in a hung jury, and Plante was not called back to give testimony at the man's second trial. In return for his testimony, a prosecutor in Maui sent a letter to the Texas parole board, acknowledging Plante's cooperation in the case. Still, the board denied him parole in 1995, and then again in 1996. When Plante was paroled in 1998, he immediately violated the terms, and according to a spokesman for the Texas Department of Criminal Justice, was listed in the system as an "absconder."

Families of the four men in custody were quick to point out similarities in the two cases.

Meanwhile, the defense team for William Labrador stumbled upon a newspaper article about Luigi Lungarini published in the Montreal *Gazette* on June 8, 1992.

The article began:

> Four years ago this month, Erica Eboli was swept off her feet. When she met Luigi Lungarini he was a perfect gentleman. The two fell in love almost immediately. Within five months they were married, and four months later she gave birth to a son.
>
> Then on May 26, 1991, during a violent argument, Eboli plunged a kitchen knife into her husband's chest, piercing his lung. Lungarini survived. Eboli was arrested and charged with attempted murder.

The story talked of a whirlwind courtship, and then a disturbing pattern of domestic abuse, with Lungarini allegedly changing into a violent and critical person on the day they got engaged. Eboli, a thirty-one-year-old manager of a commercial real estate firm in Canada, told the reporter that when she bought a black dress to wear to the couple's engagement party, Lungarini slapped her across the face to express his displeasure with the color.

At her trial, Eboli told the court that the couple's arguments over sex culminated in violence. She testified that once, when she was eight months pregnant, her husband wanted to make love, but she did not. The one-hundred-and-five-pound Eboli said that when she rebuffed his advances, he kicked her in the back with such force that it sent her flying right off the bed.

"It started with pushing and kicking," she recalled. "Then gradually, it got worse and at the end his favorite thing was to grab me by the throat and just squeeze real tight."

Eboli said she called the police at least twelve times during their thirty-month marriage because her husband was hitting her. She said Lungarini would threaten her, saying "We're married until death do us part."

The culmination of their volatile relationship allegedly occurred on Luigi's twenty-eighth birthday. According to Eboli's testimony, at a party she and her husband hosted at their apartment, Eboli was dancing with her sister and another friend in a way that her husband described as "vulgar." She said Luigi grabbed her by the arm and angrily admonished her to stop at once. When she refused, he seized her again. This time, she was frightened and retreated to the kitchen. For the rest of the night, Erica moved from room to room in an attempt to dodge her husband, who kept following her. He finally told his guests to go home.

"The way he threw everybody out, I was sure he was going to kill me," she recounted.

By then, according to Eboli, Luigi was in a rage. Terrified, she made a run for the door and had her hand on the knob when he pulled her back inside. Calling her a "bitch" and a "whore" as he chased her around the flat, he finally knocked her to the ground and then kicked her across the kitchen floor. Next, he had her by the throat and was pushing her up against the wall, Eboli testified.

"I grabbed the first thing I could get my hands on and I hit him," Eboli testified.

She told the judge that her husband fell back shrieking that he couldn't breathe. When she saw that both of his hands were covered in blood, she raced to the bathroom to retrieve a towel, and then remained with him until police and an ambulance arrived.

During the trial, Luigi claimed it was his wife who was making the threats, throwing dishes at him in the kitchen, and in the bedroom, punching him in the nose so hard that it bled.

"I looked at her and I said, 'What are you going to do?' She said, 'I'm going to kill you.' I said, 'Yeah, yeah, OK.' She said, 'I am going to kill you.' I was about to turn around, that's when she hit me with the knife."

Luigi testified that after she stabbed him, his wife blocked the bedroom door to stop him from calling 911. That's when, he maintains, he picked her up and moved her out of the way.

On March 31, 1992, Eboli's defense of "battered woman syndrome" won her an acquittal, and Quebec Court Judge Celine Pelletier found her "not guilty."

The story was chilling, yet it did little to sway Deputy Commissioner Johnston's mind about who had killed Lois McMillen. The commander was disgusted by Labrador's attempts to shine a spotlight on Lungarini—and away from himself.

"It is not uncommon for criminals to try and deflect attention by putting out other theories that cause jurors to raise questions about their own guilt," he said.

Through it all, the commander insisted that Luigi had played no role in Lois' murder, and remained confident that police had the right men in custody.

CHAPTER TWENTY-NINE

Another Investigator Joins the Fray

At least one private detective working the McMillen case believed that police had the wrong men in custody. In October of 2000, the Benedetto family had hired a former detective from the New York Police Department to look into the murder case on Alex's behalf. It had taken a number of months for Victor Benedetto to fully trust the retired cop who had contacted him after reading a newspaper account about his son's arrest.

Jay Salpeter had retired from the New York Police Department in the early 90s after twenty years of service to start his own private investigations firm on Long Island. While in the Street Crimes unit of the NYPD, he donned disguises and "got mugged" for a living. Once, to solve a case, he posed as a rabbi, another time as a woman. He also worked as a hostage negotiator, and then as an undercover investigator for the narcotics squad. When he retired from the force in 1991, he was a detective second grade, in the 104th Detective Squad in Queens. He spent the next decade investigating several high-profile cases on behalf of defendants facing lengthy prison sentences for murder.

The compactly built man with the bushy moustache and thick feathered-back hair recalled that when he flew to Tortola in October, the World Series was heating up with the New York Yankees pitted against the New York Mets. He had tickets to one of the games, but opted instead to board a plane for Tortola so he could look into the case on behalf of the Benedettos. He recalled that when he arrived in the BVI, the bars were packed with people watching the "subway series" baseball games. A lawyer named Bruce Barket had accompanied him to Tortola to act as an advisor in the case. Barket was a former prosecutor in Long Island's Nassau County. He had made a name for himself as a defense counselor to Amy Fisher, the teenage girl who had been dubbed "the Long Island Lolita" after she was arrested for trying to kill the wife of her much older boyfriend, Joey Buttafuoco.

The day after the plane set down in the balmy paradise, Salpeter and his associate accompanied Alex's Road Town attorney, Paul Dennis, to Her Majesty's Prison. There they met with Alex and learned of his ordeal.

Coincidentally, another private investigator was at the jail meeting with Evan's roommate, Umberto, that same day. The meetings between the investigators, attorneys, and their respective clients all took place concurrently in the prison's outdoor recreation area.

In the hours after his meeting with Alex at Her Majesty's Prison, Salpeter said that he and Barket toured the island, visiting a number of relevant locations, as well as the rocky beach where Lois' body had been found. During their journey, they stopped at Bomba's and Quito's and then returned to the crime scene, where they took photographs.

Salpeter's first stop when he landed on Tortola had been the Jolly Roger Inn, the last known place that Lois McMillen was seen alive. He and his colleague had spoken with the restaurant's owner, Louis Schwartz, and some of his employees, to learn what they could about Lois' final hours on the island. Salpeter also expressed an interest in finding Salo, the taxi driver who had chauffeured the men around on the night that McMillen was killed; he asked if the restaurant owner from Long Island could help arrange a meeting. Salpeter then returned to the Jolly Roger later that evening to watch another World Series game, and hopefully meet up with Salo. He was under the impression that Schwartz was going to introduce him to the taxi driver that night.

After several hours of waiting, Salpeter said that he signaled Schwartz over to the table in the upstairs restaurant where he had dined, and asked when Salo would be arriving. He was flabbergasted when the slender restaurant owner with the wavy brown hair told him that the taxi driver had been sitting at the bar for hours earlier that evening—but that he had made it clear that he did not want to speak with anyone about the McMillen case.

Salpeter was furious that Schwartz had not alerted him to Salo's presence at the bar, which was less than three feet from where he had been sitting, and went back to his hotel in a rage.

Schwartz later said that Salo told him he had no interest in speaking to anyone about the case.

The former NYPD detective said that after studying the statements taken by police, he had formulated his own theory about the crime. For example, he expressed disappointment with the local police's investigation into the murder, and felt that they had missed numerous opportunities to track down and apprehend the *real* guilty parties. He was surprised to learn that officers had not closed down the airport and ferry terminals immediately following the discovery of Lois' body to prevent a possible perpetrator from leaving the island. He was also astonished to learn that police did not do a mass canvass of people in the West End area around the ferry terminal where Lois' rental car had been found. He also pointed out that in New York, it was routine to run the license plates of all the vehicles in the vicinity of a crime scene to find out who had been in the area, but this had not been done either.

"They did not do interviews with people who might have been in the areas where Lois was last seen," Salpeter said during an interview at his Great Neck, Long Island, office. "They did not pull her phone records to see who she was talking to while she was on the island. They never established who she had been intimate with in the days before she was murdered. There are so many things that they never did in this investigation."

Salpeter's theory was that someone who was at the Jolly Roger on the night of Lois' murder was lying in wait in the rear seat of her rental car.

"She couldn't see when she gets into the car," Salpeter related. "How many people look in the back seat?"

He believed that at some point after Lois pulled out of the Jolly Roger's parking lot, she was attacked from behind, with the perpetrator reaching up and placing his hands around her throat. "That would have caused her to slam on the brakes as Beulah Romney heard," Salpeter surmised.

"She left the Jolly Roger, and at a point where she is about to almost come upon Beulah Romney's home, the person, that I feel is in the back seat behind her, now comes out and grabs her around the neck," he continued. "It's a natural reaction that when you are grabbed around the neck by surprise—it is an instinct, a body reaction—she reaches for the hands. In order for her to reach for the hands around her throat, she had to take her hands off the wheel of the car, which made her brake while driving.

"The braking sounds are consistent with what Beulah Romney hears and later testifies to," he repeated. "Subsequently, the crime scene will show that there was a palm print on the rear passenger window behind Lois.

"That print was caused, in my opinion, by when Lois brakes and this person now has to brace himself. I would say that his right hand was around Lois' throat and he braces himself until the car stops.

"Consistent with the crime scene and the autopsy of Lois, it's showing that she grabbed on to whatever weapon, possibly a pocket knife, and that reaction is consistent with the markings on Lois' hands."

"I've been to plenty of crime scenes," Salpeter concluded. "That's what I believe happened."

Officials in the case have confirmed the existence of a palm print, but said that it was found on the outside of the vehicle—along with other prints that matched "no one of significance."

There was also a shoe mark on the inside door of

McMillen's vehicle. Deputy Commissioner Johnston has alleged that any number of people who had occupied the back seat of the vehicle could have made it. He believed the print was most likely made by someone's foot hitting up against the door as a person was getting in or out of the vehicle.

Upon returning to the United States, Jay Salpeter presented his findings to Alex's father, Victor Benedetto, who believed that the private investigator might be on the right track. But, Salpeter said, the elder Benedetto expressed frustration, saying that there was little he could do to present the detective's theory to police, who seemed to have already made up their minds about his son's guilt.

The former NYPD detective would next be asked to investigate Stephen Esses—the man who had approached the McMillens earlier in the year claiming to be a private investigator.

According to Salpeter, Esses was also trying to get money from Victor Benedetto. The supposed investigator had contacted Alex's father to tell him that he needed funds to continue his hunt for Lois' killer. Esses was claiming to be a friend of Alex's. Among his many claims, Esses purported to be an FBI agent, and said that he could help Mr. Benedetto free his son. In reality, he was a security guard who did not even have a permit to carry a gun, and knew almost nothing about being an investigator, according to Salpeter.

Fearing that Alex's friend Esses would only cause trouble, Mr. Benedetto asked Salpeter to find him and put a stop to his nonsense. Yet, tracking Esses down would prove a challenge. As he had done with the McMillens, Esses had provided Alex's father with several telephone numbers—one for a cell phone, another for a pager, and even an office number at the United Nations where he said he could be reached. Some were non-working numbers, and others did not lead to Esses, Salpeter said.

In the end, Salpeter said he did locate Esses in New York. He was able to confirm that Esses did, in fact, know Alex.

Yet, the depth and length of the men's relationship was never established.

During a brief discussion, Salpeter said he communicated to Esses that the Benedetto family wished for him to steer clear of them—and the McMillen murder case.

CHAPTER THIRTY

Following up on Other Leads

In the weeks before the trial, Prosecutor Terrence Williams grew increasingly concerned that he did not have a solid case to present to the court. The skilled attorney had hoped to build his case around evidence taken from the crime scene and from Zebra House. But the preliminary lab results turned up nothing conclusive and Williams' team was still waiting for some word back on the additional testing that was being done in a lab outside London.

British Virgin Islands' High Court Justice Kenneth Benjamin had fixed an April 2, 2001, court date—choosing to schedule the men's trial at the end of his calendar for the March Assizes. Asking for yet another adjournment was not possible.

"I am not going to tolerate any excuses as to why [the trial] should not begin," Benjamin had warned Senior Crown Counsel Williams in setting the trial date.

As the date neared, it was becoming increasingly clear to Williams that Jeffrey Plante—a convicted felon—would have to be the key prosecution witness. Lab tests had not yet returned the "smoking gun" that officials had expected, and with no signed confessions and no witnesses to the crime, there was little else to hinge a prosecution on.

In an attempt to bolster the Crown's case, Terrence Williams and Alwin James, the police investigator assisting him, began to track down and talk to a number of individuals who had been linked to the case, but who had never been thoroughly interviewed by police. In fact, the men were still on the road conducting interviews less than one week before the trial was set to begin.

Williams and James began their stateside inquiries in Florida. They filed a request with the FBI for permission to interview Clifford Lefebvre, the friend of Michael's who had been vacationing at Equinox House, at the base of the driveway to Zebra House in Belmont Estates, in January of 2000.

As is customary, all requests for assistance in criminal prosecutions by foreign governments must go through the Federal Bureau of Investigation. The BVI had a particularly good relationship with the Bureau as a result of its joint police work in regard to the Colombian drug-smuggling ring that was funneling its product through the BVI en route to the United States.

On February 2, 2001, the two men, accompanied by a Federal agent, traveled to Cape Coral to meet with Lefebvre. According to one witness, Lefebvre had gone to Zebra House at about ten a.m. on the day after the murder to alert Michael and his friends to the news. When Lefebvre found no one at home, he supposedly peered in the window and observed that all of the beds had been stripped and the place was in disarray. If the information turned out to be true, it would help the prosecution's case, because it would suggest that the four men had attempted a cover-up before police arrived at Zebra House that day.

However, in his interview with Williams and James, Clifford was unclear about the exact time of his visit to Zebra House. Williams concluded that he could not use Lefebvre to buttress the prosecution's case.

Williams left the Florida residence with a brief statement from Lefebvre about his observations of Zebra House the day after Lois' murder. In it, the attorney described his trip to Zebra House:

On the morning of the 15th January 2000, I was walking past the villa of the McMillens when I was

informed by a workman that the daughter of the
McMillens, Lois, was brutally murdered. As a
result of what I had learned, I then visited the residence of K. Carpenter Doyle. I then informed her
of what I had learned. In my presence, Doyle then
tried contacting the residence of the Spicers by telephone. She was not successful. We then had a discussion and as a result I went to the Zebra House to
establish whether Michael and his friends were
there. I walked to the house and on arrival there was
no one present. I made my way around the house
and entered the same through a bedroom that was
unsecured. I discovered on entering the house, that
the bedroom in which I entered, the bed was
stripped of all lining. The room was a shamble. I
then wrote a note and left it on the kitchen counter
for Michael. I then left the house.

                                   —Clifford Lefebvre.

Just days before the trial, police would solicit yet another
statement from Lefebvre. Station Sergeant Anderson
Blackman contacted the older man in Florida by telephone,
asked him a series of questions, and instructed him to fax his
responses to the Road Town police headquarters.

In that statement, Lefebvre wrote:

In connection with your investigation of the death
of Lois McMillen, you asked me to detail my
encounters with Lois during my visit to Tortola
from Jan. 1 to Jan. 18 [sic]. I saw her briefly four
times.

(1) Shortly after my arrival walking up the
beach at Long Bay, a car being driven up
the hill by Russ McMillen stopped and Jo
in the front and Lois in the back warmly
welcomed me.

(2) Walking down to the beach, Lois driving downhill stopped long enough to be complimented on her green hat before the car behind her honked and she drove off.

(3) I took a telephone message down to Charles Bailey who was having morning coffee with the McMillens and stayed five to ten minutes to drink the coffee Lois poured me.

(4) I said hello to Lois and Theresa Bowness at the entrance to the Captain's House where the Cerritos were giving a cocktail party.

In your second call, you asked me about scratches which I didn't remember until you mentioned rock climbing. I went up to Zebra House for a drink after dinner and can now definitely recall being told an escapade (by Michael, I believe) involving rounding a rocky point near the water and being told someone had been injured. You mentioned that it was Alex. I cannot now remember who it was, or the nature of the injury. It was night when I was told and we were outdoors. Maybe you and Alex can supply details that would jog my recollection. I wouldn't have remembered being told of the matter at all if you hadn't mentioned "rock climbing."

In addition to visiting with Lefebvre, Williams and James traveled to New York on February 28, 2001, to speak with Stephen Esses, the supposed private investigator who had contacted Russell and Josephine McMillen the previous year. Again, an FBI agent accompanied the men. Williams and James had arranged to visit Esses in the United States to follow up on his alleged remarks to the McMillens about buying evidence in the case from the Caribbean labs.

Williams said that Esses was evasive and that the meeting with the supposed investigator yielded few clear answers. About all they gleaned was the fact that Stephen Esses was somehow linked to Alexander Benedetto and that his trip to Tortola had been funded by a close friend of Benedetto or William Labrador.

A subsequent meeting with the man on March 26 revealed that he was not a private investigator as he had alleged. It also appeared that he had little information of value to the investigation. Some describe Esses as "a wannabe" who was merely looking to make some money off the Connecticut woman's death.

"He was a kind of character, he was enthusiastic, and he did express a possibility that he could pervert the investigations," Williams recalled of his two meetings with Esses. "I don't think he did at all. He was somebody who was seeking fame from the case. He was on Howard Stern as a guest. He was pretending to be a private investigator. He used to install security alarms."

Williams strongly doubted that Esses had tampered with evidence in the case, as the McMillens feared. He said that police did check flight records and other data to learn if Esses had traveled to Jamaica or Barbados where the crime labs were located. Their search showed that Esses had in fact visited those islands in the past, but not during the time of the McMillen case.

The day before the men spoke with Esses for the second time, the prosecutor and the police constable had flown to Boston to speak with a man named Jeffrey Simms, an electrician aboard the Coast Guard vessel *Grand Isle*. With only a few days left before the trial, they wanted to see what Simms could tell them about Zebra House and its occupants.

Simms, a petty officer with the US Coast Guard, was the man who had accompanied Lefebvre to Zebra House on the evening of January 14, the night that Lois was murdered. He was on Tortola for just one night as his ship made a liberty call there. He met Lefebvre on the beach at Smuggler's Cove, where he intended to spend the night. Lefebvre invited him for drinks at Bomba's and then for cocktails at Zebra House, so that he could introduce him to Michael and his friends.

It was difficult to track Simms down, and authorities only located him with the help of the McMillens' private investigator. The officer was not anxious to speak with island authorities, believing he had little to add to their investigation. In fact, Simms claimed that he only learned of the murder and the arrest of the four Americans from Zebra House long after it occurred when another officer showed him a press clipping. Nonetheless, Simms' superior officers at the Coast Guard station in Massachusetts gave Williams permission to speak with him on March 25, 2001.

Williams said that the thirty-year-old man with the military-style haircut and eyeglasses provided information that he deemed "important" to his case. According to Williams, the young officer indicated that Labrador seemed anxious that evening and kept walking back and forth between the house and the patio as Simms stood talking to Benedetto. He said he and Clifford left the house when Labrador announced to the group that they had to get ready to go out.

"Mr. Labrador came out and said, 'We have to get ready to go,'" said Simms. "I heard some talk outside and Michael said more specifically, 'We have to go meet somebody.'" Williams said that Simms also told him that the men intended to meet someone on "the other side" of the island. It was unclear who that someone was, but the prosecutor suspected it might have been Lois McMillen.

The information prompted Terrence Williams to add the Coast Guard officer's name to his list of witnesses for the prosecution. The Senior Crown Counsel was also hopeful that he could bring another witness to the stand, Luis Reveiz, who would testify to a conversation that he overheard at Her Majesty's Prison in which Alex Benedetto pointed to William Labrador as Lois McMillen's lover.

Reveiz was employed by Kroll Associates, the firm the McMillens had hired to look into their daughter's case, and was working in direct liaison with the Tortola police.

According to a statement he made to the court, Reveiz said that he overheard a portion of a conversation that he claimed had taken place between three individuals, Alex Benedetto, Alex's father, Victor Benedetto, and Alex's lawyer. Reveiz had gone to Her Majesty's Prison to interview Umberto Chavez, Evan George's cellmate, to see what more he could hear about the case.

In his official statement, Reveiz said that he overheard the following that day:

> They were very concerned about David Blyden [Salo]'s statement and if he could change his statement to the police. The Tortola attorney advised them that he had not changed his statement and that it was unlikely that he would. The person with the New York accent asked if there was any other DNA evidence that was being tested other than the shoes and the shirt with blood. They did not appear to know if there was any other evidence. They discussed the possibility of having separate trials.
>
> During the course of the conversation Alex Benedetto had the following outbursts: "He had her in his room and banged her" and "he was in the car with her the night before." It should be noted that during both outbursts Victor told Alex to shut up and would not let him finish what he wanted to continue saying. It was apparent that Alex was referring to Labrador.

What the investigator allegedly overheard raised the possibility in the eyes of the prosecution that William Labrador might in fact have been Lois McMillen's lover. It was a startling revelation and one that could explain the semen that had been found on the tampon that Lois had been wearing when her body was discovered on the rocky shoreline.

Jay Salpeter, the private investigator hired by the Benedettos, later claimed that the alleged conversation between Alex and his lawyer did not occur in the presence of Alex's father, Victor. In fact, he said that the elder Mr. Benedetto was not even on the island at the time that the agent supposedly heard the statements in the prison court-yard. In fact, Salpeter insists that *he* was one of the three men visiting Alex at the prison that afternoon, and was accompanied by Alex's Road Town attorney, Paul Dennis, and New York lawyer Bruce Barket.

Salpeter also contended that what Mr. Reveiz reported to have heard differed greatly from what actually was said during the four men's conversation in the prison yard. Salpeter did not deny that Alex was speaking in a raised voice, and that Barket had admonished him to keep his voice down, but he insisted that the New York man never made the remarks that the Kroll investigator alleged to have heard.

Ultimately, the dispute between the investigators proved of interest only to the media. The evidence would never be presented to a jury. The judge in the case ruled that Reveiz's testimony about the conversation was inadmissible. He barred the private investigator from being called as a witness for the prosecution, stating that his testimony, among other things, would violate attorney–client privilege.

Yet, while the conversation would be deemed inadmissible in court, it confirmed in the minds of Russell and Josephine McMillen that the men awaiting trial for their daughter's murder had played a role in Lois' death.

CHAPTER THIRTY-ONE

The Trial

"On the fourteenth of January last year, Lois McMillen lost her life," Senior Crown Counsel began in his opening remarks to the jury on April 2, 2001. "She was forced in the late hours of that Friday night to flee from her motor vehicle in the West End area just a few hundred yards away from West End police station. There was a struggle; she was met, menaced, and cut with a knife. She suffered a beating and then was violently drowned.

"Next morning, the police went to the Zebra House in Belmont, Tortola, a house occupied by these accused men," the prosecutor asserted in a deep, confident voice over the whir of the small courtroom's central air-conditioning. "They had been with her on previous occasions in that vicinity. When the police went to the house, they saw wet and sandy shoes. You shall hear that the sand under one of those pairs of shoes matches the same sand at the place where the body of Miss McMillen was found. They were asked to explain why their shoes were wet and sandy and Mr. George and Mr. Spicer said, 'They were wet and sandy because we were walking along Cane Garden Bay by Quito's.'"

Terrence Williams told the seven men and two women of the jury that his case was largely based upon circumstantial evidence, and that it would also include testimony from a prison informant named Jeff Plante. The thirty-five-year-old prosecutor was energetic and succinct, explaining that he would introduce some physical evidence, including sand found on the sneakers of one of the men. He would argue that the sand on the sneaker came from the boulder-strewn beach where the woman's body was found.

"You shall hear that there was no sand under those shoes from Cane Garden Bay. And from Mr. Spicer's shoe was found the sand from the scene where this crime was committed," Williams continued. "You shall also hear from witnesses about things said by these accused men whilst in custody. These men were in the area at the same time, about the same time when this woman lost her life. This case is based first of all on circumstantial evidence. We also in the case will be bringing evidence of words said by the men which we are saying shows their involvement in the case.

"I ask you to look particularly at the evidence coming from the stand regarding tests made on items taken from the accused men. And particularly to match that against what is said to the police as to where they were at the time of this girl's killing."

The prosecutor's remarks were the first public statements by the Crown about the case. Ironically, the international contingent of reporters that was there to cover the trial never got to hear what Williams had to say that morning.

Outside the High Court building, police in uniform were denying admission to the more than twenty journalists who were there to cover the proceeding. Officers were telling reporters that the small upstairs courtroom was full to capacity with potential jurors waiting to be picked for the trial. Unlike in the United States, where the selection process can take days, even weeks, as defense attorneys and prosecutors weed out candidates, laws governing the process in the UK ensure a time-efficient selection. Out of the fifty or so candidates from Tortola and the other islands in the BVI, only nine were empanelled to sit on the case—three fewer than in the United States. Additionally, there are no alternates chosen to take over in case of illness or other circumstances.

Court officials had logically assumed that prospective jurors who were not selected to serve on the nine-person panel would leave the courtroom. But that did not happen. Instead they opted to remain there—leaving no room for the press corps.

Police promised admittance as soon as the courtroom had emptied a bit. But that did not happen. Instead, the reporters were ordered to line up on the sidewalk across the street from the courthouse—and outside the locked iron gates that encircle the building. There was nowhere to hide from the blistering heat, and reporters, dripping with sweat, stood holding their notebooks over their heads to seek refuge from the sun's blistering rays.

The McMillens' friends and family, however, were allowed to stand in the shade under a tent that authorities had erected in the parking lot. One reporter recalled that for much of the first morning, the police officer in charge of the courthouse security detail paced the sidewalk, slapping a brass-tipped baton against his thigh, and mumbling something about "illegal assembly" as the proceedings got under way inside.

It was only after a US diplomat from Barbados complained to the judge that officials promised to set aside seats for reporters in the small courtroom.

The proceedings in Tortola were similar to those in the United States—with some key differences. Attorneys wear black robes to court and some of the older judges still don traditional blond wigs. All witnesses stand during testimony. Jurors can take notes and ask questions of witnesses after the attorneys have completed their examinations. Defense attorneys are also prohibited from making opening statements, and defendants do not sit with their lawyers.

The judge presiding over the case was Kenneth Benjamin, a High Court Justice from the island of Antigua. Justice Benjamin had presided over a number of high-profile cases during his years on the bench. In one instance, he sentenced a beach vendor to die by hanging for the 1995 murder of a twenty-six-year-old Canadian tourist. In Antigua, hanging was, and still is, the mandatory sentence for a murder conviction.

Those in the Caribbean legal community thought him a fair and responsible judge and defense counselors and prosecutors alike were pleased that he would preside over the highly publicized case.

Because of the nature of the case, the Crown had brought in a second, more experienced attorney named Theodore Guerra, QC, to lead the prosecution's case. Tall and well-dressed, Guerra, a Senior Queen's Counsel of Trinidad and Tobago, had a glowing reputation and was known for his flamboyant, animated courtroom style. Guerra's appointment to the team surprised Williams, who had done much of the preliminary work and knew the case inside and out. The indefatigable young prosecutor was accustomed to arguing before a judge, and in fact, it was what he did best. He had always enjoyed debating at school—and at home, where he often got into healthy discussions with his father, a politician and trade unionist in Jamaica, and his elder brother, who was also a lawyer. A third lawyer, Crown Counsel David Abednego of the Attorney General's office, was also assigned to Her Majesty's legal team.

J. S. Archibald and Oscar Ramjeet were at the defense table on behalf of Michael and Evan. Paul Dennis was in court to represent Alex. William had hired yet another attorney, Richard Hector, a Queen's Counsel from Bermuda who previously served as a prosecutor and judge in Guyana. William's previous lawyer, Ralph Gonsalves, had won his bid for Prime Minister of St. Vincent and the Grenadines—leaving William without legal counsel just months before the trial was set to begin. His new attorney, Richard Hector, would act as lead counsel; Hayden St. Clair–Douglas of Road Town, who had represented him at the pre-trial hearing in July, would continue to serve on his defense team. In his search for a new attorney, Labrador's family friend and New York lawyer Michael Griffith of Southampton had recommended the attorney from Bermuda.

Labrador's mother, Barbara, had come to court with an entourage that included Michael Griffith, her oldest daughter, Honey, and two of Honey's female friends from California.

Sean Murphy, the attorney who was helping William with his case, was also there with his wife and his half-brother, Duke Thrush. Journalists complained that the group was monopolizing the seats in the front of the courtroom throughout the first days of the trial, placing personal items on the seats as a sign that the spot was "reserved."

Spicer's sister, Chris Matthews, and his brother, Lewis, known as "Casey," had found seats near the Labradors in the second row just behind the raised defendant's box where her brother and William Labrador were seated. Alex and Evan were seated on plastic chairs nearby because there was not enough room in the "box" or "dock" for all four defendants. All four men were dressed conservatively in suits their families had brought to them from the States. Labrador had opted not to wear his trademark red pants to the first day of the proceedings; instead, he came to court in the suit that his mother had bought for him at a local shop.

Fourteen months after the men had been arrested and charged with killing Lois McMillen, Spicer, Benedetto, Labrador, and George would finally hear what evidence the Crown had against them.

Spicer's best friend from San Francisco, Justin Cohen, had flown to the island to lend support. He was seated near Michael's sister, who complained that her view of the proceeding was partially obstructed by the wide brim of the hat that Michael's friend Kay Carpenter Doyle had worn to court.

The lawyer hired by the McMillens to "watch" the proceedings, Dancia Penn, was in court with her associate and sister, Astrid Penn.

Russell McMillen was seated on the left side of the courtroom in the front row behind the jury box. His wife was conspicuously absent. She had been instructed not to enter the courtroom until she was called as a witness by the prosecution. Several of the couple's friends from the Belmont Estates complex had come to lend support and occupied the seats behind Lois' father.

The journalists, all of whom would join the proceedings

after the lunch break, grabbed the empty seats scattered about the rows. Many were furious that they had missed the prosecutor's opening remarks and the testimony of the Crown's first few witnesses.

Julia Mead, a curly-haired reporter for *The Southampton Press*, said that the others had also missed the testimony of Sheena Andrews, the young girl who'd discovered Lois' body on the beach; but made it in time to hear from Beulah Romney, the taxi driver who'd heard the struggle on the road beneath her home; and Constable Jocelyn Rhymer, the first officer on the scene. Mead was a reporter for the weekly newspaper that served Barbara Labrador's hometown, and was also on the island representing the *New York Law Journal*, a daily newspaper that covered the legal community.

In response to questions by the defense, Constable Rhymer testified that she did not know *who* had placed the multicolored sheet over Lois' body at the crime scene—testimony that she would later be forced to correct. Her testimony ended with the first of several surprises from the defense attorneys—a demand that she present a complaint that Lois McMillen had allegedly filed with her in 1999.

At the urging of the defense, the judge had instructed Rhymer, who testified in street clothes, as do all police witnesses, to come back to court the next day with the report.

Rhymer's report proved unremarkable, showing only that Lois had had her purse stolen in 1999. But it proved a heart-stopping moment for Terrence Williams, who had known nothing about the incident before the trial began. He had feared that the report in question might have linked Luigi Lungarini and Lois McMillen, as the defense had alleged over the months.

Mr. McMillen observed quietly as the lead investigator in his daughter's murder case, Chief Inspector Jacob George, made his way to the front of the courtroom, and placed his hand on a cherry-red leather Bible. Like other witnesses, the lanky officer was required to stand while giving testimony before the court.

The prosecution introduced certain pieces of evidence, including the three pairs of sneakers taken from the defendants, and items found at Zebra House and the Drake's Highway location, all of which were identified by George.

The day ended with a dramatic disclosure. In response to questions from William Labrador's attorney, Mr. Hector, Inspector George revealed that he had arrested the four men on "suspicion" of murder on January 15 after finding what appeared to be blood on Spicer's shirt.

But George said that he was unaware that *initial* forensic tests performed on Spicer's shirt had failed to detect the presence of blood. It also became evident during the cross-examination that George had not stayed abreast of all aspects of the investigation even though he was supposed to be in charge of the investigating officers. What was not revealed in court was that Inspector George had been instructed to attend a police training seminar and was off island for a period of time during the McMillen investigation.

The prosecution suffered another setback when George was called back to the stand on Tuesday and asked to point out the supposed bloodstain that he had seen on Michael's pale blue Banana Republic shirt.

"Where exactly on the shirt was the stain?" the defense counselor for Labrador asked the investigator. "You're pointing to the lapel."

"My Lord, I was about to say the stain that I saw was right on the chest," George announced in a low voice.

"On the chest?"

"Right on the chest."

Judge Benjamin interrupted the exchange with his own question. "Center? Left-hand side? Right-hand side?"

"Left," the inspector replied.

"Was it a large stain?" Mr. Hector next asked.

"Not a large stain. I would say the stain was about an inch."

"An inch?" the defense counselor in the black robe shot back.

"Yes, and it was quite obvious."

"Could we have a look at the shirt?" Mr. Hector directed the court to pull the shirt out for the witness to view. But the stain that Inspector George had referred to was not apparent in court to either the witness himself, the attorneys, or members of the jury. Defense attorneys had previously argued that, if there was a stain on the shirt, it was from barbecue sauce—and not from blood. "Maybe you can show us where that stain was."

"The stain I saw was right above the pocket," the inspector explained, pointing toward the shirt. It was clear that the officer was growing uncomfortable with the cross-examination and began to sway restlessly in the witness box.

"Above the pocket?" Hector quizzed.

"Yes, right on the chest area."

"Did anybody wash the shirt?" the lawyer asked half-facetiously.

"I don't know. But I know that shirt went to the forensic laboratory," George responded.

"I'm going to suggest to you quite seriously that you are mistaken about seeing any stain of any dimensions on the front of that shirt," Mr. Hector declared.

Under cross-examination from Michael Spicer's attorney, Joseph Archibald, Inspector George also admitted that the wet, sandy sneakers belonging to Spicer were not among the initial items sent out for forensic testing. Unbeknownst to Inspector George, Sergeant Harley, the forensics expert, had determined that the pair of white K-Swiss sneakers were not wet and sandy when he received them at the West End substation, and he opted not to include them in the package sent to the lab in Barbados for forensics tests. In addition, the inspector acknowledged that he did not know what happened to the footwear once he'd turned it over to Harley. The cramped courtroom grew increasingly warm as the day wore on, in spite of the central air-conditioner to cool the hot, muggy space. The inspector was also grilled about the presence of sand on Spicer's sneakers. Though George maintained that there was sand inside the sneakers when he took them as evidence in January of 2000, there was no sand in the shoe when it was examined in court.

Reporters in the courtroom found his demeanor odd. His

seemingly casual attitude and occasional giggling on the stand troubled them. But perhaps most importantly, George admitted under cross-examination that he had not thoroughly read written statements taken from the four accused men.

For example, at one point Mr. Archibald asked George, "So how much attention did you pay to Evan's statement to the police, which you directed should be taken?"

"Well, as I said, I looked at the statement but I did not read it, as I said," the inspector responded.

"Are you telling us, Chief Inspector George, that on your thirty-one years of experience as a police officer, ten years in the CID, you arrested a man for murder on your suspicion and when you the next day direct that he give a statement—Evan George, and he gave a written statement, which took a police officer four hours and fifty minutes to write—you don't study it in detail?" the diminutive lawyer with the thin moustache and eyeglasses asked.

"I did not, My Lord."

At the end of intense questioning by counselors for the defense, members of the jury posed questions to the inspector. Jurors asked if his officers had considered Lois' former boyfriend, Luigi Lungarini, as a suspect. George said that police had not regarded him as a suspect because they had examined his whereabouts on the night of the murder and determined that he was on the adjacent islands of Virgin Gorda and Anegada. Next, the jury forewoman wanted to know why the investigator did not accept William Labrador's statement to him that the cut on his nose happened while hiking the trails around Belmont the previous day.

"Because the cut was a fresh cut," the investigator responded.

Following Inspector George's testimony would be a number of police witnesses and forensics experts who introduced additional evidence into the record, establishing a chain of custody for the evidence and detailing their findings.

On Wednesday, the jury would learn that one of the men standing trial for Lois' murder, Alex Benedetto, had had a romantic relationship with her in New York. That same day,

the young Coast Guard officer who had accompanied
Clifford Lefebvre to Zebra House on January 14 took the
stand. Jeffrey Simms described how William Labrador was
anxious to get the group ready to go out that evening, and
how Michael said that they "had to go meet somebody." The
Senior Queen's Counsel, Theodore Guerra, led the questioning for the prosecution. During the examination of the petty
officer, the prosecutor sought to focus attention on the
group's destination on the "other side" of the island, inferring that they might have been heading to the West End—
where Lois was last seen alive. As he posed his questions, he
even gestured in the direction of the island's West End, hoping his body movements would serve to convince jurors that
it was in fact the men's destination that night.

During his testimony, Simms also related how Labrador
seemed edgy. He described William emerging from a back
room, saying he "kept going outside and coming back inside.

"Alex and I were talking and our conversation was interrupted because they were getting ready to leave and because
Mr. Labrador came out and said 'We have to get ready to go,
we don't want to be late,' " Simms explained.

Reporters present at the trial have suggested that the
prosecutor wanted the jury to think that the four men had
had plans to meet Lois McMillen that evening. Oddly, when
the defense cross-examined the Coast Guard officer, they
did not ask him about where the men might have been heading, or whom they were supposed to meet. Instead, Hector
worked to dispel Simms' suggestion that Labrador was agitated that night.

The next witness, Dr. Francisco Landron, the medical
examiner from St. Thomas, testified that Lois McMillen died
as a result of drowning after a violent struggle. In response to
questions by Terrence Williams, Landron said that either an
impact or direct pressure on the area could cause the sort of
contusions found on the former model's neck.

"So if one were to put his foot on the neck of the victim,
on the right anterior neck, could that have created a contusion there?" Williams asked of the witness.

"Yes, that would be possible," the pathologist responded.

Another forensic pathologist from London who had been called in by the Crown to offer an opinion in the case testified that the defense's claim that Lois McMillen might have taken her own life was absurd.

"I think it is almost laughable," Nathaniel Roger Blair Cary replied to a question from Terrence Williams. Dr. Cary was a full-time consultant pathologist in the Department of Forensic Medicine at Guy's Hospital Campus, which is part of the University of London. "It would be the most bizarre theory imaginable. You can only look at one crime-scene photograph to see that this is no suicide, and that would be without even knowing about the individual.

"This is someone who died in relation to a trail of escape where we have her artifacts on the ground and then we have her death. We have evidence of various kinds of violence, in particular sharp injury," Dr. Cary continued. "The bottom line is, there is nothing about this case which suggests suicide."

The nine members of the jury looked on as seventy-six-year-old Jo McMillen walked to the front of the courtroom. Like the other witnesses, she had been asked to wait in a back room of the courthouse until she was called to testify. Dressed tastefully in a dark pantsuit and pearls, a pretty lace handkerchief in her hand, Mrs. McMillen stepped into the witness box and then took a seat before the court, the only one of the witnesses who was allowed to be seated while testifying. Already, the jurors had seen official crime-scene photos of her daughter's dead body on the south shore beach. It was evident from their reaction that some on the panel had been upset by the images' graphic nature.

"Do you have a daughter?" Terrence Williams stood before the older woman and inquired about Lois.

"I have a daughter. She is deceased . . . Lois Livingston McMillen." Jo McMillen remained poised throughout the testimony, identifying items that had once belonged to her daughter, like the delicate heart necklace that Lois' father had given her for Christmas.

As the prosecutor held up the tiny fragments of gold

chain, visions of Lois, seated in their Connecticut living room dressed in a red-and-white Santa hat, flashed through Jo's mind. For a split second, Jo McMillen could see her daughter's smile as she unwrapped the box that contained the necklace—the one that was now in pieces, the one that the prosecutor was dangling before the jury, the one that someone had savagely ripped from her daughter's neck.

Lois' mother was controlled as she continued answering the prosecutor's questions about Lois' activity on the night of her death, and about her former boyfriend, Luigi. She dispelled the defense's claims that Luigi was still in her life, and posed a danger to her. "They went around as boyfriend and girlfriend for a few months in 1998," Lois' mother told the court. "When their friendship ended, that was the end of it."

Mr. Archibald stood up and asked the woman with the auburn hair and designer eyeglasses if she was aware that Lois had filed a complaint against the Canadian-born Luigi to police on Tortola in 1998.

"No," she responded in clipped tones. "Are you aware of that?"

"Yes," the attorney replied without divulging anything more about the police report that had allegedly been filed by Lois.

Rising from the seat in the witness box as she finished testifying, Mrs. McMillen smiled gently at the judge and the members of the jury. On her way back to join her husband, she glanced briefly at Barbara Labrador and her son's New York attorney, Michael Griffith. In spite of the allegations against William, Mrs. McMillen had always made it a point to say hello and to be polite to his mother. As always, Mrs. Labrador was busy taking notes as she had been doing on a daily basis since the trial began. She was reportedly keeping a written log in preparation for writing a book about what she insisted was her son's wrongful imprisonment. Mrs. McMillen was offended to see that Griffith continued to whisper to Mrs. Labrador and her entourage during the proceedings.

Jo McMillen noted that, like his mother, William Labrador was constantly taking notes about the proceedings on a pad

he brought with him to court each day. She found it telling
that the dark-haired man from Long Island never gazed in
her direction. Meanwhile, she observed that Evan George
spent much of the time looking around the courtroom
absent-mindedly. Jo McMillen took a seat next to her husband in the front row of the courtroom. Russell McMillen, a
cane resting in the chair beside him, had endured three days
of testimony thus far, and more witnesses were expected to
take the stand over the next week or so.

After a series of police witnesses testified for the prosecution, the forensics expert for the Royal Virgin Islands
Police Force was called to talk of his role in the case. By all
accounts, Sergeant Julian Harley appeared to be the most
highly-trained member of the investigatory team and an
important witness for the prosecution.

Under cross-examination by defense attorneys, the tall officer with the close-cropped graying hair offered testimony
differing from his superior officer, Chief Inspector Jacob
George. According to Harley, the K-Swiss sneakers that
belonged to Michael Spicer were neither wet nor sandy when
he received them into evidence in January of 2000. He also
revealed that a wet and sandy floor mat removed by police
from McMillen's rental vehicle had gone missing at a lab in
Barbados, as had a sample of sand that Harley had collected
from the beach at Cane Garden Bay. It was at Quito's in Cane
Garden Bay that Spicer, George, and Benedetto claimed to
have strolled on the beach on the night of Lois' murder.

At one point, the defense raised questions about the Fuji
camera the four said they had used to snap pictures of their
hike around Belmont Estates on the afternoon of January 14,
2000.

Judge Benjamin listened intently as the sergeant acknowledged that he had, in fact, received the camera into evidence
the day police searched Zebra House, but had never processed the film it contained.

Without hesitation, Benjamin ordered that the forensics
expert develop the roll and return to court the following day
with the photos.

The four Americans seated in the "dock" appeared pleased with the judge's order. Alex and William, especially, were hopeful that at least one of the images would prove their claims that they had sustained their injuries—the scrapes on Alex's arm and leg, and the cut on William's nose—before Lois' murder, and not as a result of any involvement in the crime.

The following morning, Harley was back in court with the photos. He also brought enlargements that allowed the judge, jury and even spectators at a distanace to see them.

Court TV reporter John Springer looked on from the rear of the courtroom with interest as the snapshots were introduced into evidence. His attention was drawn to a blow-up of William Labrador's face, and what appeared to be a healing sun blister on the bridge of the Southhampton man's nose. The photo and what it revealed appeared to be quite favorable to Labrador, Springer thought to himself as the questioning continued.

Among the pictures were various snapshots of Alex, Michael and Evan on the veranda of a private estate that was located in the Belmont Estates section. Others showed Michael, Evan and William on a dock behind that home, and standing in the home's driveway. In the distance, there was a Club Med boat. Labrador would explain the significance of that ship when he took the stand to testify later in the trial.

At the end of Harley's testimony, jurors focused in on Lois' SUV.

They were anxious to learn if any of the defendants' fingerprints were found inside. Harley told the panel that none of the men's prints were found. In fact, police had previously indicated that the entire inside of McMillen's Daihatsu had been wiped clean. Some male DNA was found on the key left in the ignition, but Prosecutor Williams later said that it was impossible to determine to whom it belonged since several police officers had handled the key.

During one court appearance, Alex and Michael expressed condolences to Jo and Russell McMillen for the loss of their daughter. But neither man admitted to any involvement in

Lois' death. Alex's father, however, infuriated Jo McMillen when, after extending his condolences, he suggested that she use her investigator to find the person who *really* killed her daughter. It was the only time that Mrs. McMillen ever lost her composure in public, storming off and telling her husband that she was furious at what she felt were the diminutive man's rude and outrageous comments.

The following day, the judge ruled that Kroll investigator Luis Reveiz would not be allowed to testify about a conversation he'd allegedly overheard between Alex Benedetto and his lawyer at Her Majesty's Prison that past October, citing attorney–client privilege. The prosecution had been counting on his testimony to bolster its already-weak case against the four on trial.

Instead, the jury would hear from a British officer named Michael Wickerson, chief advisor to the Royal Virgin Islands Police Force. Detective Chief Inspector Wickerson was in court to testify to the "chain of custody" of key pieces of evidence that he had been collected from labs in Barbados and Jamaica and transported to the world-renowned lab outside of London for further analysis. He also addressed the issue of the supposedly missing mat from Ms. McMillen's SUV and the sand sample from the beach at Cane Garden Bay.

Under cross-examination by the attorney for Michael and Evan, Wickerson testified that the items were never lost. He explained that he and another British officer, Peter Lawton, had made a conscious decision not to submit the mat for testing because the defendants had had legitimate access to the vehicle in the days prior to the murder—rendering any evidence obtained from the mat moot. Lawton was a member of the Murder Review Board from Scotland Yard that had visited the island the previous October and was asked to be on hand in case questions as to the "chain of custody" of pieces of evidence were raised at trial.

Wickerson testified that he personally had collected the sand sample from Cane Garden Bay, thinking at the time that its chemical composition might be different from sand found elsewhere on the island. When he later found out that the chemical composition was the same, he decided that there would be no point in having the sample analyzed and held it back as a control sample that he could submit at any time in the future.

Mr. Archibald questioned the high-ranking officer about whether he had the authority to make judgments as to what pieces of evidence would undergo analysis, to which he responded that he did. He then asked the chief inspector if he had considered that his decision not to test the sand from Cane Garden Bay might actually deny important findings that could help his client, Michael Spicer. The inspector said, "No, otherwise, I would have submitted it."

CHAPTER THIRTY-TWO

Prison Informant Takes the Stand

Flanked by court officers, Jeffrey Plante, whom critics had dubbed "the Snitch of Tortola," made his way up the flight of steps leading to a back room of Justice Benjamin's second-floor chambers, smiling for photographers before stepping inside the building on the morning of April 17, 2001. Dressed in a suit and tie, his gray hair combed to one side, the Texas man with the neatly-trimmed beard flashed a grin to reporters standing below. When it was time for him to take the stand, uniformed officials led him to the witness box, which was just beside the judge's bench. There, he would offer testimony for much of the day and again the next.

Michael and the others were already inside when the man who had shared the remand wing with him and his cohorts for nearly five months made his way to the front of the courtroom.

The prosecution's star witness appeared cool and relaxed as he stood before the court and took an oath to tell "the truth, the whole truth, and nothing but the truth."

The four defendants, William, Michael, Alex, and Evan, watched from the "dock" as Senior Crown Counsel Williams rose from the prosecutor's table, his long flowing robe covering the dark suit he had worn to court. In a confident tone, he first cautioned the nine jurors that the testimony they were about to hear was coming from a man who was hardly a model citizen.

After establishing that Plante had a criminal record in the United States and had been jailed on and off since 1985 for fraud and other offenses, the thirty-six-year-old prosecutor asked him about the time he had spent at Her Majesty's Prison as a cellmate to William Labrador.

"Well, I shared the cell with Mr. Labrador for over one hundred and thirty days, and the majority of the time they kept us in the cells twenty-three hours a day, seven days a week. Towards the end of that period of time, they would let the remanded prisoners go out and recreate. And I think we were out for about four hours a day, out in the yard there, in the remanded area." Over the next few hours, Jeffrey Plante told the court how he spent a lot of time together with William and how they talked about each other's background, family, friends, and legal problems.

"[William] wanted to get separated from the other three defendants because he felt that the evidence that the police had only concerned the other three defendants, such as Mr. Spicer's bloody shirt and whatnot, and that he wanted to separate himself from the other defendants because he felt that he was putting a plan together that he might possibly obtain release, and again that all the evidence was against the other three defendants and that the police were incompetent and they didn't know his whereabouts that night," Plante told the court.

In his testimony, Plante alleged that Labrador told him that police had picked up for evidence the wrong pair of his shoes. He further told the court that Labrador's mother had come to Tortola about a week after the arrest and "took custody" of William's luggage and other personal items at Mr. Spicer's house. However, Barbara Labrador did not set foot on Tortola until March of 2000, more than one month after the men's arrest. On cross examination, Plante did not contend otherwise.

William "was glad that she took back to New York a pair of surfing gloves and generally he felt that there was not anything that tied him into the crime," Plante told the court.

Later that day, Plante detailed the alleged confession that

Labrador made to him a few days before Good Friday the previous year. He described how William asked: "did I think God would forgive him if he had anything to do with killing someone." Plante said that he referred William to a priest in Road Town, and went on to ask his cellmate point blank if he'd had anything to do with killing Lois McMillen.

"And he answered me yes," the Texas man told the court in a thick drawl. "And I asked him why, and he said that it was over money and that she was no good."

Plante then went on to describe how the fight between William and Lois started with an argument, got heated and out of control, and that ultimately he "dragged her into the water and put his foot on the back of her neck to drown her."

Curiously, this was the first time that Plante had testified that Labrador had said that he put his foot on the back of Lois' neck to drown her. In previous statements to police and prior court appearances, Plante had said only that Labrador had placed his foot on McMillen's neck—without specifying front or back.

It was only later, at the end of a lengthy cross-examination, that Labrador's attorney questioned Plante about the inconsistency. Plante said that he could not recall exactly what he had told police previously. Prosecutor Terrence Williams dismissed the matter as a "small edition" to Plante's story. Later, however, this would become an issue in the appeal.

He also described heated arguments between Labrador and Benedetto at the prison that once escalated to physical violence when Labrador threw a basketball at Benedetto so hard that he broke Alex's finger. Plante recalled that during another fight, Alex allegedly shouted at William that *he* was the one who had "the girl up at the house."

Alex's lawyer, Paul Dennis, later argued that what Plante supposedly overheard was vague, and by no means proof of murder.

"It is so vague as to be meaningless," Dennis would tell Judge Benjamin on his client's behalf. "My Lord, there is no evidence that he was speaking of the deceased."

To a hushed courtroom, Plante further testified that his

own relationship with Labrador was sometimes tense, and that at one point, William had threatened him over money. He said Labrador "took a coat hanger, twisted it and put it around my big toe, and started to twist it, and said, 'You better loan me the money.'"

When asked why he had waited a month before coming forward to police with William's alleged confession, he said he was testing his cellmate's "veracity." And Plante explained that he could "no longer live with myself."

Under cross-examination, Plante was initially calm, and even elicited laughter from jurors and spectators with some of his responses. Labrador's attorney, Mr. Hector, first sought to discredit the prison informant by asking him to detail his many convictions in the United States. He also pointed to the fraud charges that Plante was facing in the BVI for allegedly writing thirty-two bad checks while he was being reimbursed for his living expenses by the local government. Hector suggested that he found it hard to believe that Plante had repented when, soon after getting out of prison in Texas for one crime, he flew to Tortola—and immediately went back to his old ways as a con man.

Plante grew increasingly uncomfortable as the questioning by Hector continued. Still standing, at times he swayed and fidgeted, involuntarily placing his hands on the wood bar of the witness box for balance. He even tried to shift some of the blame for his current predicament on his wife, Shannon, who, he said, had written some of the "hot" checks that he was now charged with passing.

Terrence Williams sat at the Crown's table listening carefully to Mr. Hector's questions so that he could later rebut. He had spent months working on the McMillen case, carefully researching case law, studying the police files, and traveling to the States to interview potential witnesses. Yet he was unprepared for the response his star witness was about to give to a question Hector posed about Plante's marital status.

"And you are a good Roman Catholic, are you?" Hector began.

"I am Catholic."

"You were divorced how many times?"

"I am sorry?"

"You were divorced how many times?"

"Ten."

"Ten times?" Hector repeated, pausing for a moment to contemplate the number.

Williams recalled that he nearly fell off his chair when he heard Plante divulge the stunning number. He was equally surprised by how well the Texas man was able to shrug off mention of the multiple marriages amid laughter from many in the courtroom. The prison informant wore a sheepish grin as he explained that some of the marriages had been mistakes—he had followed his heart and it had not worked out. Others, he said, were just paper marriages so that his "wife" at the time could handle his legal matters while he was incarcerated.

"Six of those wives were by proxy when I was locked up, to do my business," Plante clarified. "I never even kissed these people. It was strictly business. It was strictly done by paperwork and was done for business purposes, which I am sure you knew."

It was evident by the expressions on the faces of the nine jurists that they found the Texas man oddly amusing. They would be brought to laughter again when Labrador's lawyer detailed Plante's foray into an Internet chat room while he was on the island waiting to testify in the McMillen case. Somehow, this soft-spoken middle-aged man had managed to lure a Parisian woman to Tortola, telling her tales of great personal wealth, multiple residences, and even his own private plane—that just happened to be unavailable because it was in for service.

The men and women in the jury box chortled as Hector confronted Plante about his weeks-long island romance with the French woman to whom he quickly become engaged. They sat rapt as the attorney next described how the European woman had even approached local authorities with accusations that Plante was attempting to charge up her credit cards before she fled the Territory for home. Despite all the discussion about his serious run-ins with the law, Plante appeared to charm the nine people who sat in the jury box with his wit and sensitivity.

Michael and Evan's attorney, J. S. Archibald, next took the floor.

"Mr. Plante, I have just a few questions to ask you," the lawyer began. "Yesterday, you said, 'Mr. Spicer had asked me at one point whether or not the police were capable of tracing some twenty-one phone calls that morning'?" The lawyer was referring to Plante's testimony in regard to a conversation about Salo the taxi driver that he'd purportedly overheard.

"Yes, sir," Plante responded.

"Now are you sure it is Mr. Spicer who mentioned to you about twenty-one phone calls, or somebody else mentioned that to you? Are you sure? That is all I am asking."

"Well, Mr. Archibald, actually it was Mr. Spicer and Mr. Benedetto who were together. Three of us were out in the yard together."

"My question is, are you sure it was Mr. Spicer?"

When Plante evaded answering directly, Archibald produced a copy of the evidence Plante had given before Her Worship the Magistrate, Gail Charles, on July 25 at the men's Preliminary Inquiry, and read it aloud for the court:

" 'They mentioned to me that there was evidence of twenty-one phone calls made to Salo on the morning of the murder. I believe it was Mr. Benedetto who said this.' "

"Is that accurate now?" Archibald asked.

"Yes, sir. I believe my memory at the time of the P.I. would probably have been better than today. But they were together and concerned about the twenty-one calls."

Next, Archibald produced a telephone bill from Zebra House for the month of January 2000 and asked that it be passed around the courtroom so that "everyone" could view it. ". . . I want to suggest to you that not a single call was made from the Spicer house on the fifteenth of January," he announced.

Addressing statements that Plante made in relation to

Evan George, the diminutive attorney in the wire-rimmed glasses pulled out a sheet of notes.

"Evan George said he never told you that he saw Labrador when they came back home the morning of the fifteenth." Archibald looked directly at the Texas man. "He said he never told you that he saw Labrador in any wet shoes."

"Well, Mr. Archibald, I stand by what I said," Plante responded. "What he said is that he went into the pool house and he went to where Mr. Labrador was. Mr. Labrador was laying fully clothed on the bed and he had wet shoes."

"The other things he said . . . He never said to you that Alex Benedetto or William Labrador, or both of them, left the place that evening, that time when they came back. He never told you that," Archibald continued to read from his notes.

"Again, I stand by what I said, Mr. Archibald."

"Now did you ever show Mr. Spicer a newspaper report referring to the taxi driver, Salo?"

"No, sir, I have never seen a newspaper report referring to the cab driver Salo."

"I put to you that with respect, Mr. Plante, that Mr. Spicer never told you that he had paid Salo a lot of money. What do you say to that?"

"He did tell me that, Mr. Archibald."

"I want to put to you that Evan George never told you that when he got back to the house on the night after coming in from Cane Garden Bay that he was stoned on drugs."

"Sir, he told me that and they, all three of them, told me that."

After questioning Plante about his hearing problem, Archibald next asked Plante if he knew Lois McMillen.

"Yes."

"From when?"

"I met her for thirty minutes on Norman Island a long time ago. Didn't know who she was," Plante said. He told the court that Lois was with a girlfriend at *The Willy T*, a floating bar, when he saw her on the nearby island in September of 1999.

"We talked for about thirty minutes . . . She seemed like a nice woman. I didn't know her name."

"How did you come to know that you met her?"

"When I eventually saw a picture of Lois McMillen, that's when I knew I met her. I believe I saw it off of some kind of fax or something that Mr. Labrador, one of his friends had sent, smuggled into the prison."

"When did you see the picture? Did you know where she lived?" Archibald was attempting to show that Plante had been reading news accounts and may have even known Lois' address when he came forward to police with his startling information. The lawyer closed his cross-examination by asking Plante when he'd learned of her death.

"I believe in late January when they [the defendants] first came up there [the prison]."

Alex's attorney, Paul Dennis, picked up the questioning after a short recess. Through a series of questions, he worked to show the jury that the fraud charges against Plante had been dropped within weeks of his three statements to police.

"Yes, sir," Plante responded.

"I am suggesting to you, Mr. Plante, that it was in recognition of the serious charge you were facing which opened you to the possibility of imprisonment that you decided to make these statements implicating the defendants?" Dennis asked.

"Absolutely not."

Alex's lawyer next mentioned a letter that had been entered into evidence in which Plante told his wife Shannon: "I will tell you this, Shannon, I will not go back to prison no matter what! I could not take that again, love, not here or anywhere."

"My state of mind was that I could not live with myself without coming forward and giving a statement as to what I knew to be the truth. That was my motivation."

At the end of Mr. Dennis' cross-examination, it was the jury's turn to question Plante. The group was anxious to pose questions to the Crown's key witness. Before they adjourned for the day, the jury forewoman inquired about a car accident that Plante had alluded to in his testimony. He had told the jury that the crash in front of Long Bay hotel had involved Labrador, Benedetto, and Lois McMillen.

The sturdy Tortolan woman was interested to hear more details of the incident, and about Plante's allegation that William boasted that after the accident the three—he, Alex, and Lois—had "gone back to the house" where both men supposedly made love to the former model. Already, Labrador had admitted knowledge of an intimate relationship between Lois and Benedetto. But he maintained that he never told Plante about a three-way sexcapade with his business partner friend and Lois McMillen.

Outside the courthouse, Russell McMillen felt compelled to say something to the man who had just spent several hours under grueling cross-examination by defense attorneys. Throughout it all, the McMillens had never spoken a word to Jeffrey Plante. They were grateful that Plante had shown the personal fortitude to come forward with his statements to police and to endure hour upon hour of questioning on the stand as defense attorneys sought to poke holes in his story and cast him in a bad light. For the McMillens at least, Jeff Plante had proven to be a credible witness on the stand, and one who never ducked questions about his own checkered past.

A gentle breeze swayed the palm trees as Lois' father ambled over to the Texas man, who was standing in the courtyard near the fountain. Extending his hand, Mr. McMillen said, "I want to thank you for the courage you showed."

"Yes, thank you," Mrs. McMillen remarked.

"Jeffrey Plante was very credible on the stand," Jo McMillen later said. "He endured hours of grueling testimony and did not get disturbed by it. He answered all the questions directly, even the ones about his criminal past and his ten wives. He was honest. He said he never murdered anybody and he never would. Stealing people's money is one thing, but murder is quite a different category."

The following day, the defense counselor for William Labrador wanted to further question Plante about the car accident, and to dispel jury speculation about the "alleged" three-way romp back at the house.

"Yesterday you gave evidence when you said that

Mr. Benedetto—that Mr. Labrador told you that Benedetto and himself were involved in an accident at Long Bay where they ran into a concrete wall or something, and that after that accident, they both went back to the house and both of them had made love to Lois?" Mr. Hector demanded.

"Yes, sir," Plante replied.

". . . He told you there was an accident and he never told you anything about both having sex with her. That was your addition of filth to this whole escapade," Labrador's lawyer insisted.

"Did Mr. Labrador ever admit to you that he was having an affair with Lois McMillen?" another juror asked.

"He said that he made love to her one time."

"What was your reaction when Mr. Labrador told you that he had drowned Miss McMillen?" was the question posed by another of the nine panelists.

"I guess shock. I guess, I mean, I felt really bad for her because I didn't feel like he gave me any kind of justification. I mean, not that there ever is. It just seemed so senseless, so unnecessary. I really felt bad about what he did, and I guess I had a lot of disgust, too."

"Can you tell me how long it took you before you told anyone about it?"

"Actually a while. At least a month or so."

"Can you tell us if Mr. Labrador stated when that, when was the one time he slept with Miss McMillen?"

"Yes, ma'am," Plante responded, referring to the day in 1997 that he and Alex met her at Bomba's Shack.

"No further questions," the jury forewoman announced.

"You can step down," the judge announced.

Dr. Kenneth Pye was next to be escorted to the witness box. The professor of environmental geology had earned a Masters at Oxford University and a doctorate at Cambridge, and was currently a professor in the Geology Department at the University of London. During his two decades in the field of geology, he had been called to testify as an expert at numerous trials in the UK, including twenty murder cases.

He had come from the United Kingdom to present his

analysis of chemical and microscopic tests he'd performed on sand and soil samples given to him by police, and other samples that he had collected from various locations around the island. Police had brought Pye in to see if he could link sand found on the sneakers of three of the defendants, on the patio, and in the trap of the outdoor shower at Zebra House with sand samples taken from the crime scene.

Before Pye could begin presenting his findings, Mr. Archibald interrupted and asked permission of the court to allow his own sand expert from the United States to sit in on the professor's testimony. He explained that he would need the geologist's "specific specialist advice" to formulate some of his questions to the witness. He also indicated that he might call his geologist as an expert to rebut Pye's findings.

After listening to arguments from both sides, Justice Benjamin ruled to allow Nicholas Albergo, a geologist from Florida, to be in court while the professor gave evidence.

Much of what Professor Pye testified to was technical in nature and lost on the jury, as well as many of the spectators in the courtroom. But his key point was not. According to Pye, there was a "high probability" that sand found on Michael's footwear did come from the area where Lois' body was found. He based his finding on a detailed analysis of the material's color, chemistry, grain size, polish, and composition.

Pye indicated that he was able to identify sand from the West End shoreline because of the polish found on the grains of sand, and because of the presence of numerous fragments of volcanic material and quartz grains. He stated that even a layperson with an untrained eye could differentiate the sand found at the crime scene from sand on other island beaches. Pye explained that the West End shoreline is largely protected by offshore reefs, which limit wave action there and result in sand with a different polish from grains found on other less protected beaches ringing the island. He further testified that he also found a second type of sand on Spicer's sneakers that was consistent with samples taken from Smuggler's Cove or Long Bay on the island's north coast, adjacent to Belmont Estates.

The prosecution witness told the court that he could find no links between the sand found on sneakers belonging to William Labrador and Evan George to the murder scene. For reasons that are unclear, Pye was not asked to analyze yet another pair of sneakers belonging to Alex Benedetto.

The professor had also tried to determine whether or not any of the four men had walked on the beach adjacent to Cane Garden Bay through his sand analysis. He testified that the sand found in all of the sneakers he analyzed was not consistent with samples taken from Cane Garden Bay.

Pye's finding conflicted with statements taken from Michael and Evan indicating that they had gotten their sneakers wet and sandy while walking along the beach near Quito's at Cane Garden Bay.

The defense argued that Pye's testimony was irrelevant. Under cross-examination by Spicer's attorney, Joseph Archibald, Pye acknowledged that his staff had made errors during the testing and admitted that geology is not an exact science.

It also became apparent in court that the geologist had never seen Spicer's sneakers before the trial and, in fact, had limited his work to the study of the sand that was supposedly found inside the footwear. Spicer's attorney sought to hammer that point home when he asked Pye to remove the sneakers from an evidence bag and physically examine them. Archibald was trying to establish that Spicer's sneakers were old, beat up, and had holes in the soles. He argued that Spicer could have walked along the West End shoreline weeks or even months before the murder, and picked up sand in his sneakers well before Lois' body was found on the beach in January of 2000.

Pye acknowledged that he had no way of ascertaining how long the sand had been in Spicer's sneakers. And further questioning revealed that only about fifteen percent of the small sample he'd found on the tattered white canvas sneakers appeared similar to sand and sediment near the Drake's Highway crime scene.

A member of Britain's Forensic Science Service laboratory,

Michael Paul Jonathan Appleby, was also called to the stand to testify about the results of his intensive Low Copy Number DNA (LCN DNA) analysis of dozens of pieces of evidence. Williams had previously won a five-month adjournment from the court to permit the LCN DNA analysis as well as the sand analysis done by Professor Pye.

In his forensic report dated February 22, 2001, and again in court, Appleby stated that "two areas of tiny blood spots were detected on the left and right shoulder areas" of Michael Spicer's pale blue Banana Republic shirt—the same shirt that Inspector George had taken into custody after noting what "appeared to be blood" on the chest area of the garment. But the scientist reported that the sample size was so small that he had been unable to determine whether it was the blood of Lois McMillen or not.

Commenting on the "tiny blood spots" found on the shoulders of Spicer's well-worn shirt, Appleby acknowledged that he had been able to identify just two of the twenty variable characters normally found in a full DNA profile. He determined that the "cellular matter" that he'd located on the left shoulder of the garment could have come from Michael Spicer. But he admitted that he could not even say for certain that the source of the DNA detected there had come from the small number of blood spots. The person wearing it could have transferred the cellular matter to the shirt during normal contact.

Tests of the "tiny stains" he'd found on the right shoulder of the faded blue shirt revealed that their profile was somewhat similar to Lois McMillen's DNA—and one out of every four women in the UK.

Though Appleby's testimony was far from conclusive, Deputy Commissioner Johnston still regarded it as significant. After all the debate about whether the spot on the shirt was blood or barbecue sauce, the forensics expert was for the first time confirming that there was indeed blood on Spicer's garment.

Appleby also told the court that DNA tests he'd conducted on other evidence given to him by police failed to link the four men to the murder. The blood found on William's sneaker matched the DNA of Alex Benedetto, he said. No testing had been performed on samples taken from Evan George.

On April 20, Station Sergeant Anderson Blackman was in court to testify to his role in the investigation. Blackman was the officer who first focused police's attention on the men from Zebra House. In a hushed voice that was nearly inaudible, he testified to his part in the first hours after Lois McMillen's body was discovered.

In response to questions from attorneys, the sergeant, in a low mumble, said he was aware that a Jamaican dressmaker named Winsome Manning had first spotted the body on the beach more than one hour before police were finally able to find it. The defense later argued that the police's failure to locate the body until a second person arrived at the substation to make a report was further evidence of the department's sloppy police work.

On April 23, Constable Jocelyn Rhymer was back in court for a third time to correct her earlier testimony about the sheet that had been placed over McMillen's body at the crime scene. The officer was dressed in plainclothes, a natty suit and heels, her hair in neat braids. Woman Constable Rhymer told the court that it was she who had in fact placed the sheet there. Previously she had testified that she had no idea who'd covered Lois' body. The thirtyish police officer explained that she had confused two cases, the other involving a woman from St. Vincent who had also been found dead on a beach.

Later that day, the judge, jury, and others left the courthouse to visit the crime scene and other locations discussed during the trial. The nine-person panel spent Monday afternoon visiting the rocky beach where Lois' battered body was found, and more than a dozen other relevant locations. The spectacle was reminiscent of recent high-profile cases in the United States such as the O. J. Simpson murder trial. Under bright sunny skies, the judge, jurors, defendants, and others boarded about fifteen vehicles, including government vans and police cars for the trip. The McMillens were among the participants.

The group first stopped adjacent to the pink-and-white hilltop home of Beulah Romney, the taxi driver who'd testified to hearing a car come to a screeching halt on the roadway and then screams for mercy. From there, the group traveled a short distance down Drake's Highway to the crime scene where McMillen's body had been found. A small cross had been placed on the roadside a short distance away. As the group examined the rocky beach, Lois' father stood by the makeshift memorial. While the crowd studied the boulder-strewn location, Russell McMillen stared pensively out at the sea, steadying himself with a wood cane. His wife, dressed all in black with a wide-brim hat, was by his side.

Climbing back into the vehicles, the jurors continued to Soper's Hole where they would visit the ATM machine where the men had withdrawn money before setting out for Quito's that night. Then it was on to the Jolly Roger Inn, the last place that Lois had been seen alive. They would also be shown the hiking trails behind Belmont, and Quito's, the beachside bar on Cane Garden Bay. The visit to the north coast provided the four defendants with their first opportunity to walk on a beach since being incarcerated in Her Majesty's Prison in January of 2000. Officials allowed them a few moments to soak up the sun and enjoy the surf on the sandy white stretch adjacent to Quito's, once the others were safely ensconced inside their vehicles.

On Tuesday, the Crown rested its case and the fate of the men was now in the hands of the defense attorneys.

CHAPTER THIRTY-THREE

William Will Stand Alone

For the next two days, Judge Benjamin considered the merits of the evidence the Crown had presented against the four men and reviewed defense motions for a dismissal of the charges.

Hour after hour, the High Court justice listened to lawyers for both sides present their arguments—the defense asking for dismissal, the prosecution asking that the case be turned over to the jury for a verdict.

Benedetto's lawyer, Paul Dennis, stood in the balmy upstairs courtroom for nearly two hours, laying out for the judge why the case against his client should be thrown out.

"There is no evidence," the tall, slender Dennis said countless times during his lengthy dissertation. "My Lord, this is the totality of the Crown's evidence. In that testimony, there is no evidence that this accused [Benedetto] committed the crime alleged. It is so very tenuous, so very vague and unreliable that no jury, properly directed, could convict upon it."

On Thursday, April 26, the seventeenth day of the trial, the judge was again hearing arguments for dismissal from the defense attorneys. The lawyers had filed "no case" submissions—legal motions asking that the murder charges against Michael, Alex, and Evan be dropped on grounds that the prosecutors had failed to make their case in court.

Earlier in the day, attorney Joseph Archibald had presented a case for dismissing the charges against Evan

George, who sat fiddling with his tie during the lawyer's fifteen-minute legal argument. Evan was at once conservative and stylish in his dark-colored suit and trendy black shoes with thick rubber soles.

Mr. Archibald argued that there was absolutely no evidence to link the young Oregonian to the crime, and insisted that his four hundred and sixty-eight days of confinement should end immediately.

After spending the entire morning in chambers listening to the lawyers state their grounds for dismissal, the judge decided that he would let the jury go for an early lunch. Just before eleven forty a.m., he left the bench to alert the group to his decision. Since Tuesday, the jurors had been sequestered in a back room where they had been instructed to remain while lawyers for the four defendants presented their arguments to the judge. Under rules of the British court system, jurors hearing evidence in a case are obliged to stay together while court is in session.

The day took an unexpected turn when Benjamin learned that two of the jurors had violated his order and had left the courthouse during the lunch break in the company of a police officer. At about noontime, the pair returned to court with the uniformed constable. One of the jurors told Benjamin that she had misunderstood his instructions and had left the building with a fellow juror to run an errand.

In response to the pair's violation of the court rules, the judge announced that he would hold a hearing that afternoon to determine whether the action of the two jurors would make it necessary for him to "abort" the trial. Benjamin's declaration stirred worry among the defendants' family members and friends: Would the judge declare a mistrial and force all involved to go through the proceedings a second time?

Now, the indiscretion of the two jurors was threatening to halt the trial and block the men's chances of having a verdict rendered. Behind closed doors, Archibald and Ramjeet explained the magnitude of the situation to Michael and Evan. The attorneys advised them to proceed with the case, saying they were close to a dismissal. They next advised the men to sign a legally binding paper acknowledging the jurors' violation and waiving their right to declare a mistrial.

The incident with the jury was not the first one to threaten the case. Earlier in the trial, a fire had broken out in the records room adjacent to the Magistrate's Court, where the men's Preliminary Inquiry had been held, and speculation whirled around the island that the four accused men had paid someone to set it to destroy potentially damning evidence in the case. In reality, there was nothing in the second-story room that was linked to the men's trial. All of the items associated with the case had been moved from that location several days prior. But the rumors added a dramatic touch to the ongoing proceedings. The men would later claim that police had deliberately set the fire to make it look like the four of them were trying to pervert the course of justice.

Once the jury matter was resolved and all parties had agreed to move forward with the proceedings, prosecutors argued against the defense's "no case" submission and asked that the case go to the jury. Senior Queen's Counsel Guerra and Senior Crown Counsel Williams insisted that they had presented enough "circumstantial evidence" to tie the four men from Zebra House to the crime. They argued that Plante's testimony, plus a witness statement that Spicer and the others were "going to meet someone" on the night of Lois' murder were sufficient to send the case to the jury to decide.

Williams also noted that Michael Spicer had failed to call the McMillens to offer condolences after learning that their daughter was found dead on the beach—even though he had known the couple and Lois for nearly twenty years. He pointed out that it seemed odd in light of the fact that Michael had courteously apologized to Mrs. McMillen on a prior evening that same week for keeping Lois out late.

Spicer shot the prosecutor an angry look for inferring that his decision to wait to place the call somehow pointed to murder, and later half-joked that the only thing he was guilty of in this case was "bad manners."

The defense argued that the Crown's twenty-one witnesses had presented no physical evidence to tie the men to Lois or the crime scene, and insisted that it would be legally wrong for the judge to send the case to the jury.

Meanwhile, the prosecutors continued to push for the case go to the jury, where the nine men and women would decide on the merits of the Crown's evidence. Williams and Guerra argued that Plante had made statements about all four of the men that, if believed, contradicted their signed statements to police.

Senior Counsel Guerra went so far as to ask Benjamin to consider allowing the jury to decide three of the men's fates on the lesser charge of accessory—and not murder—even though he had made it clear from the onset that he only intended to argue the murder indictment.

Judge Benjamin expressed surprise at the Crown's shift in position. Curious how the defense would react, he later asked the lawyer representing Spicer and George how the trial might proceed if he threw out the charge of murder and let the jury deliberate on charges of accessory after the fact.

Archibald told the High Court judge that he believed the Crown had given up its right to seek convictions on the lesser charges when it told the court that it would prove only the murder charge at the opening of the trial.

On May 3, the men would learn the judge's decision. Benjamin directed the jury to acquit three of the four men of murder, citing insufficient evidence in the case. "Michael Spicer, Alexander Benedetto, and Evan George, you are discharged," Benjamin said after instructing the jury to formally enter "not guilty" pleas for the three. "You are free to go. Step out of the box." The judge found that the prosecution had not presented the case as promised in its opening arguments. The decision was met with applause from family and friends of the men, and gave hope to the Labrador camp that William, too, would be free soon. In his twenty-six-page ruling, which he read aloud, Benjamin called the evidence against the three men "less than thin."

Benjamin also ruled that the case against William

Labrador could lawfully go to a jury in light of the alleged confession he had made to Jeffrey Plante.

"Three down, one to go," a cheerful Barbara Labrador later told the pack of reporters who encircled the family for comment.

A bespectacled Michael Spicer emerged from the courtroom and flashed an ear-to-ear grin to the crush of journalists waiting at the base of the staircase for comments from him and his two friends. With an air of relief, he told the group that he just wanted to jump into the Caribbean Sea and wash the ordeal from his body.

Alexander Benedetto wiped tears from his eyes and embraced his father, Victor.

For a brief while on Friday, it appeared as though Michael and Alex may have been headed back to Her Majesty's Prison. They had been ordered to remain in the Territory after the judge's directed verdict to enter pleas on the lesser charge of perverting the course of justice that the men were still facing. The lesser charges had not been made part of the men's murder trial, so technically, they were still outstanding. In court, prosecutors asked Judge Benjamin to order the two men held until October to give them time to pick a jury to consider a charge of conspiracy to pervert the course of justice. The misdemeanor charge against the two men was contained in a separate indictment.

"The issues are still alive," Senior Queen's Counsel Theodore Guerra argued to Benjamin. He implored the judge to direct that the two Americans report at once to a local police station to confront the minor offense. The elder prosecutor indicated that he did not intend to further pursue charges against Evan George.

Alex's lawyer, Paul Dennis, did little to hide his fury at the lead prosecutor's pronouncement, calling the maneuver "outrageous" and suggesting that the Crown was trying to "ambush" the defendants. "My Lord, this is simply vindictive."

The judge told the lawyers that the only factor for him to

consider was bail. Alex and Michael each posted $10,000 and were liberated for a second time.

En route to the ferry on Friday afternoon, Michael and Evan passed the small white cross that marked the place where Lois McMillen's battered body had been discovered. No one said a word as they drove along Drake's Highway. But the eerie silence was soon broken when Evan, dressed breezily in shorts and a colorful Hawaiian shirt, pointed to the West End police substation across the road and said, "That's where it all started."

As the men climbed aboard a ferry at West End for the US Virgin Island of St. Thomas, where they looked forward to setting foot on US soil for the first time in nearly sixteen months, Alex and his father were heading to Tortola's Beef Island Airport. Amid departing passengers and flocks of chickens roaming the inside of the terminal, the Benedettos waited for a plane to the US Territory of San Juan, Puerto Rico. There, they would check into a five-star hotel and luxuriate on the Caribbean island for one night, hitting the restaurants and casinos, before returning to New York the following day. Alex loved to visit the casino and, when in New York, often jaunted to the Mohegan Sun Casino complex in Connecticut to gamble and catch the shows.

The ticket agent who checked Alex in for his flight recalled how the fair-haired man with the soft blue eyes stood gazing around the terminal. At first, Andrew O'Mar Mullin, an airline employee from the island of Jamaica, did not understand why the tall, slender man in the sport coat was acting so oddly. He said that he was glancing in every direction and proclaiming "how beautiful" it all seemed. But once Alex announced that he had just been released from the prison, Mullins said that his behavior began to make sense.

The judge's ruling was no victory for the McMillens, who had lost their only daughter and now sat watching as the men they believed to have taken her from them walked free. It would be even more difficult for them to return to court the following day to listen as William Labrador testified before the court.

CHAPTER THIRTY-FOUR
The Verdict

After learning the judge's decision on Thursday, May 3, William Labrador's mother and members of his defense team returned to the Prospect Reef hotel optimistic about William's fate and celebrated with food and drinks at the restaurant beside the boat basin. When they arrived at the waterside resort, Mrs. Labrador was alerted to the check-in of a key witness in her son's case.

In the months leading up to the trial, family friend and lawyer Sean Murphy had done extensive research on behalf of his brother's childhood friend and had found two people whom he believed would help William win his freedom. One was Shannon, the tenth wife of Jeffrey Plante. The other was a woman named Tisha Neville. Neville had been Plante's parole officer in Texas for nearly one year, and had agreed to fly to Tortola to testify to what Neville described as his "constant lying" while under her supervision.

Honey Labrador, the older of William's two sisters, had arranged and paid for Shannon's ticket, and the family had also reportedly picked up the tab for Neville's flight to Tortola, and her expenses while on the island.

The Labrador women also made arrangements when it came to their own accommodations. Barbara had agreed to be interviewed—by select members of the media. The producers of the CBS program *48 Hours* intended to dedicate an entire show to the presentation of her son's case.

William's mother said that she knew the executive producer, who lived only a few miles away from her home in Long Island, and felt confident that the popular news program would portray her son in a favorable light.

It has been claimed she struck a deal that included her participation on the show. In exchange for her cooperation, the program agreed to foot the bill for her airfare, hotel accommodations, and meals while on the island. Mrs. Labrador allegedly refused to grant a similar interview to the producer of a British documentary being prepared on the case, telling the producer that she would not appear on the show unless she was paid for her interview. She had mounting legal bills and extensive travel expenses, and needed money to float her until her son's release, she told the producer.

Already, she said she had doled out $15,000 of the more than $100,000 owed in attorneys' fees. William had been hoping that Jeff Plante would make good on his promise to make a $25,000 donation to the William Labrador Defense Fund when Plante went to police with his allegations the previous summer.

William's sister Honey was a movie producer in Hollywood and was employed by singer Michael Bolton's production company, Passion Films. Before joining Bolton's company, the attractive woman with the short dark hair and glistening teeth had tried her hand at acting. Like Lois McMillen, Honey had landed several bit parts. But she ultimately decided she preferred to be behind the camera, and claimed to be quite successful as a producer in California.

Honey had convinced her mother that she knew the movie industry, and could get a film produced on her brother's case. She even went to her boss and asked if he could help her brother in his plight. Bolton was reportedly a good friend of Hillary Clinton and it has been rumored that the singer asked the New York senator to look into the matter on Honey's behalf.

The Labrador women were in for a disappointment when the *48 Hours* segment would air in the United States on May 24, 2001, just three weeks after her brother's case had been decided by a jury. The broadcast would not be at all what they had expected. In fact, an online poll after the broadcast found that more than 70% of the viewers felt that William and the others were guilty. William had been featured on the segment in an on-camera interview from Her Majesty's Prison.

When Shannon arrived at the Prospect Reef hotel on May 3, she quickly learned about the judge's dismissal of the charges against the three other men standing trial with Barbara's son. She was exhausted after taking a series of connecting flights from Alabama to Tortola. Her luggage was chock-full of paperwork about Jeff Plante—paperwork the defense could use to discredit the con man. All she wanted to do was check into her room and ask Barbara Labrador one question: Was William really innocent?

The front desk had given her the room next to Barbara's. When Shannon stepped out onto the terrace to survey the view, she could hear the Long Island woman talking on the phone to a reporter. Shannon had expected a warm welcome from Mrs. Labrador—after all, she'd invested substantial time and effort to get to Tortola with all her paperwork. But their first meeting was a big disappointment. She felt that Barbara Labrador was dismissive, and tersely signaled that Shannon should be in contact with the lawyer in the case. Before turning away to complete her phone call, Barbara instructed her to join the group—and another defense witness who had flown in from the States to testify on William's behalf—for a dinner at the hotel's waterside restaurant.

But Shannon was in no mood to socialize, especially after she received an anonymous phone call within hours of arriving at the hotel. She recalled that when she picked up the receiver, she'd heard a man's voice on the other end. He asked her to identify herself, and then quickly hung up. Dialing the front desk, Shannon alerted the clerk on duty to the strange call, and then asked if she could please change her room. Next, she telephoned Mrs. Labrador to tell her what had happened. A hotel assistant escorted her to another

accommodation, and Shannon said she tried her best to settle down and relax.

Shannon claimed that Barbara Labrador was more concerned with her testimony about Jeffery Plante than addressing other questions Shannon claimed she raised about
William's innocence. Ultimately Shannon was not called
upon to testify.

William Labrador's defense team was confident that the
judge's decision to dismiss charges against Spicer and the
others was a good indication that Labrador, too, would soon
be free. Yet members of the jury noted that William's three
friends did not stick around to provide moral support. They
were on their way home to the United States to reunite with
their friends and family.

In response to questions from his lawyer, Labrador denied
any involvement in Lois' murder and testified that he'd had
no reason to harm her. During his five hours on the stand, he
even told the court that Lois had been driving a different
vehicle, and not the one police found at the ferry dock, when
she drove him and his friends around the island in the days
before her murder. He also testified to his desire to separate
from his friends, as his cellmate had told police.

"Mr. Plante said that you were talking to him about separation," William's lawyer, Richard Hector, asked his client.
"Do you remember his evidence in that regard?"

"Yes, I do," William answered.

"Did you speak to him about separation, and what did
you speak to him about separation?" the attorney continued.

"Yes . . . I figured since, on the evening of the fourteenth of January where I had been dropped off at Sebastian's and I had gone home and went to bed, for myself I
could be held accountable for my whereabouts and in turn
separation for me seemed the proper course of action,"
Labrador said.

"I see," said Hector, pausing to formulate his next question. "There was some talk about, you were heard to say,

Mr. Benedetto was heard to say you owed his father three hundred and fifty thousand dollars. First of all, did Alex Benedetto tell you anything about that?"

"Alexander would have made that statement, yes," William admitted under oath.

"Did you owe Victor Benedetto any money?"

"No, I did not."

William's statement contradicted Alex's assertion that Labrador was responsible for half the money his father had loaned them to start their business, Bella Management.

". . . Mr. Plante also said that Benedetto had said that you had the girl up to the house that night, all night. . . . First of all, did Benedetto make any such statement?"

"No, he did not."

"You also heard Mr. Plante say that he heard Evan George say that you had been, on the morning of the fifteenth, lying on your bed with wet shoes, awake. . . . What is your comment about that? What was your position on the early morning of the fifteenth?" he said, referring to the day after the murder was committed.

"I was sleeping."

William next testified that the cut that Jacob George had seen on his nose was a fever blister from too much "Tortolan sun." And he pointed to photographs that had been tendered into evidence by the defense from the Fuji camera that police had taken from Zebra House during their search. The photos, taken by Alex and William, showed the four men on the hike they said they had taken on the Friday that Lois McMillen was murdered. There were several photos of Alex on the roll, but none that showed the areas of his body where he had sustained scratches as a result of a fall he said he had taken during the hike.

One shot was of William, Evan, and Michael posing in front of an estate in Belmont. In the background was a Club Med cruise ship that William insisted only visited the island on Fridays. Labrador pointed out the "sun blister" on his nose. "That injury, and for the jury, as you see, on my lower lip, it would be a fever blister from too much Tortolan sun," the Southampton man said. He reasoned that, since Evan had arrived that previous Wednesday, the photos could only have been taken on the afternoon of the 14, well before Lois McMillen was murdered. Another photo showed William, Michael and Alex pointing to a sign posted at the base of the driveway to the Conaught Estate. PRIVATE, NO TRESPASSING it read. A final photograph featured a West End location called Gun Point in Smuggler's Cove, and showed seawater rushing through a cave-like rock formation.

"The photo where you and Benedetto and Spicer are pointing to the private driveway, what shoes are you wearing?"

"My Adidas aqua sport hiking shoes," Labrador replied.

"And were those shoes taken by the police?"

"Yes, they were. They were."

During his testimony, William also responded to questions about his business involvement with Jeff Plante. He told the court about the power of attorney that Plante had given to his mother, Barbara, so that she could handle his affairs in Texas concerning his divorce from Shannon. William testified that it also enabled her "to assist in the process of wiring money from his account in the Cayman Islands not only to my defense fund, but also for his own use."

"In March, did anything happen which was significant to you and to Mr. Plante?" Hector asked the deeply tanned man in the witness box.

"Yes."

"Could you tell this court what that was?"

"Yes," William began obligingly. "During the course of those two months prior to the twenty-third of March, he was assisting me obviously with my Web site and obviously I was assisting him, me and my mother, with his Dallas proceedings, and in *The BVI Beacon* of which we would share, actually the wing would share, in reading, because we only got one paper up there, so each cell will go through the reading. There was a police brief concerning his status with his case here. And in that it had mentioned the possibility of extradition back to Texas."

"Who being extradited?" Hector posed.

"Mr. Plante being extradited. . . . At that very point, Mr. Plante became very concerned and actually with that article coming out on the twenty-third . . . he wanted me to assist him in pursuing some avenues to not only Immigration, but him avoiding deportation."

Mr. Hector was working to establish, as the defense had alleged throughout the case, that it was this information about Plante's possible extradition to the States and a lengthy prison sentence for his parole violation that had prompted the con man to "fabricate" the alleged confession by William Labrador.

Under cross-examination by the Crown's lead prosecutor, however, Labrador did not hold up as well as he had during the morning session with his lawyer. Theodore Guerra pressed him about his statement to police, in which he told officers that he was an investment banker.

In response to questions, William listed a number of occupations, ranging from businessman to model manager. At one point, he announced that he was self-employed as a financial manager and consultant. Again, the prosecutor hammered at him to list his credentials to the court. He insisted that the Long Island man did not hold a license and had not taken any test to qualify him to work in the field to which he was claiming, and that he was not, and never was, qualified to practice such a profession.

Labrador also testified under oath that he was in fact aware that Alex Benedetto had had an intimate relationship with Lois McMillen in 1997. His testimony was startling, in light of the fact that he had told police in his official statement the day after the murder that he had no knowledge that any of the men from Zebra House had had an intimate relationship with the deceased.

On the stand, Labrador said that it was "last year" that he had learned about Benedetto's relationship with Lois, after he and the others had run into her on the twelfth or thirteenth of January 2000.

"And you knew that on the fourteenth of January, because

having been told that by Benedetto on the thirteenth, you
knew that on the fourteenth of January 2000?" Guerra asked
the witness.

"Correct," Labrador replied.

"You knew that on the fifteenth of January 2000?"

"Yes."

"But on the sixteenth of January 2000, you gave a statement to the police?" the prosecutor asked.

"Correct."

". . . Did you tell the police in your statement, 'to my
knowledge, none of the guys ever had or was having an intimate relationship with Miss Livingston'?" Guerra asked
William Labrador, having just produced his original police
statement in court.

"Yes," William replied.

"You told the police that?"

"Yes. Intimate. Intimate."

"So you said Alex told you that he was having a relationship with Miss McMillen?"

"That he had had a relationship with Miss McMillen, yes."

"You also answered to me that you said Alex told you
that he had an intimate relationship with Miss McMillen."

"He had a relationship."

"You will answer my question," Guerra snapped.

". . . Alexander had an intimate relationship with Miss
McMillen," William responded.

"We're talking about intimate?" the prosecutor asked
Labrador.

"I was not aware of an intimate relationship with
Miss McMillen and Mr. Benedetto," the Long Island man
answered.

"If you said that he told you that he had an intimate relationship with Miss McMillen, that would not be true? Will
you answer the question?"

"I did not say that he had an intimate relationship. They
had a relationship."

"Thank you. I'll pass on," the gray-haired Guerra said
with exasperation in his voice.

Pressed about his conversation with Mr. Plante while at Her Majesty's Prison, William Labrador next told the court that "separation from the others" was a concern he raised with his cellmate.

"What separation did you want from the others?"

"I figured since I was dropped off from Sebastian's at eleven twenty, I could be accountable for my whereabouts and I felt the separation procedure would be the best to take."

"Yes. You did not want to be lumped with the other three?"

"I couldn't be held responsible," Labrador responded.

"No, I'm asking you, you did not want to be lumped with the other three?" the attorney asked.

"No. No, sir."

". . . You were concerned with protecting yourself?" the Senior Counsel asked.

"Of course."

". . . And you told Plante that you were not concerned about the others. You were number one and you're taking care of you?"

". . . I was accountable for myself," Labrador replied, his eyes darting from the prosecutor to the jury to the ground. "In turn, I had separated myself from the others. Regardless of what their concern was for the situation, my concern was for myself."

At one point, he appeared annoyed with Guerra's line of questioning, and responded to the prosecutor with a question of his own, to which Guerra snapped, "You will not ask me any questions. You will just answer me when I ask you questions."

"Yes, sir." William shrank back on the stand. His hands folded behind his back, he continually shifted his position, rocking back and forth in the witness box as he looked down at the ground, and then back at Theodore Guerra, who continued his probe.

The prosecutor's inquiry next shifted to the testimony given by prosecution witness Jeffrey Simms, the Coast

Guard officer who had testified to hearing Michael Spicer say, "we have to meet someone on the other side" on the night of Lois' murder.

Guerra began by asking Labrador, "Simms said that Spicer said they had to meet someone on the other side. Is that true?"

"The other side of Quito's? The other side to West End?" William replied with more questions for the prosecutor.

"Look, Mr. Labrador, just answer my question," the gray-haired counselor admonished.

". . . Mr. Spicer said we had to meet someone on the other side," William agreed.

"Was that true?"

"Yes."

"And you all went to the other side?" the prosecutor asked, motioning in the direction of the island's West End.

"First we went to the ATM machine."

"Was that on the other side?" the prosecutor continued.

"The ATM machine was in Soper's Hole, so we went to it."

"Standing with your back to the hill when you are in Zebra House and you point into the hill, that would be the direction of Soper's Hole?" Guerra asked, pointing to what would be the island's West End.

"Correct. Actually, to be exact, the direction close to Big Ben's Superette," William responded, referring to a supermarket in the same general area. When pressed further, William told the prosecutor that the men's meeting on "the other side" was with "nobody I knew of."

On Friday, it was more of the same—intense questioning by the prosecutor and a steady stream of confusing and often argumentative responses from the witness in the box. William's mother and sister looked on from the second row of the courtroom as William admitted to the senior counselor that he had in fact advised Michael not to phone the McMillens on the morning their daughter's body had been found on the beach.

"I told him that he should not interfere in a criminal investigation by the police and it was best not to call the McMillens," the strapping man in the double-breasted suit told the jury.

"No one up to that time had informed you of the manner in which she had died," the white-haired prosecutor in the black robe declared in a loud voice. "I put it to you that the reason why you said it was a criminal investigation is because you knew what you had done to Ms. McMillen."

"No, sir," William replied.

Later in the day, Labrador would be asked a question about the same topic—this time by a member of the jury.

"Did the police on their first visit to the Zebra House indicate to you that you were a suspect in the death of Lois McMillen?" the juror asked Labrador.

"No, not at the first visit."

"Can you explain why then, why did you deter Spicer from calling the McMillens to express sympathy?"

"Well, he wasn't calling to express sympathy. He wanted to contact the McMillens not knowing whether the McMillens had been contacted. There was no reason for Michael to interfere in that," Labrador explained.

Before lunch, William shrugged off the prosecutor's questions about his involvement in the "concerted media effort" in the United States to bring his case into the headlines. He denied any direct role in the campaign, and said that he was unaware "what *they* were doing in New York."

"Now, tell me something," Guerra next asked Labrador. "I understand you to be referring to Lois McMillen as Lois Livingston."

"That is her middle name," William responded.

"Is that the name she was referred to in modeling circles?"

"I don't know, sir," William replied. "I have no idea about her modeling career."

". . . And you have been in the industry for quite a while?"

"Yes, sir." William was compliant.

"Now you were involved in the following modeling agencies?" the prosecutor began. "Woman Direct."

"Yes, sir."

"Whom were you involved with in Woman Direct?" the attorney asked.

"I can't recall," William replied.

"How long ago was it that you were involved in Woman Direct?"

"It would have been during the Woman Management years, so between '90 and '95 I believe, sir," William replied.

"Woman Direct was a different organization to Woman Management?"

"Yes, sir," the witness said.

"Whom were you involved with in Woman Management?"

"That is confidential, sir."

"Will you answer the question?" Guerra asked.

Hector objected to the line of questioning, but the judge ruled that Guerra could proceed. Labrador again refused to reveal anything about his employers or detail the reasons why he left another of the companies he had worked for, Women Model Management.

"That's all covered by confidentiality agreements," he said time and again in response to a series of questions about his departure from the firm.

"You refuse to answer the question?" the prosecutor demanded.

"It falls under a confidentiality agreement, so I cannot discuss that."

"You were then involved in the I Group?"

"Yes, sir," William replied.

"With whom were you involved with that?"

"That falls under a confidentiality agreement."

"Do you refuse to answer my question?" Guerra cracked, as jurors looked on in disbelief. ". . . When did you sever your ties with Woman Direct?"

"All of that falls under a confidentiality agreement, sir."

"All right. Let me ask you, why did you sever your ties?"

"All that falls under a confidentiality agreement, sir."

William Labrador's responses were clearly beginning to frustrate the prosecutor and others in the courtroom. The exchange would also raise questions in the minds of jurors as to what this witness might be hiding from them.

After lunch, Guerra picked up the case with more questions about Labrador's employment. The air in the stark white courtroom was stagnant; the central air-conditioning had suddenly stopped working and as the day wore on, the temperature inside the second-floor room continued to rise. Officials turned off the overhead lights and swung open the double doors in an attempt to keep the room cool and help circulate the humid, muggy air. Guards in uniforms were posted as a measure of security.

After responding to nearly nine hours of questioning from attorneys over two days, it was the jury's turn to question a weary, sweating William Labrador in greater detail.

"Can you think of any reason, any reason at all, why Mr. Plante would make accusations against you?" one of the nine members asked the accused.

"The only incident that would come to mind would be the fact that extradition proceedings which was made aware in the *Beacon,* the twenty-third March issue, not necessarily to the public, but to the wing up there, because nobody did know that he was going to be extradited, and it was not for me to determine why but, from that stage moving forward, different personalities started to kick in."

"So, in other words, you are saying because he was being extradited, that is why he talked against you? That is what you are saying?"

"Yes," William Labrador responded.

"Why were you dropped off at Sebastian's when you were the one in a hurry to leave the house to go out?" another juror asked.

"I was too tired from hiking during the day and I said that to Mr. George. I felt that I wanted to go home." The dark-haired man held his hands clenched behind his back, and continued to bow forward and then stand fully erect as he addressed the court.

"If you were so tired, why didn't you ask the cab driver to drop you at the Zebra House?" the juror asked.

"To save time," Labrador responded. "The others managed to get to Quito's . . ."

Throughout his testimony, William Labrador continued to refer to the deceased as Lois Livingston, the stage name she used for her acting and modeling career. The reference seemed odd, especially since he'd testified to having only seen her once during the vacation—on the Thursday before her murder—at Pusser's in Soper's Hole where they had shared a plate of chicken wings and some wine with Michael and Evan. He testified that he had only met her once before, on the night that he and Alex met her at Bomba's Shack in 1997. What made William's repeated references even more curious was that neither Michael nor Alex—who both admitted to knowing Lois—referred to Lois by her stage name, ruling out the possibility that he had been introduced to her by one of them using her middle name. Could it be that William knew Lois during her days as a model, when she used Livingston as her stage name?

The peculiarity would not be lost on the judge, who asked William about it at the close of the jury's examination.

"Mr. Labrador, throughout your statements, you have been referring to the deceased lady as 'Miss Livingston,'" Judge Benjamin asked the accused. "Why is that so?"

"Just a middle name, sir," William Labrador replied. "Lois Livingston as opposed to saying Lois McMillen Livingston."

William's response did little to clarify the oddity for the judge or others in the courtroom.

Mr. Hector had his own frustrations. He was upset at the way his client had behaved on the stand. Racing up to the window of the car that was being driven by journalist John Springer, Hector confronted William's mother, who was in the passenger seat waiting to be taken to the Prospect Reef. The lawyer wanted to know why William had refused to answer questions put to him about his past employment. According to the reporter, Barbara Labrador defended her son, telling the attorney that *he* was the lawyer and that *he* should have better prepared William to take the stand.

Court officials and others present at the trial said in interviews that it became clear to them that the case turned after the three defendants had been released and Labrador was left as the only man facing charges. It suddenly became easier to examine the prosecution's case against Labrador and determine his guilt or innocence. At that point, the case became largely focused on the testimony of just two individuals—Jeffrey Plante and William Labrador. And while few people in the courtroom found Plante a trustworthy character, what observers believe ultimately swayed the jury was Labrador's own testimony on the stand, including Labrador's refusal to answer even simple questions about his job history and his vague responses to other questions.

Next it would be Jeffrey Plante's former parole officer Tisha Neville's turn to take the stand. But her testimony would have to wait until Monday as lawyers from both sides argued as to precisely what she would be permitted to testify to.

Meanwhile, police had picked up Plante's tenth wife over the weekend for passing bad checks. Shannon's arrest stemmed from checks she had written against the couple's joint account during her previous visit to Tortola. She insisted her arrest had been perfectly orchestrated to coincide with her anticipated testimony in the murder case —and to prevent her from taking the stand.

Shannon claimed that police had no way of knowing that she did not intend to testify, and that she had actually been preparing to leave the island when she was brought to headquarters in Road Town on the charge of passing a bad check for $300. Much to her dismay, her ex-husband was occupying a cell in the same filthy locked unit where she was about to be detained.

Throughout the day, Jeff Plante shouted taunts at her from his unit, she recalled. While she could not see him from her cell, the sound of his voice was almost too much to bear. She had deep disdain for the man she claims stole her heart and her money. Since returning to the States in October of 2000, she had contacted several of Jeff's former wives and had heard their equally hair-raising stories of his trickery. Now, as she sat in the cell at the Road Town police station, she felt that she had become a victim once again, this time for trying to do a nice thing for another alleged victim of her con-man ex-husband.

"Ha, ha, ha. What goes around comes around, huh, baby?" Jeff derisively yelled from his cell.

Worse still, she recalled that no one from the Labrador camp came to the jail to see her. She said that Honey did alert William's lawyer, Mr. Hector, to her situation, and that the attorney agreed to hold her money while she tried to find an attorney to take her case. It seemed that every lawyer on the island had a conflict of interest, since most were somehow linked to the McMillen case.

Two days after her arrest, Shannon was brought before a magistrate, where she was formally charged with passing six bad checks totaling less than $600. She said she offered to make restitution, but was taken instead to Her Majesty's Prison where she came face-to-face with William Labrador for the first time.

Through an open window in her cell, she spoke briefly with the Southampton man, who was in the prison yard for exercise. As she ranted about her innocence and about her hate for Jeff Plante, she expected William to join in. She was surprised when he lowered his head, and in a low voice said, "Well, you know how Jeff can twist the truth." He then offered to give her some telephone numbers for the American Embassy before excusing himself, saying that he had to go and pack.

Shannon recalled that later that day, William's mother and sister arrived at the prison with an empty suitcase for William. They, too, were confident he would be coming home.

Plante's parole officer took the stand on Monday, the final witness before the defense rested its case. Tisha Neville told the court that the Texas man under her supervision had lied about looking for work and other such things while she was his parole officer. She also produced a report that she had obtained from authorities in Hawaii where he had testified as a jailhouse informant in a murder in 1995. She had gotten hold of the report to illustrate the similarities in his statements in that case and the one she was now participating in.

The prosecution worked to discredit Neville as a witness, asking if she had been compensated for her testimony, and then pointing out that the Labradors had paid for her expenses on the island by picking up the cost of her flight and accommodations. They also found certain discrepancies with what Neville, who was now a homemaker after having left her job with the Board of Prisons, said on the stand. For one, it became clear that she had not been granted permission by her former superior at the Board of Prisons to testify in the case. And for another, the Crown suggested that she had obtained a case report from Hawaii through dubious means, although the judge had already ruled that she would not be permitted to testify about the case in which Plante had participated in Hawaii. Under cross-examination from Guerra, Neville admitted that Plante had filed an application to have her removed as his parole supervisor. He suggested that she might be holding a grudge.

As the jury began its deliberations, the Labrador family was confident that William would soon be on his way back to New York. Shannon was at the prison listening to the verdict being delivered over the radio that evening with other female inmates in the remand wing. She recalled the screams and cries from the Women's Unit when the announcement was made at eight fifteen p.m. on May 10.

The jurors had first appeared in chambers after deliberating only a few hours to alert the judge that they could not reach a unanimous verdict—they were split seven to two. But Benjamin admonished them to go back and try again. Later, the nine-member panel re-emerged to say they had come to a decision.

William appeared unsteady, his body trembling as he stood before the court to learn his fate. He watched as the nine members of the jury rose before him to deliver their verdict.

"Guilty!"

The declaration was met by a blaring, guttural scream from Barbara Labrador, who doubled over in court and then began shouting at the McMillens.

"You've done your daughter a great disservice!" she cried. "The person who did this to her is still out there." Inching toward Russell McMillen, Barbara continued to shout and waved her fist in the stunned man's face, according to McMillen. Her daughter Honey, following closely behind her mother, yelled angry accusations at a visibly shaken Jo McMillen.

In an effort to defuse the situation, Judge Benjamin quickly imposed sentence on a stunned and shaking William Labrador—he was to remain incarcerated at Her Majesty's Prison for the remainder of his natural life with no chance of parole. "Take him away immediately," the judge barked from his perch on the bench.

As armed police officers in paramilitary garb escorted the van transporting a handcuffed William Labrador back to prison, Barbara Labrador lingered in the courtroom with Honey.

Police Commissioner Vernon Malone later said in an interview that he actually wanted to have Labrador's sister arrested for her outburst, but other officials advised against that. Instead, police posted round-the-clock uniformed officers outside the home of the McMillens.

"Members of the drug squad escorted us home and searched the villa before we were permitted inside," recalled Mrs. McMillen. "They were around our villa all night long."

While the guilty verdict gave the couple a sense of peace that justice had been served, it did little to answer questions they had about why William Labrador might have killed their daughter.

"I believe Labrador did not set out to kill Lois that night when he went out," Mrs. McMillen later speculated. "I think they were arguing over something and things got heated and he lost his temper."

The "something" that Mrs. McMillen was referring to remains a mystery to her—Lois' mother speculated that they could have been arguing over money, "or he could have asked her to do something she did not want to do. Maybe he wanted her to drive him somewhere, or he wanted to go and buy drugs, or he wanted her to take drugs. I just don't know.

"I do know that she was very much against drugs," Mrs. McMillen said. "Lois was also very naïve, and she might have threatened to go to the police, not realizing that by saying that, she was putting herself in danger."

To remember Lois, the couple's friends took up a collection and purchased a Hong Kong orchid tree that they planted in the island's Botanical Garden with a plaque dedicated to Lois McMillen.

"Lois' death hasn't soured us on Tortola," Lois' mother said in an interview at the family's villa in Belmont Grove. "She loved it here. To her, Tortola was heaven on earth."

CHAPTER THIRTY-FIVE

Free in Paradise

About one hundred residents had gathered outside the court-house to hear the verdict and thousands more were glued to their radios to learn the outcome of the sensational trial that had put "Nature's Little Secret," as the BVI bills its cluster of islands, on the international radar screen.

It had taken the two men and seven women of the jury seven and a half hours to deliberate the case and ultimately find William Labrador guilty of murder. They had listened to the closing arguments of Mr. Hector and Mr. Guerra, and then the judge's four-hour charge.

After deliberating for nearly five hours, jurors had come to the judge to say that they were deadlocked seven to two, and could not reach a unanimous finding. The Honorable Justice Kenneth Benjamin acknowledged that the trial had stretched out over many weeks, and requested that the jurors go back and try again to come to a collective decision in the case. At the request of the nine-person panel, the judge read back a portion of the testimony that had been given by Plante.

Judge Benjamin had instructed the panelists to look closely at the evidence. He explained that if they did not believe the testimony that was presented by Jeffrey Plante, it was their task to review the evidence presented by the Crown and determine if they could reach a verdict beyond a reasonable doubt. Benjamin also advised the group that they should examine the alleged lies of both men, not just Jeffrey Plante. He focused their attention on Labrador's testimony about his knowledge of an "intimate" relationship between his friend Alexander Benedetto and the deceased. Under oath, the Southampton man testified that he became aware of that aspect of the relationship two days before Lois was murdered. But he then admitted in court that the day after her murder, he told police in his official statement that he had no knowledge of any intimate relationship between Lois and any of the men staying at Zebra House.

But Judge Benjamin's failure to "give an express warning to the jury to regard Plante's evidence with caution" would later have an impact on appeals in the case.

Upon returning to Her Majesty's Prison after learning the verdict, William Labrador was reportedly melancholy. Shannon, Jeff Plante's ex-wife, was at the prison the night that Labrador's verdict was returned and recalled that he said little, but remained optimistic about his situation.

"Look around, the sea, the climate. It's paradise here," William told her.

Meanwhile, the following day, his mother filed a petition for an appeal of the jury's verdict. After the verdict had been read in court, Barbara Labrador had jumped into the waiting van hired by the CBS crew and was taken to the prison to be with her son. As William's mother reached for the door handle, she reportedly shouted out to reporters, "They bought this conviction. This is a world of corruption."

The jury verdict would be just one in a series of blows to the Labrador camp. In 2001, the three judges who sat on the Eastern Caribbean Court of Appeal denied William Labrador's appeal.

"Plante's vivid and unequivocal admission of guilt by Labrador was supported with circumstantial evidence presented by other witnesses," wrote Justice Satrohan Signh of Guyana. "The jury heard all the evidence, saw the witnesses and came to their conclusion, obviously accepting the testimony of Plante."

The three-judge panel also refused to admit items of fresh

evidence being offered by the defense in order to reinforce Labrador's argument about the unreliability of Plante's testimony. Among the items were a notarized declaration by a court reporter in Hawaii verifying the transcript of the trial at which Plante had given evidence of a confession allegedly made by a fellow prisoner, a statement from the Deputy Superintendent at Her Majesty's Prison stating that prison records did not indicate the finding of a knife in Labrador's cell as Plante had testified at trial, and a statement from the prosecutor at the Hawaii trial, giving as his reason for not calling Plante as a witness at the retrial in Hawaii that he had not found Plante to be a credible witness. Also denied by the appeals court was a statement from a Roman Catholic priest who reported that he had first met Labrador at Her Majesty's Prison in January of 2000. Since Labrador had already met the priest in January, the statement contradicted Plante's testimony that at the time of Labrador's alleged confession in April of 2000, the Texas man had offered to introduce Labrador to this priest. The judges' decision not to admit these items would later be called into question by London's highest court.

The three judges also overturned Judge Benjamin's dismissal of murder charges against Alex Benedetto. The appeals court held that Plante's testimony about conversations involving Benedetto that he claimed to have overheard while jailed at Her Majesty's Prison constituted sufficient evidence for the case to be presented to a jury for its verdict.

Benedetto, who opted not to return to Tortola after the ruling, had technically been a fugitive from Tortolan authorities since that time. Instead, on the day that he was supposed to be appearing before a Magistrate in Tortola to answer charges in connection with the case, he was in a CNN studio taping an interview with Larry King that aired several days later. His appearance and what he said during the hour-long program infuriated the McMillens and authorities on Tortola. The show's producers denied the government's subsequent request for equal time.

In February of 2003, Labrador's appeal went to London's

Privy Council, the final court of appeals for British Territories and former British colonies. On April 7, 2003, the British court quashed the conviction of William Labrador on the grounds it was based on the unreliable testimony of a jailhouse informant—and William Labrador walked out of Her Majesty's Prison a free man.

"It would be hard to imagine a witness who was less deserving of belief than Jeffrey Plante," the Council wrote. "Even those facts about his background which he was prepared to admit to while he was giving his evidence were more than enough to show that he was not to be trusted.

"He had numerous convictions for theft, cheque fraud, and other crimes of dishonesty. They had culminated in a conviction for theft in Texas, for which he had been sentenced to 45 years imprisonment. He admitted to two violations of parole, for the first of which he had been returned to prison to serve a further period of custody. He also admitted to pleading guilty to overstaying the time allowed to him in BVI in breach of the immigration rules. It was plain that the reason for this was his desire to avoid being dealt with by the authorities in Texas for his second parole violation.

"He was a thief and he was a liar. The fact that he had been married ten times added further weight to the argument that he was utterly cynical in his dealings with others, and totally unscrupulous."

The Council ruled that the lower court had erred by not informing jurors that Plante had reason to benefit from his testimony against Labrador.

"The omission of the necessary steps from the summing up was in itself such a fundamental defect that on this ground alone Labrador's appeal must be allowed and this conviction quashed on the ground that it is unsafe," the panel ruled.

In further comments on Plante's evidence, the council wrote, "There is no doubt that by 19 April 2000 when Labrador was alleged to have made his confession it was common knowledge that the deceased had met her death in tragic circumstances and where the body had been found.

There was evidence at the trial that the incident had been reported in the press and that Plante had read about it. But the alleged confession contained some elements, which at first sight were not previously known to the witness and might have been known only to the perpetrator.

"Labrador is alleged to have said that he dragged the deceased into the water, put his foot on the back of her neck and drowned her. He is also alleged to have said that it took him about 45 minutes to get from the ferry landing where the car was left to Mr. Spicer's house.

"The trial judge told the jury that the pathologist had not yet reached the conclusion that the cause of death was drowning by the date when the confession was alleged to have been made. He was wrong about this, as Dr. Landron had concluded as a result of his post mortem examination on 18 January 2000 that his findings were consistent with death by drowning and this had been announced by the police press officer and given extensive press coverage. This was, in the circumstances, a serious misdirection as its effect was to suggest that there was an element of special knowledge which the jury would be entitled to take into account in their assessment of whether or not the confession was genuine.

"No attempt was made at the trial to show that by the time when the confession was made the fact that the deceased had been drowned had already been reported in the newspapers. Plante claimed that he did not know that the deceased had met her death by drowning before he gave his statement to police. He sought to evade the issue by saying that, while he had seen newspaper articles, he was not familiar with everything that had been published."

The Council also questioned the Court of Appeal's unwillingness to acknowledge Labrador's attempt to enter into the record copies of various newspaper articles, including one which appeared in the *BVI Beacon* on March 16, 2000, stating that Lois McMillen had died of unnatural causes related to drowning. Labrador's attorneys were trying to show that Plante could have learned of McMillen's death from the newspaper article.

"Then there is the detail which Labrador is alleged to have mentioned, that he put his foot on the back of the deceased's neck as he drowned her," the Council wrote in its decision. "The prosecution did not attempt to relate this to any of the findings at the post mortem of the deceased's injuries. No mention was made of any bruising to the back of her neck. But there was mention of bruising at the base and anterior side of the neck.

"This suggests that the pressure was applied to her neck from the front and not the back, and that the detail which Labrador is alleged to have given was inaccurate.

"Dr. Landron said in cross-examination that there were no injuries to the neck to indicate that the deceased had been drowned by putting a foot on the back of her neck. There was also a significant omission from what Labrador is alleged to have said.

"Nothing in the alleged confession can be said therefore to reveal special knowledge of facts which Plante could have learned about only from the perpetrator," they concluded. The Council further discredited Plante's testimony by citing his initial failure to recall the evidence he gave against his fellow prisoner in Hawaii, his lies about his past convictions, and his claims that he had been given permission by his parole officer to leave Texas in 1999 to visit the BVI.

The Privy Council ultimately concluded that "no value whatever can be attached to Plante's evidence." Apart from Plante's testimony, the Privy Council decided, there was no other evidence that could support Labrador's conviction or a retrial of any of the defendants. The Council also ruled that the acquittal of Alexander Benedetto would be reinstated. The trial judge was "right" to throw out the case against him, the Council ruled.

After serving 1,179 days of a life sentence for murder, William Labrador walked out of Her Majesty's Prison a free man and into the open arms of his mother. Mrs. Labrador had flown to Tortola to be near her son when the decision was delivered.

"I can't tell you how overjoyed I am," Barbara Labrador

told a reporter for the *New York Post*. "This is a miracle."

She blamed "abuse of prosecution" for what she said was a shoddy investigation and an unfair trial. "They picked up four Americans and never did any investigation," Barbara Labrador said. "All of a sudden, the system gets ahold of you and wrings you dry."

William told the *Post* that he had done his time in a jail cell that had ocean views, a DVD player, books, and six pet cats to keep him company.

He said he spent most of his time in incarceration working on his computer, writing court appeals and applications for his fellow inmates, and enlarging their family photos. As part of a prison work program, he tended a small garden on a hillside just above one of the prison buildings. But despite his rather comfortable accommodations in Tortola's Balsam Ghut Prison, Labrador was relishing his freedom.

"It's a great sense of relief. I took a jump in the ocean and I'm eating a yogurt," Labrador said. The Southampton man said he kept a journal in jail and intended to write a book about his ordeal.

"I came out of it fifteen years younger and I could have come out of it thirty years older," Labrador said. "In an idyllic setting like this, something like this should never have happened. All through this ordeal, my prayers were with her [Lois]."

After clearing out his cell and finishing up paperwork, Labrador flew back to New York to spend the next six months relaxing at his Southampton home with his family and friends.

"For the first time, I can walk outside without waiting for someone to turn the key," William Labrador told the *Post* by phone from the Lambert Beach Hotel the following morning.

But not everybody was pleased with the Privy Council's decision. In an interview, the McMillens said they were "very deeply disappointed."

"We had felt that justice had been served," Mrs. McMillen said. "There was just no question in our minds that they were responsible."

Ignoring her heart condition and a doctor's orders not to travel, Mrs. McMillen had gone to London in January to be at the hearing before the Privy Council.

"I wanted to be there for Lois," Jo McMillen explained. "It was important for Russ and me to have somebody there to represent our daughter."

Jo McMillen said that the acquittal of Labrador was a miscarriage of justice, and she would always believe that William Labrador murdered her daughter.

"We've done everything we could to get justice for Lois and we thought we did. So now we'll have to live with that."

EPILOGUE

After months of research, hundreds of interviews, and close scrutinizing of more than 2,000 pages of court documents and other materials, can I tell you with certainty who is responsible for killing Lois McMillen? No, I cannot.

We may never know exactly what happened that night. One thing seems evident: that William Labrador himself bears some of the responsibility for the Tortola jury's initial decision to convict. What appears to have hurt William Labrador in the courtroom was not the physical evidence that was presented or the testimony of the many witnesses called by the prosecutor. It was his own testimony. William Labrador displayed a mystifying unwillingness to answer even simple questions about his background and employment, skirted questions about who he had arranged to meet on the night of Lois' murder, and was seen as displaying a contempt for the island's justice system, prosecutors, and police alike. As one court official viewed the proceedings, it wasn't that the jury found Jeffrey Plante so believable, it was that they couldn't believe William Labrador.

Judge Benjamin had focused the jury's attention on Labrador's conflicting testimony about his knowledge of an "intimate" relationship between his friend Alexander Benedetto and the deceased. Another factor that could have contributed to the jury's decision was the confusion over

footwear that William said he was wearing on the night of
the murder. On the stand, he testified that the sneakers he
had turned over to Inspector Jacob George—and said he had
been wearing the previous evening—were not, in fact, the
shoes he had been wearing when he went out with his
friends on the night of Lois' murder. In court, Labrador testified that he was wearing another pair of sneakers—a pair
of Fila brand shoes—on the night that Lois McMillen was
killed. When asked why he did not tell police they had taken
the wrong shoes, he said that nobody had ever asked.

It seems likely that jurors reacted negatively to Labrador's
refusal to answer questions about his past business associations, and to his claim of being an investment banker. It's
also likely that jurors reacted to Prosecutor Theodore
Guerra's remarks about Labrador's lack of allegiance to his
childhood friend, Alex Benedetto. "We here in the Caribbean know what boyhood and girlhood friends mean to us,
especially when you are claiming that the four of you were
arrested for nothing," the prosecutor said. "You are in prison
for nothing, is it not the time when you would give, lend
your support to your boyhood friend?

". . . If there is no loyalty to a boyhood friend, how much
more would he not try, as he said he was trying, to save himself?"

London's Privy Council suggested that Mr. Guerra may
have gone too far. The Council faulted his remarks as "xeno-
phobic" and "inflammatory."

In a telephone interview some months after the trial, Alex
Benedetto expressed disappointment over Labrador's unwillingness to remain united in the men's defense of their innocence. He also rebutted several of the statements that Jeffrey
Plante had made to police and at trial.

In commenting on Plante's statements to police, Alex
confirmed that he and William *did* indeed have a heated
discussion over culpability while at Her Majesty's Prison—

but that it had nothing to do with Lois McMillen. The conversation was to determine who was responsible for paying back his father the money he had loaned them to start their model management business, he said. Alex said he felt that William, as president of the company, should be the one to take responsibility for repaying the loan, or at least a portion of it. He was angered that his friend and business partner was refusing to even entertain the idea of repaying the loan, and worse, that he had cut off all contact with Alex in prison.

When asked about Plante's testimony on the mock trials, Alex explained that he and William had decided to conduct mock trials as a way of "mocking" the officials on Tortola by play-acting the men's murder trial. He said they used the exercise to imagine what evidence the authorities would present. He admitted there was also a "sinister side" to the mock trials, and acknowledged that he and William—at first unsure of Evan George—wanted to use the forum as a way of determining how Evan would act, and what he would say, if the case went before a jury.

Since the trial, Evan George has avoided publicity and has rarely commented on the case. Since leaving Tortola, he has moved to San Francisco, where he's enrolled at a local college and is working to start a new life. In an e-mail, he wrote:

> I think it is good for other people to know what can happen when traveling to a place that seems very nearly America and uses American money but is not protected by our beloved Constitution.
>
> Of course, this experience on Tortola is not an issue for most people when traveling overseas, but the fact that it can happen indiscriminately to anyone is scary in and of itself. Especially when being an innocent person, you find it all the more frustrating that you cannot convey that to your captors in such a way that they believe, or are willing to acknowledge, your innocence, even if every rational

view of so-called evidence or circumstances on intensive examination point to no other interpretation except of your absolute innocence or knowledge of any crime.

It still often frustrates me to recall my Caribbean vacation because it was a real live nightmare that I, for sixteen months, could not awake from.

I have become a fairly private person who just wants to put these memories of captivity behind me. I also try to remember there is another victim in this tragedy who lost infinitely more than sixteen months of her life.

While being in no way responsible for what happened to her, I feel it is not fair to blame everyone and try to portray her or her family as culprits in this situation. Nor do I want to be seen as a victim craving pity or attention at the expense of anyone else's life. However, I do believe after a certain point I did become a victim of a corrupt system.

I have for the most part put this ordeal behind me. I am in college and will be transferring to a university in the fall. I have not yet declared my major but am leaning toward psychology.

I don't know if my life deserves too much sympathy, since most of the adversity I have encountered has been a direct result of poor choices I have made in my life. However, in the instance of Tortola, the only poor choices I could be accused of, in retrospect, is taking a vacation with people I didn't know well (excluding Michael of course) and not investigating my vacation destination. I hope one day I will be able to overcome all of the obstacles I have put in my life's way, such as dropping out of high school and deciding to be an independent individual too young. Now, I am no longer living for instant gratification, but have a clear established plan that includes college.

I like volunteering at the animal pound because

> the animals give an unconditional love and as I
> remember how I disliked being caged, I like rescu-
> ing and visiting them, for a time, so they are not
> always in their cages.

The day after the trial judge dismissed the case against
Michael Spicer, Alex Benedetto and Evan George, Michael
returned home to Charlottesville, Virginia. Soon after, the
three men headed to New York City, where they booked a
suite at New York's ritzy Plaza Hotel in May of 2001.
Charges had been dropped against the three of them and
they figured that it was only a matter of time before charges
were dropped against William, too. They wanted to be
together to celebrate William's anticipated release. Armed
with bottles of champagne, they waited anxiously for the
phone call from Tortola, telling them that William, too, had
been exonerated. They had even agreed to appear on a
national television program to talk about their ordeal.

News that the jury had found William guilty as charged
sent them into a tailspin, and they quickly cancelled their
television appearance.

As Labrador sat at Her Majesty's Prison awaiting his
appeal, Michael continued to proclaim his own innocence.
To prove that he had no involvement in Lois' murder, he
returned to Tortola in March 2002 to answer the then-
pending charge of perverting the court of justice after the
fact. Alex Benedetto chose not to accompany him after
learning that an appeals court had re-indicted him on the
charge of murder.

Michael's return to Tortola surprised court officials, who
did not expect either man to return to face the charges. Magistrate Gail Charles postponed Michael's case and issued a warrant for Alex's arrest. Both cases were postponed again
pending a ruling from the Privy Council. In May 2003, following the Privy Council's determination, the lower court finally
threw out all the remaining charges against Michael and
Alex.

In June of 2003, Michael said that he and his mother had

put Zebra House up for sale. It remains unclear if they will buy another vacation house in Tortola or not.

Spicer said that he intends to keep taking the Bar Exam until he passes. He then hopes to practice law. Like Alex, he, too, avoided commenting on William Labrador's behavior while the four men were being detained at Her Majesty's Prison. He did say, however, that William stopped talking to him shortly after they arrived at the facility at Balsam Ghut.

In an interview with a reporter from his hometown paper, upon his return to Charlottesville, Spicer fashioned himself a thirty-something cross between Thurston Howell III, the fictitious millionaire from the '60s sitcom *Gilligan's Island,* and journalist Hunter S. Thompson, the left-wing writer of the late '60s best known for his outspoken advocacy of illicit drugs. When asked about the characterization, he said that he was just being sarcastic.

In regard to the case, Michael Spicer said:

> I know every word is true in mine and Evan's state-
> ment and I believe the same for certainly Alex's
> and William's as well. We told the truth from the
> beginning and to the end. We respected the process
> out of respect for Lois. The other side told lies from
> the beginning and concluded their case with one of
> the most notorious liars in the world.

In an interview in Tortola before the Privy Council's ruling, Police Commissioner Vernon Malone of the Royal Virgin Islands Police Force said that he was "one hundred percent convinced of William Labrador's guilt" based upon evidence collected by his men. Malone has since retired from the force, after serving thirty years as an officer, the last seven in the role of commissioner.

The new police commissioner of the Royal Virgin Islands Police Force is Barry Webb, a British officer, and a former member of Scotland Yard. One of his roles with the force in the United Kingdom was as a member of the department's Murder Review Board. His specialty—reopening and solving crimes languishing in the department's "cold case" files.

The governor of the island, Frank Savage, has also retired from his post. At a farewell ceremony, he was lauded for his efforts while holding the two-year position in the BVI.

Terrence Williams continues to serve as Senior Crown Counsel in the BVI. He said he hopes to some day practice law in the UK or in Canada. "I have no second thoughts about bringing the case," Williams said in late 2002. "We had a good case against all of them. My only criticism is that they [the police] should have interrogated the men."

Deputy Commissioner John Johnston has since returned to his home in Scotland. Notwithstanding all the failures of physical proof in the laboratories and in the courtroom, Johnston maintains his belief that at least three of the men from Zebra House played a role in Lois' death.

Johnston maintains his belief that Lois McMillen was killed by William Labrador, either alone or acting in concert with Alex Benedetto. He said he also continues to believe that Michael Spicer went back to the beach at some point after the crime to see if Lois was really dead. He believes that it was Spicer who turned over the body, getting sand in his sneakers and blood on his shirt in the process.

Johnston theorized that Spicer was a law school graduate and someone who liked to "fix" things for his friends, and this was one of those cases in which he would want to find a "fix." Johnston argues that Spicer wouldn't have given much thought to disposing of the clothing that he wore that night because he did not participate in the actual murder and had no reason to think that there would be any links between him and the crime scene. The commander was not convinced of Evan George's participation and said it is quite possible that he played no role in the murder.

"Whilst the decision demonstrates the rigorous standards required within the criminal justice system pertaining to British Territories in the Caribbean to sustain a conviction, it does not in any way alter my personal opinion that all of the individuals arrested were responsible for the death of Lois

McMillen. Unfortunately the highest court of appeal decided that the strength of the evidence provided against them was insufficient. I am afraid my sympathies at this time lie with the McMillen family."

"I didn't go back to where the body was found, that's just not true," Michael Spicer said in response to questions about Johnston's theory of what occurred on the night of Lois' murder.

Michael has repeatedly denied any involvement in Lois McMillen's murder.

"I was not there that evening," Spicer said. "I was aware of Alex's whereabouts until dawn, we all [Michael, Alex and Evan] stayed up watching *Vertigo* and I could hear him knocking around in the living room until first light, and then I went to sleep."

Alex, too, insisted that he played no role in the former model's murder, and suspects that her killer is still at large. He insisted that he, Evan, and Michael were together that entire evening and they have witnesses to corroborate their story. Alex said he could not account for William Labrador's movements once William stepped out of the taxi in front of Sebastian's hotel that night. Nevertheless, he remains convinced that William is innocent.

After the trial, Alex Benedetto revealed in a telephone interview details of an alleged hour-long conversation he had with Lois McMillen at Bomba's Shack on the Wednesday before her murder. The publishing heir claimed that Lois told him that people on the island were being hostile toward her, and that she was concerned for her safety. Alex also said that Lois had revealed to him that she had solved a murder on the island, and that she was going to report her findings to police. Alex maintained that he had counseled Lois to go back to Connecticut if she felt that she was in danger. Lois reportedly wanted to stay on the island because her father was ill and she wanted to be by his side for what she feared might be his last holiday.

Furthermore, Alex also claimed to have had a "strange" encounter with Bomba Callwood, owner of Bomba's Shack, in the first days of his vacation on Tortola when he was at the beach adjacent to the bar surfing the waves. He indicated that he was surprised when Bomba recognized him from his previous visit, and even more taken aback when Bomba asked if Lois was coming down for the holidays. Alex said that he'd told the bar owner that he did not know if she intended to visit the island.

"She better not. She's not welcome here," is what Bomba allegedly said to him.

Alex also said that he had opted not to tell police about the matter prior to Lois' death because he had feared reprisal from the bar owner.

Later, Benedetto claimed that he did not want to get involved in Lois' business and so said nothing more about the conversation—even to his friends. When asked why he did not tell police about the exchange with Lois, or the alleged "veiled threat" from Bomba, he insisted that he did, in fact, tell police about Lois' fear for her safety. He claimed that he wanted them to include the information in his official deposition to police, but said that one of the officers taking his statement had discouraged him from doing so because the officer regarded the exchange as either unimportant or irrelevant.

Under cross-examination, defense counselors asked Sergeant Anderson Blackman if he recalled having a conversation with Alex Benedetto in which he was told about Lois McMillen's fear for her safety. Blackman said he "could not recall."

When asked about Alex's claims, Deputy Commissioner John Johnston said: "My recollection is that the first time Benedetto made the claim that Lois told him she feared for her life was at the trial. At the time we, me, Blackman and all others involved, were of the opinion that it was a red herring thrown in by Benedetto in the knowledge that it could not be proved or disproved even if the police denied he ever said it. Just another lie in a catalogue of lies put forward to sow doubt in the minds of the jury," said Johnston.

Michael Spicer also claimed that Lois had mentioned a

recent murder on Tortola during their outings to Road Town in the days before she was killed. He remembered that on the two nights that he and Evan had accompanied her to Road Town, she had pointed out the gas station where Jason Bally had been gunned down in October of 1999 and then announced, "That is where Jason Bally was murdered."

Bally was the young promising athlete from Trinidad who was shot and killed as he stood talking on a pay phone outside of a gas station along Drake's Highway. Police suspected that the thieves who had just burglarized the gas station killed him, fearing that Bally was calling cops to alert them to the heist.

The Bally murder occurred less than two miles from where Lois' body had been discovered in an area called Sea Cow Bay. In April of 2000, another man named Euan Watkins was brutally murdered, shot multiple times as he stood tending bar at the pub adjacent to his home in the same area.

Alex and William suspected that Lois' murder might somehow be linked to the other two murders in Sea Cow Bay—and speculated that she might have been killed to stop her from coming forward to police with information in the Bally case.

Like Alex, Michael failed to put the information regarding what he claimed were Lois' references to the site of Jason Bally's murder in his official police deposition.

Later, Alex would claim that a man named Patrick, who worked at a roadside stand opposite Sebastian's hotel, had confided a conversation that he had with Lois on the eve of her murder. Alex maintains that the reed-thin black man told him that Lois had come to the stand anxious to tell him something important, something about cyclist Jason Bally's murder. But the conversation between Lois and Patrick was reportedly cut short when a customer arrived at the stand, and began to ask questions about the art items on display.

Alex claimed that Patrick told him that Lois waited for a while, but that after several minutes she waved him good-bye, saying only that she was in a rush, and would "be back tomorrow" to continue the conversation. Lois was murdered later that evening.

When approached and asked about Alex's account, Patrick denied any knowledge of the cryptic conversation with Lois that Friday night.

As of this writing, the Jason Bally case remains unsolved. In June of 2002, two detectives from England's Scotland Yard came to Tortola to assist local police with the Bally investigation. In late 2002, police arrested a local man and charged him on suspicion of murder, but the magistrate presiding over his preliminary inquiry set him free, citing insufficient evidence to try him for the crime.

A second pair of detectives from Scotland Yard came to Tortola in late 2002 to help police in the Euan Watkins investigation. In May 2000, police arrested two men in the Watkins case, but they were later released pending further investigation.

There has been no allegation by police of any linkage between the Bally or the Watkins case and the McMillen murder.

"I can say to you from my professional judgment there is no link whatsoever between the Watkins case and the Bally case, and there is no link whatsoever between either of those cases and the McMillen case," said Police Commissioner Barry Webb.

"At the present time, the police have reviewed the McMillen case and there are no additional investigative opportunities available at this time, particularly as forensic opportunities were limited from Day One," the Commissioner said.

In May of 2003, Commissioner Webb asked the McMillens to come and see him on Tortola. Tragically, Webb's meeting with the McMillens was not to be.

Shortly after the couple arrived in Tortola in late May of 2003, Josephine McMillen was hospitalized on Tortola. After three days, she was airlifted to Baptist Hospital in Miami. Doctors there diagnosed her with viral pneumonia.

On Sunday, June 29, 2003, Josephine McMillen passed away. Her husband was by her side. Her sister, Phyllis Cobb, reported that she died of a rare lung disease. It is this author's belief that she died of a broken heart.

More than two hundred people attended her memorial service at the Middlebury Congregational Church in Connecticut, where friends and family said goodbye to the seventy-eight-year-old McMillen. In a private graveside ceremony, she was laid to rest next to her beloved Lois at the family's plot in Long Island.

"You know, I think most of her died about three years ago after Lois' death," Russell McMillen commented by phone from Florida.

"I was always impressed with her nobility in a trying situation," said prosecutor Terrence Williams of Josephine McMillen.

"She maintained her dignity throughout this entire ordeal," said Commissioner Webb of Mrs. McMillen. "It is such a terrible tragedy. She lost her only child."

In an interview in June of 2003, Webb said that police have no plans to reopen the McMillen case.